The South
Is Another Land

**Recent Titles in
Contributions in American History**
Series Editor: Jon L. Wakelyn

Congress, Courts, and Criminals: The Development of Federal Criminal Law, 1801-1829
Dwight F. Henderson

Radical Beginnings: Richard Hofstadter and the 1930s
Susan Stout Baker

Organize or Perish: America's Independent Progressives, 1913-1933
Eugene M. Tobin

The Absent Marx: Class Analysis and Liberal History in Twentieth-Century America
Ian Tyrrell

"Co-operation with Like-minded Peoples": British Influences on American Security Policy, 1945-1949
Richard A. Best, Jr.

The Antislavery Rank and File: A Social Profile of the Abolitionists' Constituency
Edward Magdol

The Paradox of Professionalism: Reform and Public Service in Urban America, 1900-1940
Don S. Kirschner

American Frontier and Western Issues: A Historiographical Review
Roger L. Nichols, editor

Continuity and Change in Electoral Politics, 1893-1928
Paul Kleppner

Arms at Rest: Peacemaking and Peacekeeping in American History
Joan R. Challinor and Robert L. Beisner, editors

Close Neighbors, Distant Friends: United States–Central American Relations
John E. Findling

American Urbanism: A Historiographical Review
Howard Gillette, Jr., and Zane L. Miller, editors

THE SOUTH IS ANOTHER LAND

Essays on the Twentieth-Century South

EDITED BY
BRUCE CLAYTON AND
JOHN A. SALMOND

CONTRIBUTIONS IN AMERICAN HISTORY, NUMBER 124

GREENWOOD PRESS
NEW YORK • WESTPORT, CONNECTICUT • LONDON

Library of Congress Cataloging-in-Publication Data

The South is another land.

(Contributions in American history, ISSN 0084-9219 ; no. 124)

Bibliography: p.
Includes index.
1. Southern States—Civilization—20th century.
I. Clayton, Bruce.   II. Salmond, John A.   III. Series.
F215.S684   1987   975'.04   86-29625
ISBN 0-313-25556-3 (lib. bdg. : alk. paper)
British Library Cataloguing in Publication Data is available.

Copyright © 1987 by Bruce L. Clayton and John A. Salmond

All rights reserved. No portion of this book may be reproduced, by any process or technique, without the express written consent of the publisher.

Library of Congress Catalog Card Number: 86-29625
ISBN: 0-313-25556-3
ISSN: 0084-9219

First published in 1987

Greenwood Press, Inc.
88 Post Road West, Westport, Connecticut 06881

Printed in the United States of America

The paper used in this book complies with the Permanent Paper Standard issued by the National Information Standards Organization (Z39.48-1984).

10 9 8 7 6 5 4 3 2 1

For
Dick and Ruth Watson

Contents

		ACKNOWLEDGMENTS	ix
		INTRODUCTION *Bruce Clayton and John A. Salmond*	xi
Part I		**THE POLITICAL SCENE**	1
	1	The "Unrewarding Stone": James F. Byrnes and the Burden of Race, 1908–1944 *Winfred B. Moore, Jr.*	3
	2	A Last Gasp: Clyde R. Hoey and the Twilight of Racial Segregation, 1945–1954 *Susan Tucker Hatcher*	29
	3	Southern Senators and Reform Issues in the 1920s: A Paradox Unravelled *Erik N. Olssen*	49
Part II		**THE WORLD OF WORK**	67
	4	Sectional Influences on National Policy: The South, the Labor Department, and the Wartime Labor Mobilization, 1917–1918 *William J. Breen*	69
	5	"Big Enough to Tell Weeds from the Beans": The Impact of Industry on Women in the Twentieth-Century South *Marion W. Roydhouse*	85

6	"Miss Lucy of the CIO": A Southern Life *John A. Salmond*	107
Part III	**THE WAY OF THE LORD**	**123**
7	After Scopes: Evolution in the South *Willard B. Gatewood, Jr.*	125
8	Dry Messiah Revisited: Bishop James Cannon, Jr. *Robert A. Hohner*	151
Part IV	**THE SEARCH FOR THE SOUTH**	**169**
9	A Southern Modernist: The Mind of W. J. Cash *Bruce Clayton*	171
10	With Pen and Camera: In Quest of the American South in the 1930s *Burl F. Noggle*	187
	BIBLIOGRAPHICAL ESSAY	205
	INDEX	209
	ABOUT THE EDITORS AND CONTRIBUTORS	215

Acknowledgments

Many hands go into the making of a book such as this. We would like to thank each of the contributors, not only for their essays, but for their constant enthusiasm, advice, and support of the project from the beginning. Special thanks also to Barbara A. Sayers, administrative assistant to the History Department, LaTrobe University, and Lyn Trace, secretary to the History Department, Allegheny College, and Dorothy Jeanne Smith, Reference Librarian, Allegheny College. All were invaluable. We also greatly appreciate the wise counsel and kind words we received from our friends and fellow historians, Professor Lawrence Curry, of the University of Houston, and Dr. M. E. R. Bassett, Minister of Health and Local Government in the New Zealand Labour Government. In addition, we are indebted to LaTrobe University and Allegheny College for unstinting support and encouragement. And last, a warm word of appreciation to Richard L. Watson, Jr., Professor of History Emeritus at Duke University. To all of us, and many, many more, he has been a friend and mentor, the very embodiment of humane scholarship, dignity, and decency.

Introduction

BRUCE CLAYTON and JOHN A. SALMOND

"There exists among us . . . a profound conviction that the South is another land, sharply differentiated from the rest of the American nation, and exhibiting within itself a remarkable homegeneity." So wrote W. J. Cash in launching his great work, *The Mind of the South*, in 1941. There was, Cash admitted, considerable conflict as to what the South's "singularity may consist in, . . . But that it is different and that it is solid—on these things nearly everybody is agreed." Occasionally, Cash conceded, someone would argue zealously that the South was a mere geographical expression, a lot hotter in the summer, of course, and made different from the rest of the nation by the larger number of blacks. But no one took such arguments seriously. "And rightly," Cash quipped.

The historians represented here, rightly eschewing Cash's audacity, are committed to a dispassionate research of the sort that held few blandishments for the Tar Heel writer who cut his literary teeth on H. L. Mencken. Yet their—our—conclusions, arrived at independently after researching various topics in the history of the twentieth-century South, point to the conclusion that the South was another land, different—at its core, in its identity and its self-consciousness—from the rest of the nation.

We begin not with the weather, as U. B. Phillips did, but with "The Political Scene." Winfred B. Moore, Jr., explores the life of James F. Byrnes, South Carolinian who rose to be secretary of state under President Harry S. Truman in the late 1940s. During the early years of the New Deal, he was one of President Franklin Delano Roosevelt's most ardent supporters; later during the war he served with distinction as Director of War Mobilization. But in 1944 Byrnes' lifelong espousal of his state's commitment to white supremacy cost him what he coveted most: the Democratic party's—

his party's—vice-presidential nomination. Byrnes understood, Moore explains, but "understanding did little to cushion the blow for, in many ways, it was a verdict on his whole career." He went to his death embittered; angrily aware that it was impossible "to be both a loyal defender of white southern interests and a fully accepted leader of the nation at large."

One might say that no one forced Byrnes to accept white supremacy. But his region had: to get elected, to get to be somebody in South Carolina politics one had to endorse, publicly and passionately, racism. Yet as Susan Tucker Hatcher shows in analyzing Clyde R. Hoey's senatorial career (1944–1954), no one had to lift a finger to convince Hoey to embrace the white supremacy movement that swept North Carolina during his youth in the late 1890s. An ambitious man, a man of substantial political power from the 1920s on, Hoey exploited the race issue. That combined with his flowing mane, swallowtail coat, and stentorian, but empty, rhetoric prompts one to dismiss him as a kind of Senator Foghorn. Yet Hoey embodied the white South as much as did the more accomplished and better known Jimmy Byrnes.

They were uniquely and distinctively "southern." This is not to say that the rest of white America did not share much of their racism. But in the South their racism was mandated. The assumptions of white supremacy might flow naturally from within, but in the South in the first half of the twentieth century the imperative to accept racism was absolute. That everyone knew.

Erik N. Olssen's study of "Southern Senators and Reform Issues in the 1920s," however, should serve as a caution to all generalizations. Basing his conclusions on sophisticated analysis of voting rolls, Olssen argues that southern senators were more liberal, particularly on nonracial issues, than we have thought. Yet even the most liberal senators—such as Tennessee's Kenneth McKellar or Alabama's Hugo Black—had no intention of attacking white supremacy. Moreover, many southern Democrats had devious reasons for supporting reform, Olssen writes. In addition to being "adept at exploiting racism and sectional pride, at blurring prospective social divisions, they also became remarkably flexible in devising programs designed to weaken Populist appeals." Like Byrnes and Hoey they were all self-consciously "southern." But all of them paid a price for it. While southern Democrats in the 1920s "helped define the agenda for reform in their region they were not, in general, involved in defining the national agenda."

The South's values, its self-consciousness, its determination to remain different, particularly wherever race was involved—in other words, the region's identity—were ever present in what we have called "The World of Work." William J. Breen focuses on the way southern business leaders and industrialists responded to the federal government's attempt to mobilize labor after America entered the war in 1917. Did the war years, as some prominent historians argue, see a significant nationalization of the South?

Doubtless it did in some areas, but Breen contends that whenever self-interest was involved, particularly in racial matters, "southerners consistently placed regional interests above national interests." And as Marion W. Roydhouse shows in " 'Big Enough to Tell Weeds from the Beans,' " a study of working conditions for women in North Carolina's tobacco plants and textile mills, values from the past were unalterable. Women got lower pay than men; men got the best jobs. Black women got the dirtiest jobs, and the lowest pay. Gender and race, as they intertwined with religion and politics, were central to southern history. That history determined how people lived their lives—who got what, and how much, or how little. Some of Roydhouse's factory and mill women, many barely literate, understood that.

So did Lucy Randolph Mason, a Virginia lady (the term is used advisedly) who broke free from the "cult of true womanhood" to become an effective organizer for the Congress of Industrial Organizations, the CIO, the militant wing of the American labor movement. As her biographer John A. Salmond shows, "Miss Lucy" could understand both factory girls and greedy, insensitive mill and factory owners. Both were products of history. That is why she stepped down from the pedestal and fought tirelessly for better working conditions, feminism, even equal rights for blacks. Northern liberals urged her to join them in their crusades, and she succumbed once to their blandishments. But, says Salmond, for all her emancipation from southern traditions and prejudices—and she was one of the region's few truly unprejudiced minds—"she was always a southerner." She lived and died in Dixie—a redeemed Dixie, that is.

The South bows to no section in vying for the honor of being the godliest part of America, for walking in "The Way of the Lord." If fighting against evolution and for prohibition are true indicators of religion, the South deserves to be called the Bible Belt. Willard B. Gatewood, Jr., a leading student of the evolution controversy in the South, here demonstrates that the South's hostility toward evolution in no way ended after the celebrated Scopes ("monkey") trial in 1925 in Dayton, Tennessee. "Only in the South did fundamentalists achieve their aims by statutory means," Gatewood writes. Even in those states such as North Carolina that prided themselves on thwarting the more rabid fundamentalists the feeling was almost universal in southern schools that evolution was a subject not to be discussed. For the great majority, being "southern" meant being antievolution, or, more recently, being for "creation science." There were dissenters, but they were a minority.

Methodist Bishop James A. Cannon, Jr., of Virginia spent most of his waking hours fighting for Prohibition. Nearly forgotten today, he was, as his biographer Robert A. Hohner shows, "the most powerful and best known American clergyman of his time." To Cannon's many critics, he was a bigoted, self-serving, self-promoting, self-appointed "Dry Messiah," whose bitter campaign against Al Smith in the 1928 presidential election was a disgrace to his clerical collar. But to Hohner, the bishop's busy public commitment to a range of reforms when combined with his private friendships with such northerners as Mencken and Harry Golden points to a complex and intriguing personality.

But to W. J. Cash and most writers and intellectuals who led "The Search for the South," our concluding section, Cannon symbolized the narrow, fanatical, holy men whose battle with Darwin and the other gods of modernism was doomed to defeat. Yet Cash's modernism, however personally liberating and essential to his mind and psyche, cut him off from his countrymen, the people whose "mind" he tried desperately to understand. It was an irony, says his biographer Bruce Clayton, Cash understood.

Cash was in a small minority. But as a critic, a prober, an intellectual in passionate search of the South, he was in good company. Burl F. Noggle's survey of the writers and photographers who swarmed over the region in the 1930s attests to the presence of an imaginative, undaunted minority, from novelist James Agee to sociologist Rupert B. Vance, and serves as a fitting conclusion to these essays. It does not, however, escape Noggle's eye that a significant number of those seeking to capture and define the South—people like the photographers Walker Evans and Margaret Bourke-White—were northerners. Northerners or southerners, though, they came to record a region they knew to be distinctive. They knew that "the South was another land."

PART I

The Political Scene

The "Unrewarding Stone": James F. Byrnes and the Burden of Race, 1908–1944

WINFRED B. MOORE, JR.

James F. Byrnes was "Almost a President," Frank Freidel once said, in reminding Americans of a southern politician most of them remembered only vaguely if at all. Indeed, Freidel might have added, the presidency was about the only missing page in Byrnes's career, a career that otherwise read like a classic American success story. The grandson of Irish immigrants, he was born in Charleston, South Carolina, on May 2, 1882, six weeks after his father died of "consumption." To help support his mother, a dressmaker on the "wrong side" of town, he quit school at age thirteen and took a job as an office boy in the law firm of Benjamin H. Rutledge, a blue-blooded Charleston aristocrat who eventually came to treat him like a son. Over the next five years, Rutledge guided his office boy through an extensive reading program and, in 1900, helped him to acquire a better job as a court stenographer in Aiken, South Carolina. There, he went on to become an attorney and a newspaper editor before launching a political career in 1908.

Emerging from a childhood rooted in both the needs of the "New South" and the traditions of the "Old," it became Byrnes's goal to reconcile the two. Politically, that meant seeking moderate reforms designed to modernize the South and take it again to national leadership without abandoning the region's historic values and institutions. With the help of an uncommonly quick mind, an ingratiating Irish charm, and an uncanny ability to win consensus on difficult questions, he often seemed close to reaching his ambitious goal through the course of a long journey through twentieth-century America. But on that remarkable journey, there was always one obstacle, more than others, that impeded his progress and ultimately blocked his way. That obstacle was the same racial dilemma that had stymied generations of southerners before him. This chapter will examine the way Byrnes addressed racial issues from the time of his first political victory in 1908 to that of his greatest political defeat in 1944. It is hoped that this examination will help to illuminate how one southerner affected, and was affected by, American race relations from the Progressive Era through the New Deal.[1]

As he came of age in the South at the turn of the twentieth century, Byrnes was exposed to the orthodox racial faith of the region. From his mother to Ben Rutledge to the "courthouse crowd" of Aiken, everyone he admired informed him that blacks were naturally inferior to whites. Using the "dark days" of Reconstruction as their evidence, they taught him that any misguided attempt to impose artificial equality of race could only lead to disruption and disaster. Whether childlike or savage, therefore, the Negro had to be controlled by the superior race if southern civilization was to advance. This reality, they explained, was what made statutory disfranchisement and segregation the great reforms of the day for, by removing volatile legal uncertainties, those measures defined the boundaries of a stable racial peace that worked to benefit all. Freed from the threat of black encroachments, whites could turn their attention to solving other serious problems. Purged of the notion of ever being equal, blacks could now be treated more fairly and develop to their maximum potential with the aid of newly benevolent whites. In essence, his elders assured him, the racial problem had been solved as long as everyone stayed in his place and respected the terms of the peace. Like other young southerners of his day, Byrnes accepted those teachings as gospel and never seriously questioned them for the rest of his life.[2]

But unlike some of his contemporaries, Byrnes seemed to take seriously the notion that blacks had to be provided a certain amount of fair treatment within the prescribed limits. As coeditor of the Aiken *Journal and Review* from 1904 to 1908, Byrnes never wrote an inflammatory editorial on the "race question" even though such editorials were a stock in trade of the day. Indeed, the few times he mentioned the subject, the editor mildly criticized wrongs committed by whites. One such occasion came in 1906 when he wrote that the violence initiated by whites during the Atlanta race riot was "wrong and criminal" and "no matter how great our resentment [of the alleged rape of a white woman] may be, we must admit it." By the same token, he also argued that it was wrong for juries in Aiken County to pass out harsher sentences to blacks than to whites convicted of the same crime. If social progress was to be made, he implied, order had to be preserved; and that meant policing white abuses on the right just as much as black abuses on the left.[3]

In 1908, Byrnes got the chance to put his beliefs into practice when he was elected solicitor (prosecuting attorney) of South Carolina's second judicial district. Located in the heart of the black belt, the district ran from Aiken in the south-central part of the state to Beaufort on the coast. Known for its bloody racial violence during Reconstruction and for producing the state's leading white supremacist, Senator Benjamin R. Tillman, it was often said to be "the damndest, gamecockingest, liquor-drinkingest, nigger-shootingest, sinfullest place in South Carolina." True to form, the second district kept the new solicitor busy with a number of sensational cases, many of which touched on the raw nerve of race.[4]

In the first such case, Byrnes prosecuted C. F. Baker, a white resident of Barnwell, for the murder of a Negro barber named Julius Green. At the trial, Byrnes produced several eyewitnesses who testified that Baker had first quarrelled with Green in the barber shop, then left in a rage, and finally returned with a gun which he used to pump four bullets into the unarmed barber's chest. "If you decide not to convict this man," the solicitor told the all-white jury, "I want you to be courageous enough to say why; just write on the verdict 'Not guilty'—because it was a negro he killed." Three hours later, the jury found the defendant not guilty on the grounds of self-defense. As the jurors filed out of the courtroom, one of them paused to give Byrnes some friendly advice. "I think you have one of the best futures politically of any young man I know," he whispered. "But if you keep talking to juries like you talked . . . this morning, some day a jury will convict a white man of killing a negro and then you will have ruined yourself."[5]

Apparently unconvinced, Byrnes tackled a similar case a few months later in Aiken. There, local authorities had charged Levi Chavous, a black fisherman, with the murder of a white farmer named C. S. Pringle. The charge was based on evidence that the two men had waged a long feud over a repossessed rowboat during the course of which Chavous threatened to kill Pringle if he ever caught him fishing in the Savannah River again. Shortly after the threat was made, Pringle disappeared and his hat was eventually found lying beside an unidentifiable human skull on the banks of the river. Finding the evidence in that condition, Byrnes asked the court to dismiss the charge, pointing out that the lack of a corpse made it impossible to prove that Pringle was even dead, much less that he had been murdered. The court agreed in a ruling that was probably correct but notable nonetheless. In a district known to lynch blacks on flimsier grounds, Byrnes had asked for, and somehow persuaded, the court to grant Chavous's release.[6]

Attracting more attention was the way the solicitor handled a complicated case centering on the murder of Perry Ussery, a white businessman in Barnwell. The self-confessed killer was Quitman Johnson, a Negro whom Byrnes got convicted and sentenced to death. But a few days after the sentencing, Johnson, who had perhaps heard of Byrnes's reputation for fairness, asked to see the solicitor in private. There, for the first time, Johnson explained why he killed Ussery: Chester Kennedy, one of the most prominent men in Barnwell, had hired him to do it. He would have told the story at the trial, Johnson explained, but the sheriff had promised him leniency if he took full responsibility and Kennedy had threatened to harm his family if he did not. Byrnes believed Johnson's story and quickly hired Pinkerton detectives not connected with the sheriff's office to reopen the investigation. Based on the new evidence those detectives uncovered in the black community, the solicitor got Johnson's sentence reduced to life imprisonment and Kennedy indicted as an accessory to murder. At Kennedy's ensuing trial, Byrnes somehow persuaded the court to allow his black witnesses to testify against the white defendant, a practice that was unusual in Barnwell County. Largely because of their testimony, Kennedy was convicted and, like Johnson, sentenced to life in prison. Byrnes's performance, said the district's leading newspaper, was one of the "most memorable events in the annals of the court in Barnwell County which hailed the beginning of a day when even prominent white men can be convicted of cowardly crimes." Capitalizing on that progressive reputation for law, order, and fairness, Byrnes won a seat in Congress in 1910 which he held for the next fourteen years.[7]

During his first years in the House, however, Byrnes's racial stance underwent a significant shift in emphasis, a shift that may have been partially rooted in a bitter reelection battle he had with Harry D. Calhoun of Barnwell in 1912. Throughout that summer Calhoun campaigned against Byrnes's vote for the Seventeenth Amendment to establish the direct election of U. S. senators. By agreeing to let the national government meddle in state affairs, claimed the Barnwell native, Byrnes had helped to open the floodgates for federal registration of black voters, a "revival of negro influence," and an "intermingling of races." As an abject "surrender to the nigger and the nigger-lover," Calhoun asked, "Doesn't this scare you? Vote for Harry D. Calhoun . . . and against negro domination." Dumbfounded by the absurdity of his opponent's charges, Byrnes nonetheless found it necessary to proclaim his innocence. Before he would support any measure that smacked of "negro rule," Byrnes announced for the first time, "I would pray that 'my tongue would cleave to the roof of my mouth and my right hand lose its cunning.'" Absolved by his constituents of committing the cardinal sin, Byrnes was reelected rather handily. But in the process he seemed to have drawn an important conclusion, namely that any successful southern politician not only had to believe in white supremacy but also to let his people know it.[8]

Beginning in 1913, certainly, Byrnes took steps to prove beyond doubt his commitment to white supremacy. As part of that effort, Byrnes made pilgrimages to numerous Confederate reunions to reassure the old warriors that the present generation had, indeed, learned the lessons of the past. Yes, the congressman acknowledged, evil men had once misled "a race of negroes only a few years removed from savagery" and "for a while the future looked dark indeed but gradually the influence of the mighty and mysterious army of the Ku Klux made itself felt in the land, the scalawag and the negro were overthrown and the right of the white men to rule in this country was established—established, I pray to God for all time." To keep it established,

Byrnes publicly pressured the incoming Wilson administration to remove the last legacies of Reconstruction in South Carolina. Among them were the black railway mail clerks who, Byrnes complained, could "barely read and write," and who had been "appointed solely for political reasons at the request of negro politicians," and ought to be stripped of Civil Service protection to make room for whites with "superior intellect and . . . educational advantages." Furthermore, he said, a decent respect for civilized opinion dictated that Robert Smalls, the black hero of the Civil War and Reconstruction and current Collector of the Port of Beaufort, be removed from his Republican patronage post three months earlier than originally scheduled. On both counts the administration agreed in what became part of its general policy of removing most blacks from federal jobs and rigidly segregating the rest.[9]

Although he knew the president took a pro-southern view on such matters, Byrnes nonetheless kept up his racial guard throughout the Wilson administration. In 1914, for example, Byrnes and a host of other southerners insisted on a more restrictive immigration bill than the president wanted to accept. Such a bill was necessary in part, said Byrnes, because otherwise residents of "southern Italy, Greece, and Turkey" who "have no capacity for assimilation with our white people" would come to America, "turn to the negro race, mingle with them, and so aggravate our race problem as to make it hopeless." In like fashion, one reason the Carolinian opposed the Child Labor Act of 1916 was his fear that it might be used as a precedent for federal regulation of labor practices by future administrations to ban "segregation of the races or discrimination against any race" in southern textile mills. And he also initially opposed the Military Conscription Act of 1917 at least partially because it did not prohibit the War Department from "assigning a boy from South Carolina . . . to serve . . . by the side of a negro from Indiana." "If they did this," warned Byrnes, "they would not have to go to Europe for war." Such remarks were a very minor part of years in which Byrnes worked for nearly every progressive reform of the day, earned a reputation for uncommon legislative skill, cultivated a small army of friends on both sides of the aisle, and won plaudits from the president on down as a Democratic star of the future. Still, they were unmistakable proof that the man who had defended Jim Crow's racial peace from the local threats on the right was now equally sensitive to potential national threats on the left—even under a friendly Democratic administration.[10]

In 1919, the year the Republicans recaptured control of Congress and a more militant "new Negro" came home from war, Byrnes started to perceive much greater national threats to the racial status quo in the South. Suddenly, the Aiken Congressman, like other white Americans, was confronted with multitudes of northern blacks demanding their rights and bloody racial confrontations sweeping the land. Worse, from his perspective, the contagion seemed to be spreading into Dixie. Record numbers of black Carolinians were leaving the state to search for a better life in the North. Of those who stayed behind, small but increasing numbers were joining the South Carolina chapter of the NAACP where they demanded nondiscriminatory voter registration as part of a general "magna carta of the rights and aspirations of the race." In the wake of those developments, Byrnes was sure it was no coincidence when a race riot broke out in Charleston in May. Altogether, the return of the party of Lincoln and the resurrection of black assertiveness seemed to combine in Byrnes's mind to raise the fear that a new attempt at Reconstruction might be in the making.[11]

Determined to stop such a movement before it gained any momentum, Byrnes rose from his seat on August 25, 1919, to deliver one of the most belligerent speeches ever heard in the nation's Capitol. How was it possible to explain the massive race riots taking "place in cities so widely separated and within so short a time," Byrnes asked his colleagues. Since the overwhelming majority of blacks was "prospering as never before in the history of their race" and knew that they needed "neither political . . . nor social equality" for happiness, the sole answer had to be "the incendiary utterances" of people such as W. E. B. DuBois, who were misleading "ignorant negroes" into thinking they were being treated unfairly by whites. Using that subterfuge, Byrnes continued, DuBois and other black editors were fomenting a "deliberately planned . . . campaign of violence" whose real objective was to further the "nefarious purposes" of the I. W. W. and the Bolsheviki of Russia." Accordingly, the congressman demanded that all radical black publications be banned from circulation in the U. S. mail and that their editors be investigated for possible prosecution under the Espionage Act.[12]

Having disposed of Negro radicals, Byrnes shifted his attention to their would-be allies, the white northern liberals whose sermons against southern lynchings he blamed for contributing to racial unrest. Of course, all reasonable men deplored mob violence, said the congressman, but if northerners were sincere in wanting to solve the problem they should "join us in condemnation of the criminal assaults upon white women, which is generally the cause of lynching." Perhaps now that blacks were flooding north of the Mason-Dixon line some of the Yankees' self-righteousness would be "swept away by that which is greater than constitutional or legislative enactments, namely the natural instinct of the Anglo-Saxon." "God Almighty never intended that a white race and a black race should live in terms of social equality," he declared, "and that which the Creator did not intend man can not make possible."[13]

Byrnes finished with a chilling sermon of his own:

If the two races are to live together in this country it may be well understood that the war has in no way changed the attitude of the white man toward the social and political equality of the negro. . . . If by reason of his experience he seeks social and political equality with the white men but refuses to consider leaving for parts where it will willingly be given to him, and cherishes the hope that by violence it can be gained here, he can not too quickly realize that there are in this country 90,000,000 white people determined not to extend... equality to 10,000,000 negroes and a resort to violence must inevitably bring to the negro the greater suffering.

"This is a white man's country," he warned, "and will always remain a white man's country."[14]

Judged even by the unrestrained standards of the day, Byrnes's speech was a high-water mark in postwar racial tensions. Speaking for much of the black leadership, DuBois icily observed that the congressman had just, unwittingly, exposed the real source of the nation's troubles: militant white racism. If anyone was guilty of subversion, said the black editor, it was Byrnes for trying to nullify, at a minimum, the First, Fourteenth, and Fifteenth Amendments to the Constitution. Meanwhile, less restrained black citizens flooded Byrnes's office with hundreds of angry letters, the most ominous coming from a secret organization called "the borgia" which threatened to assassinate him. Fortified with secret service protection, however, Byrnes refused to yield his ground. These new black leaders are "so radical," he insisted, "that they are making anarchists resort to new methods in order to avoid being called reactionaries."[15]

Although he calmed down a bit in the next few months, Byrnes continued to fear that Republicans might grow sympathetic to some of the black's demands and he thus remained in a heightened state of racial alert for the next five years. Fairly typical was his concern that the Women's Suffrage Amendment might eventually be used by the GOP as a pretext for registering black voters in the South. Southern congressmen always have to be on the lookout for such a move, he privately admitted, because, "It is certain that if there were a fair registration they (blacks) would have a slight majority of voters in our state," and "we cannot idly brush these facts aside. Unfortunate though it may be, our consideration of every question must include the consideration of this race question."[16]

In 1921, that "question" surfaced again in the form of the Dyer antilynching bill, a measure designed to combat lynching by making it a federal crime. Such legislation, Byrnes told the House, was unnecessary because local officials just about had the problem under control, impractical because southerners would never cooperate as well with federal agents, and unconstitutional because it proposed to usurp state jurisdiction over what was simply one form of murder. Indeed, by impugning the South's good intentions, the bill would inflame the very passions that produced lynching. Since all enlightened men were surely aware of that fact, what possible motive could the sponsors have in mind? The answer, he deduced, must be that cynical Republican congressmen, in their greed for black votes, were trying to "please a few misguided Negro leaders" in the North at the expense of racial peace in the South.[17]

Three years later, long after the lynching bill had died in Congress, Byrnes tried to get revenge against some of those "misguided Negro leaders." He took as his occasion a routine House debate on the annual appropriations request for Howard University, a major center of black student activism in the 1920s. It was time, said the Carolinian, to put an end to this ill-advised appropriation designed only "to secure Negro votes." Federal funding of any private university was an unsound practice, he argued, and especially one like Howard that taught "the essentials of socialism" and "racial equality." If the sponsors of the bill really wanted to help black higher education, then Hampton, Tuskegee, or other colleges with a self-help, nonprotest orientation would be a more responsible choice for federal aid. And if the Republican majority continued to fund Howard, as he suspected they foolishly would, then they should at least permit the Congress to "exercise some control over the institution and prevent the preaching of sermons the only effect of which can be to poison the minds of their students, arouse their prejudice against the white people of the country, make them discontented with their lot in life, and disturb the harmonious [race] relations now existing." To Byrnes's regret the funding of Howard continued.[18]

As it became apparent that he could not stop the racial "poison" being unleashed in the North, Byrnes increasingly focused on preventing its spread into the South. In 1923, for example, he asked the Justice Department to stop the circulation of advertisements soliciting southern blacks for industrial jobs in the North. Most of these ads were fraudulent, he claimed, and they should therefore be seized to prevent a lot of gullible blacks from being hurt. Moreover, white landlords were losing a lot of money from black sharecroppers who fled North without paying their debts. An unspoken but perhaps more important reason for the request was the congressman's concern that an unrestrained tide of black migration might lead both to a serious labor shortage in the South and an unmanageable growth of black voting power in the North. By spawning larger numbers of "outside agitators" such power might eventually set off tremors of protest among the black masses of his own state. With that thought in mind, he made a special trip to the South Carolina College for Negroes at Orangeburg to caution students "against allowing northern radicals to mislead them and awaken impossible aspirations of political power."[19]

In 1924, some of that posturing carried over into Byrnes's first bid for the U. S. Senate when he ran against Coleman L. Blease, the state's most flamboyant demagogue, and Nathaniel B. Dial, the incumbent. During the first weeks of the campaign, Byrnes implied that Dial was soft on white supremacy because he had proposed to recruit Italian immigrants as replacements for black workers who left the state. "I'd rather have one big black nigger working on my cotton farm," the congressman snorted, "than half a dozen Italians." Later Byrnes's campaign manager circulated a political advertisement that reminded readers that Blease had made something of a conciliatory speech to black students at Columbia's Allen University in 1916. In contrast, Byrnes reminded the crowds how he had fought black radicals in Washington and warned them not to "drift down South and create trouble." Perhaps he was still worried about black unrest or perhaps he was merely willing to use any available weapon in a hard-fought contest; in either case Byrnes had just come as close as he ever would to trying to "outnigger" an opponent to win an election.[20]

By the middle of the summer, however, Byrnes seemed to have lost his taste for racial demagoguery. Whatever the danger at the national level, he knew that there was simply no internal threat to white supremacy in South Carolina. To pretend otherwise would only disturb the "racial peace" and make it more difficult to address other questions. With such thoughts apparently in mind, the congressman discarded appeals to race and went back to his traditional method of campaigning on his superior grasp of national issues. Perhaps trying to atone for his earlier remarks, Byrnes even endorsed equal bonus payments to black veterans because "we must treat them justly and right." Similarly, he refused a Grand Kleagle's offer to become a secret member of the Ku Klux Klan. In the process, he provoked a negative reaction from the powerful Carolina Klan that may have been a significant factor in his razor-thin loss to Blease in a runoff primary.[21]

At any rate, Blease apparently thought it was, for he certainly tried to bludgeon Byrnes with the race question during their rematch in the Senate primary of 1930. Blease started at a stump meeting in Union, the site of a recent lynching, by pronouncing a blessing on the recent actions of the city's mob. "Whenever the Constitution comes between me and the virtue of the white women of South Carolina," he yelled, "I say 'To hell with the Constitution.'" "When you catch the brute that assaults a white woman," he continued, "wait until the next morning to notify me." Before the old rabble-rouser finished, one witness remarked, "the crowd went wild and they were about to tear the courthouse up. . . . Blease had swept all before him . . . the atmosphere was electric that day. . . . Blease was riding the crest." To boost their man over the top, Blease's supporters quickly followed up with a flyer, obviously aimed at Byrnes, which proclaimed that "Negroes Pray for Blease's Defeat, How will S. C. Democrats answer?"[22]

Echoing positions he had first voiced as a young editor and solicitor, at least one "S. C. Democrat" answered calmly and admirably. "We've had too much talk about lynching," said Byrnes while the crowd was still buzzing from Blease's speech. "Hanging them [blacks] to a telephone pole" accomplished nothing but a mutually destructive breakdown of order. Besides, "why talk about white supremacy and the virtues of womanhood? Of course we all believe in that and we ought to" and certainly it was sometimes necessary to protect them from outside threats. But the time had come to recognize that some men were manipulating racial fears to win office and conjuring up nonexistent internal threats to white supremacy as a means of suppressing discussion of other serious issues. "Too much thought is being given to Negroes, Liquor and personalities," he insisted, "and too little to economic problems." Hoping that a depression-era electorate was ready to help him make a change, Byrnes summed up the theme of his campaign in a statewide radio broadcast on election eve. "I have endeavored," he said:

> to appeal to the reason and intelligence of the people instead of their passions and prejudices. I have discussed economic problems and national issues instead of indulging in personalities. . . . My pledge is to give you the best that is in me . . . in an earnest effort to restore South Carolina to the place she once held in the councils of the Democratic Party.

The next day Byrnes defeated Blease by 4,500 votes. "Let us hope," wrote the editor of the Greenville *News* "that it augurs a new day when we shall select men not for the noise they can make and the cussin' they can do but for the service they can render the state."[23]

Over the next six years, Byrnes probably served his state as well as any senator in its history. After playing a key role in Franklin Roosevelt's presidential campaign, he blossomed into a highly effective "cloakroom operator." Variously labeled as the "balance wheel between the conservatives and the liberals," "the President's favorite senator," and "the brains of the Democratic Leadership in the Senate," he supported and played a key role in passing every major piece of New Deal legislation from the Emergency Banking Act through the National Labor Relations Act. Yes, said one Republican on behalf of his colleagues, Arkansas's Joe Robinson was the titular head of the Senate Democrats, "but the closest thing to a Democratic leader we recognize on our side of the aisle is Jimmy Byrnes. . . . There is nothing the Administration wants of Congress that . . . Jimmy does not have a major but inconspicuous share in steering over the shoals." Simply put, George Mowry later asserted, Byrnes became "certainly the most influential southern member of Congress between John Calhoun and Lyndon Johnson."[24]

Byrnes built that reputation while publicly addressing the race question only once. He did so with little apparent enthusiasm as part of the southern filibuster against the Wagner-Costigan Anti-Lynching Bill of 1935. "Lynching, like any other form of murder, is a violation of the law of God and of man," he sighed. "For it I have never made and will never make an apology." Unlike his nasty remarks a decade earlier, he proceeded to give a restrained, erudite explanation of why he thought federal legislation was not the proper approach to the problem. Indeed, his remarks suggested a general weariness with the subject and a wish that people on both extremes of the question would simply leave it and him alone. The race problem could not be solved quickly through militance either of the left or right, he pleaded, but only by the gradual "education of our people and the development of a sentiment that will uphold men in public office who courageously perform their duties."[25]

In the South Carolina Senate primary of 1936, however, both Thomas P. Stoney, a former mayor of Charleston, and William C. Harlee, a retired Marine Colonel, challenged Byrnes's seat on the grounds that he had been too "courageous" in performing the duties of a "socialistic" administration which was clearly soft on race. For Byrnes the immediate trouble started at the Democratic National Convention, from which his state's senior senator, "Cotton Ed" Smith, took a celebrated "walk" after discovering that the New Dealers were allowing blacks to participate. Capitalizing on Byrnes's conspicuous failure to join his colleague, Stoney told the folks back home that "Little Jimmy is not the same man we sent to Washington or he would have walked out along with Senator E. D. Smith." "Coat-tail-swinging Jimmy Byrnes," Harlee agreed, seemed to have become one of the "harpies who consort with colored people to control the government" and sanction White House dinners where "a black woman sat so close to Mrs. Roosevelt that their bodies touched."[26]

On July 7, that train of thought reached its logical conclusion when Byrnes's opposition circulated a postcard throughout the state. It labeled the New Dealers as "a Roosevelt-Nigger Democratic Party . . . not at all like the party of your fathers." "Help kick Roosevelt and Byrnes out of power forever," it demanded because:

a vote for Roosevelt and Byrnes means the day is coming closer when dirty, evil smelling negroes will be going to church with you, your sister, your wife, or your mother. Busses, trains, hotels, picture shows, bathing beaches, will all see the negroes rubbing shoulders with your beloved ones. From this it will only be a step when negroes will be allowed to propose wedlock to white girls. All under Roosevelt laws.[27]

Despite the smear tactics, Byrnes stayed calm on his way back home from the convention. "This sort of stuff . . . defeats itself," he wrote his friends. No, he had not walked out of the convention with Smith; to have done so would have been both illogical and counterproductive. "Under our doctrine of States' rights," he argued, "I do not know of any way in which we can claim for ourselves the right to determine, without outside interference, who will represent us and then force these negroes in Chicago to elect a white representative." Besides, if the South walked out of the Democratic Party where did it have to go? Unlike the Republicans, the Democrats "at least assured" the state "that the delegates from South Carolina will all be white." Yes, he said of his opponents' other charge, "F. D. R. has done more for the negroes than all other Presidents" but that was simply because "one could not help the poor people of the country without . . . helping the negroes." "The wage earner who was formerly appealed to along this line," he concluded, "now realizes that the hatred of the negro has been used by demagogues to prevent the advancement of the interests of the laboring people."[28]

Carrying that belief to the campaign trail, Byrnes stressed the need to pursue reform without fear of illusory racial threats. "They accuse me of being a New Dealer," he hooted after listing the massive benefits the administration had poured into his state. "Well, I admit I am a New Dealer, and if it takes money away from the few who have controlled this country and gives it back to the average man, I am going to Washington to help the President work for the people of South Carolina and of the country." As for the race question, the little Irishman dismissed it in an eloquent paragraph. "My friends," he said,

I have been campaigning in South Carolina for many years. It seems to me that during the past quarter of a century... some of us have put too much stress upon personalities, upon prejudice and upon arousing of racial hatreds. That is wrong and the sooner we get away from it the better for our state and our people. We have devoted too much time to discussion of "likker" and "nigger" and too little to those matters which vitally affect the welfare of the people. In your heart and mine there are certain prejudices. It is the duty of a good man to subdue these prejudices. I have no respect for the man who, for political gain, will seek to arouse the prejudices of the people. I believe the time has come in South Carolina when a man can appeal to the best that is in us instead of the worst.

If Byrnes represented the best that was in them, then he was correct for on primary day he carried every precinct in the state save one. "Never in the history of the primary elections," observed the leading authority of the subject, "had a public official received such a mandate" or "more overwhelming approval of a position that he had taken in the exercise of his duties."[29]

From 1930 through 1936, Byrnes's liberalism on domestic issues had been largely based on his lifelong conviction that the national Democratic party was a safe haven for southern interests; but in 1937 major doubts began to plague that conviction and as those doubts grew it became apparent that the senator's willingness, perhaps even his political ability, to support the New Deal had its limits. The first sign of serious trouble came in the general elections of 1936 when blacks and organized labor won much more powerful voices in party affairs. Soon, their rising prominence in Democratic policy making convinced a growing number of Carolinians that the president had begun to cater to political forces alien to the white South. "Please watch Roosevelt, [Committee for Industrial Organization leader] John L. Lewis, and [Postmaster General] Jim Farley," pleaded one of the senator's constituents. "That triumvirate would gladly sell and sacrifice the entire white population of the South and put the Negro over us politically and economically if by doing so they could carry the Negro vote in America." "While South Carolina gave Franklin Roosevelt the greatest majority of any state," warned another, "the people are beginning to believe that he is deserting them for a cause the people down here don't believe in. Is there not someone close to the President who can call him to his senses before it is too late?" Because he believed the president was being misled by northern advisers and because he knew that he, as the state's New Deal senator, would be held responsible for any dangerous change of administration policy, Byrnes quickly took that task upon himself. From 1937 to 1939, the result was a series of sudden, dramatic disputes with the administration that Byrnes seemed to view as part of a broader battle for hegemony in the Democratic party that the South could not afford to lose.[30]

Nearly all of Byrnes's disputes with the administration were at least partially rooted in race. In the spring of 1937, despite strong objections from the White House, Byrnes pushed for an official Senate condemnation of the sit-down strike as means of curbing the power of the CIO. If left unchecked, he reasoned, the CIO would try not only to organize southern workers but also to implement its policy "that there can be no discrimination . . . because of color." By the same token, Byrnes soon thereafter voted against the Fair Labor Standards Act in part because its minimum wage provisions "would have to be paid to every negro . . . as well as to white employees." And, from there, he launched a crusade to reduce and reform relief programs. "As long as human nature remains the same," he said in explaining his action, "the individual in charge of distribution, whether he is a Republican or a Democrat, will be tempted to be more liberal in the states that are doubtful than in the states that are politically certain." Since "our negro problem prevents us from dividing politically" and this ever being a "doubtful" state, "we must set forth in law how any relief funds are to be distributed" and "put it on a basis which will be better for the interest of the nation as a whole and certainly for the South."[31]

While those skirmishes ran their course, one incident in particular demonstrated how sensitive Byrnes was becoming to the rising status of blacks in the Democratic party. It occurred in the fall of 1937 when he received a tip that the director of the Farm Security Administration, Will Alexander, was about to appoint a black member to the state boards that set policies for his agency in the South. Confident that "there had been no discrimination against the negro by representatives" of any New Deal agency, Byrnes asked Alexander to reconsider the proposed change. "I greatly fear," he said, "that for you to insist that your advisory committee must have a negro member would be regarded as an effort to please the negro voters in the politically doubtful states" and to "disturb the friendly relations now existing between the races in the South." As such it would prove a serious handicap to the success of your work in those states" and "the negro will be the one to suffer." When Alexander ignored that warning, Byrnes fired a second one a bit closer to his bow. "The responsibility is yours—not mine," cautioned the senator whose committee funded Alexander's agency. "I have done my duty in calling your attention to the great danger of impairing the effectiveness of your program and arousing unfortunate feelings between the races where today in South Carolina only the best feeling exists." That last remark caught the attention of Alexander's superior, Secretary of Agriculture Henry Wallace, who quickly intervened to squelch the whole matter. Apparently Byrnes thought "we were making war on white supremacy," Alexander said in disgust, for the senator's epistle was "the most abusive letter . . . I almost ever read and it scared Henry Wallace. He just tucked his tail and turned to the high timber right away, and I never did get my negroes on the state committees."[32]

Steadily provoked by that and other developments of the previous year, Byrnes's deepest fears about the current direction of his party rose to the surface during consideration of the Wagner–Van Nuys Anti-Lynching Bill of 1938. Carrying out a prior agreement with Walter White, executive secretary of the NAACP, Senate Majority Leader Alben Barkley scheduled the antilynching bill to be the first order of Senate business in January of 1938. When he read the Senate calendar, Byrnes, as manager of the administration's controversial "Government Reorganization Bill," asked the majority leader to give his bill priority instead so it could be addressed before the pressures of an election year jeopardized its passage. He was sorry, Barkley said, but he could not make the switch unless White released him from his earlier pledge. "Barkley can't do anything," Byrnes exploded, "without talking to that nigger first." For the South Carolina senator, it seemed to be the final straw, proving that blacks were capturing his beloved party.[33]

A few days later, Byrnes stalked onto the Senate floor to deliver a biting exposition on the current state of party affairs. In "the hope of securing votes from Negroes," he announced, northern Democrats had abandoned principle to put forward a bill that could only "arouse ill-feeling between the sections, inspire race hatred in the South, and destroy the Democratic Party." "His voice tense with passion," the little senator then turned, pointed at the gallery, and shouted "angry tribute" to the black man he held responsible:

If Walter White . . . should consent to have this bill laid aside its advocates would desert it as quickly as football players unscramble when the whistle of the referee is heard. . . . Now that he has secured the balance of the voting power in so many states . . . what legislation will he next demand of the Congress . . . ? Will he demand that Congress enact legislation where white persons are entertained . . . ? Will he demand the enactment of laws providing for the supervision of elections within the States? I do not know but I know he will make other demands and that those who are willing to vote for this bill because he demands it will acquiesce in his subsequent demands.[34]

Through all sorts of difficulties on all kinds of issues, he continued, white southerners had always been the bedrock of Democratic strength. Their loyalty "has been due to the belief that when problems affecting the Negro and the very soul of the South arose, they could depend upon the Democrats of the North to rally to their support." But "Mr. President," he concluded, the chamber silenced by his candor,

> southern Democrats may as well realize now that a change has taken place.... Today 90 percent of the Negroes of the North ... are voting for Democratic candidates.... The Negro has not only come into the Democratic Party, but the Negro has come into control of the Democratic Party.... Today the South may just as well know that ... it has been deserted by the Democrats of the North.

By the time he finished, Byrnes had stopped just short of declaring war on the national party.[35]

Although he correctly foresaw long-range trends in racial policy, Byrnes soon realized that he had overstated at least the immediate danger in the Democratic party. Under his threat to filibuster "until the year 2038" and the president's lifting nary a finger to stop him, the supporters of the Wagner–Van Nuys bill withdrew it as they had each of its predecessors, proving, said one political veteran, that you still had to see southerners like Byrnes "if you want to get anywhere in the Senate." That fact, nodded William O. Douglas, "was the real reason why FDR soft-pedaled all racial issues."[36]

Indeed, for the next three years, the President increasingly soft-pedaled virtually all domestic reforms to muster support for his defense and foreign policies; and on that basis Byrnes gladly resumed his old place in the president's camp. From repeal of the arms embargo through adoption of Lend-Lease, marveled one New Dealer, the prodigal senator once more demonstrated himself to be "the most adroit man on the Democratic side." In helping to get the nation ready for the impending crisis, added columnist Joseph Alsop, "there are few men in Washington" to whom the president "owes more than Mr. Byrnes." Despite vigorous opposition from the NAACP, Roosevelt repaid Byrnes with an appointment to the U. S. Supreme Court in the summer of 1941. Maybe, the new justice must have thought to himself, there was still hope for traditional white southerners in the party of their fathers. But despite the lull in intraparty conflict it was increasingly clear that the white South had to show liberal movement on the race question if it hoped to avoid being further isolated from the nation at large.[37]

Perhaps with that in mind, Justice Byrnes, when removed from the pressures of electoral politics, took positions that may have surprised some of his liberal critics. As he conducted some of his legal research, the justice seemed genuinely shocked to discover that South Carolina "negroes have not served as Jurors ... for a number of years." In *Hill v. Texas*, Byrnes responded by voting with a unanimous court to overturn the conviction of a black man tried under those conditions. Reacting to a similar case not brought before the Court, he privately asked the governor of Virginia to commute the death sentence of a black murderer who had been misled into waiving his right to a jury trial. Meanwhile, Byrnes also wrote two majority opinions upholding the rights of black defendants. The first ruled a Georgia sharecropping law to be in violation of the Thirteenth Amendment and the Federal Anti-Peonage Act of 1867. The second reversed the conviction in an interracial murder case from Texas because of the strong-arm tactics that had been used by white authorities to extract a confession from a black defendant. Speaking for the Court, Byrnes said, "the effect of moving an ignorant Negro by night and day to strange towns, telling him of threats of mob violence, and questioning him continuously" made the "confession" a clear "product of coercion" as well as a flagrant "denial of due process." Such reasoning, the justice later told the Illinois Bar Association, was grounded in the belief that "we must by all means avoid developing a Hitler-like contempt for other groups and creeds and races." Perhaps Byrnes was also trying to say it was both possible and desirable for southerners to promote some type of progress on the "race question" without constant prodding from people outside the region.[38]

At any rate, the justice's move back toward a more moderate racial position probably made it a bit easier for Roosevelt to elevate him to politically more sensitive posts during World War II. Restless on the Court after Pearl Harbor, Byrnes gladly resigned to accept a presidential appointment as director of Economic Stabilization in October 1942 from whence he moved on to become director of War Mobilization in May 1943. In that latter job, Byrnes was given general supervision of virtually all phases of the domestic war effort. Informally known as the "Assistant President," he exercised, in the words of the *New York Times*, "more power than any non-President in American history." While steering clear of most racial issues, he also performed his duties well enough to thrust himself into the middle of vice-presidential speculation for 1944.[39]

Certainly there was ample cause for the speculation. The president's apparent first choice as running mate, Secretary of State Cordell Hull, firmly declined to run. The incumbent vice-president, Henry Wallace, was generally thought to be too liberal and too unpopular with the mainstream of the party to go on the ticket again. Justice William O. Douglas, Senator Harry Truman, and the others mentioned for the post were all "dark horses" clearly less experienced than Byrnes. Adding fuel to the speculation was the president himself, who frequently told his top aides that Byrnes was the best qualified for the job "because he knows more about government than anyone else around here." Via Harry Hopkins, the president's close friend, the word leaked to Byrnes that FDR "would rather have me on the ticket in 1944 than anyone else." The *Washington Post* concluded that Byrnes had "vaulted into the position of front runner" by the dawn of the election summer.[40]

A cautious man, Byrnes listened to the rumors warily. As a traditional southerner to the right of his party's center, he knew he would draw opposition from blacks, liberals, and organized labor. He also knew that the White House was simultaneously floating trial balloons on behalf of other candidates and that the wily president's flattering words had always fallen just short of an official endorsement. Nonetheless, Byrnes was powerfully attracted by what he heard. One "day I have dreamed for," he wrote a friend, "is when some man from the South can be nominated as President or Vice-President with hope of success." Having "no false modesty," he conceded, "I would even be willing to admit that. . . . I would be as well qualified as other individuals" to make the attempt when the proper time presented itself. As he rode the crest of his career and kept receiving words of praise from a wartime president almost assured of reelection, Byrnes began to think that if his time had ever come it was now. Probing for more information, Byrnes learned from Hopkins that FDR "wanted him to run . . . and would be the happiest man around here if he won," but, of course, could not say so in public because of his affection for other men who wanted the job. That would be all right, Byrnes thought to himself, as long as FDR did not endorse anyone else. Based on personal assurances from the president that he would not express a "preference for any candidate" but would rather leave the selection completely open to the delegates, Byrnes decided to take the plunge and by the second week of July was unofficially running for the vice-presidential nomination "like a house afire."[41]

The more Byrnes's candidacy came into the open, however, the more his racial history came back to haunt him. Throughout 1944, South Carolina made national news with its angry protest against the Supreme Court's decision to outlaw the "white primary." Further agitated by the movement to incorporate planks for abolition of the poll tax and endorsement of an antilynching law into the Democratic platform, many Palmetto state delegates openly threatened not to support the national ticket if they had to acquiesce in such measures demanded by the "coalition of city bosses, CIO, and Negroes which has been cooperating to promote dictatorship, socialism, and other un-Americanisms." In turn, those embarrassing reminders of where many southerners stood seemed to intensify the inevitable black opposition to Byrnes's candidacy. Carrying with him a documented history of the positions Byrnes had taken on racial questions, Walter White told Democratic officials that a southerner on the ticket would mean they "could kiss the Negro vote good-bye." "Negroes," affirmed a huge placard hanging on the convention hall in Chicago, "will not support a ticket with Byrnes." Armed with that intelligence, "Boss" Edward Flynn of New York warned the president that a Byrnes nomination would cost the party enough black votes to lose the critical Empire State in the general election. Other northern mayors gave similar warnings. In response, FDR privately admitted a week before the convention opened that, indeed, "the negro question was acute."[42]

Aware of the developing storm, Byrnes defended himself as best he could. From January through June, he kept publicly silent during the controversies over the white primary, the poll tax, and the antilynching law. Conveniently, he found excuses not to participate in the South Carolina Democratic Convention or associate himself in any way with the white militants back home. In the six days prior to the national convention, he spoke to Roosevelt on at least three occasions, each time countering the racial arguments against his candidacy. "Mr. President," he complained, "all I heard around this White House for the last week is negro. I wonder if anybody ever thinks about the white people." "You can't tell me," he argued, "that the fact you have a Southerner on the ticket that those negro people are going to turn against Mrs. Roosevelt and the President who has done more for them than anybody else in the history of the world." And besides, he said in making a tantalizing proposal, "If Mr. Wallace or Mr. Douglas says he is against the poll tax that is not news and they can not change the views of Southerners. But if I say I am against the poll tax, that means something."[43]

Perhaps it would have but the offer proved to be too little too late. A few days earlier FDR had privately concluded "that a southerner could not go on the ticket" because it "would cost heavily in those states with a large negro population." Nothing Byrnes said in the last days before the convention seemed to change his mind. Still, it was difficult for the president to deflate the ambitions of an extremely valuable lieutenant and risk alienating his southern base of support, especially when he knew that he bore a great responsibility for getting Byrnes interested in the nomination in the first place. Unwilling or unable to tell Byrnes he was now unacceptable, the best Roosevelt could do was to pass along some weak reminders that a lot of party officials were worried about his poor standing among blacks and organized labor. Apparently hoping the whole mess would somehow resolve itself without the President soiling his hands, FDR let Byrnes go to Chicago to line up delegates under renewed assurances that he was happy for the Carolinian to run in what he promised again would be an open contest for the vice-presidential nomination.[44]

But when it became clear on the first day of the convention that lack of an explicit presidential directive to the contrary might actually allow Byrnes to win, Roosevelt was finally forced to show his hand. He told Party Chairman Robert Hannegan that before the Carolinian could be put on the ticket his name would have to be "cleared" with Sidney Hillman, the chairman of the CIO's Political Action Committee and a man known to have little affection for Byrnes. The veto, said FDR quietly, was proof that Byrnes had become a "political liability." He wanted Senator Harry Truman as his running mate instead. "The words 'political liability,' " said one of Byrnes's closest friends, "knocked JFB cold. His face flushed and it was apparent that this statement from the man he has served politically and faithfully cut him to the quick." Immediately, Byrnes withdrew his name from consideration "in deference to the wishes of the President." The next day, Truman became the nominee and, nine months later, the president.[45]

Many writers seized on Hillman's dramatic veto as the reason for Byrnes's rejection and surely the opposition of organized labor was a critical factor, but while recognizing its impact Byrnes seemed to think that "the negro issue" was more important. "When (Ed) Flynn insisted that I would lose 200,000 Negro votes in New York," he concluded, "it was too much to expect that President Roosevelt should continue to urge my nomination." Although having different reactions to his defeat, Byrnes's conservative and liberal friends alike seemed to agree that race was the greater obstacle in his quest for the nomination. Accordingly, Hillman may well have been the convenient instrument for, rather than the underlying cause of, Byrnes's rejection. At any rate, understanding did little to cushion the blow for, in many ways, it was a verdict on his whole career. It also shattered any final hopes he had of ever achieving his fondest dream: to be both a loyal defender of white southern interests and a fully accepted leader of the nation at large. Indeed, the Charleston *News and Courier* wondered whether that was not a fate shared by the South as a whole. Since "every public man in South Carolina holds exactly the same opinion about the race question that Byrnes holds," it editorialized, "are not all Carolinians . . . in the boat with Byrnes?" "It was a hell of a note," Byrnes said with that thought in mind, "that a Southerner could not get a place on the Democratic ticket."[46]

Off and on, that melancholy note seemed to ring in Byrnes's ears for the rest of his life. In the weeks after the convention, he steadily distanced himself from FDR before finally resigning as "Assistant President" ahead of schedule in March 1945. After Roosevelt's death, Byrnes thought Truman might return the party to its southern roots and, accordingly, was eager to serve as the new president's secretary of state, a post he held from July 1945 to January, 1947. But when Truman embraced civil rights initiatives, the final die was cast. Breaking with his former chief's domestic policies in 1949, Byrnes was elected governor of South Carolina in 1950. There, for the next four years, he used all of the accumulated prestige and influence of his celebrated career in the efforts to resist desegregation, dump Truman, and create a politically independent South. Even after he left public office in 1955, the aging warrior continued to rail against the Supreme Court, denounce the measures of the "Second Reconstruction," and oppose every Democratic presidential candidate. Active until incapacitated by illness in 1969, Byrnes died in 1972, most commonly remembered, if at all, as "an embittered apostate" who fought a rearguard action for segregation and against the party he had once served so well.[47]

In large measure, that fate was foreshadowed by the way Byrnes addressed racial questions from 1908 to 1944. Embracing white supremacy as "the very soul of the South," he could never bring himself to see the terrible toll it took on blacks or the way it inevitably prevented any lasting solutions to the region's woes. Preferring instead to view Jim Crow as the only possible terms of a southern "racial peace," he never hesitated to defend it vigorously when he perceived a serious outside threat. While pursuing that course, he did much to earn the contempt of black leaders such as Walter White who branded his career as "consistent in only one respect—that of unrelenting, skilled... opposition to every measure sought by Negroes," based on a "conviction that they should be content to submit meekly to whatever status they were assigned by white men." Because he stayed on that course long after it ceased to be publicly acceptable in the nation at large, Byrnes contributed to the persistence of racial discrimination and bore considerable responsibility for driving himself away from the America he so wanted to lead.[48]

And yet, one of Byrnes's liberal friends hastened to add, "I just hope he won't be solely remembered for this because most of his life was much better than that." Never a demagogue in the classic mold of Cole Blease, he resisted northern liberals but he also resisted southern race-baiters. From editor and solicitor to Senate candidate and Supreme Court justice, there were many times when he spoke admirably, perhaps courageously, on behalf of a certain amount of paternalistic consideration and fair play for blacks within the Jim Crow system. Coupled with the important, constructive roles he played in addressing many problems under Wilson and Roosevelt, Byrnes's behavior lent credence to the many people who regarded Byrnes as a southern "liberal."[49]

Speaking on his own behalf, Byrnes liked to call himself "a conservative liberal" trying to restrain the extremists of the right and left. "Fellows on the extreme get into ditches oftenest and quickest," he once chuckled. "Damn if you don't ride longer if you continue in the middle." If one defined "conservative liberal" as a segregationist of the relatively more humane variety, then Byrnes's self-portrait was reasonably accurate. Certainly, while staying clear of southern Negrophobes in one ditch and northern race reformers in the other, he deftly steered his way along a middle road that enabled him to enjoy political success in the South and the nation for most of his life. But eventually time ran out on his middle road as it gradually narrowed to a fork. When forced to choose between the path of his native region and that of America at large, Byrnes went the way of countless southerners before him.[50]

Whatever one chose to call him, Byrnes's exceptional talent took him to higher positions than any other southern politician of his day. Perhaps he embodied the best that Dixie's political system could produce. Because of the opportunity that status gave him, one can surely fault Byrnes for not trying to lead his people faster and farther on race than he did. "It is the tragedy of the South," said one historian of such a mind:

> that Byrnes's racial liberalism triumphed too late... and when his kind of liberalism finally came into power, it offered so little. It is Byrnes's personal tragedy that he, who almost alone of southern politicians had the expertise and prestige to lead his

people toward a racial solution for the second half of the twentieth century, thought it sufficient to encourage them to be content with a solution that had hardly been adequate for the 1890's.[51]

But given the weight of the southern past and the special pressures it exerted on those who needed popular approval for success, was it reasonable to think that Byrnes could have successfully navigated a racial course much more liberal than the one he chose? While wishing it were otherwise, one weary Atlanta newspaper editor had his doubts. Out of a "melancholy deterioration" in race relations, said Ralph McGill, there

> came a Greek tragedy that never left the South's political stage. . . . The South has continued to send a number of really able men to Congress. Once there they invariably found themselves caught up in a dilemma which continually confronted them with the need to compromise along the lines laid down by their forebears. To survive politically they were required to conform to the mores of their states. They could never fully attain the national respect and stature for which they were so admirably equipped. The most excellent of these were fully competent to have become Presidents of their country. Yet, their states demanded of them that they . . . publicly, and with vigor, go counter to the mainstream of national life and values; and proclaim, instead, the virtues of white supremacy . . . including the evils and injustices so plainly seen and condemned by national and world judgement. The most able and honorable of them were condemned to be bound to a Prometheus rock, or like Sisyphus, eternally to push an unrewarding stone up the hills of bitterness.

As one who carried that stone, it was Byrnes's triumph that he went as far as he did. It was his tragedy that he went no farther and perhaps could not have done so even if he had tried.[52]

NOTES

1. Frank B. Freidel, "Almost a President," *The New Republic* 139 (December 15, 1958): 26–27. For a more detailed treatment of Byrnes's early years and his congressional career, see Winfred B. Moore, Jr., "James F. Byrnes: The Road to Politics, 1882–1910," *South Carolina Historical Magazine* 84 (April 1983): 72–88, and the same writer's "New South Statesman: The Political Career of James F. Byrnes, 1911–1941." (Ph.D. diss., Duke University, 1975).

2. For excellent discussions of race in the thought of the "progressive" South, see Jack T. Kirby, *Darkness at the Dawning: Race and Reform in the Progressive South* (Philadelphia, 1972); Bruce Clayton, *The Savage Ideal: Intolerance and Intellectual Leadership in the South, 1890–1914* (Baltimore, 1972); and, most recently, Joel Williamson, *The Crucible of Race: Black-White Relations in the American South Since Emancipation* (New York, 1984). For the New Deal era, see John T. Kneebone, *Southern Liberal Journalists and the Issue of Race, 1920–1944* (Chapel Hill, 1985).

3. Beaufort *Gazette*, October 20, 1904; Aiken *Journal and Review*, passim 1904–1908, and especially July 20, September 25, 1906.

4. Frank P. Jordan, *The Primary State* (Columbia, 1963), p. 144; Joseph Alsop and Robert Kinter, "Sly and Able," *Saturday Evening Post* 213 (July 20, 1940): 42. For a detailed analysis of this colorful district, see Orville Vernon Burton, *In My Father's House Are Many Mansions: Family and Community in Edgefield, South Carolina* (Chapel Hill, 1985).

5. Barnwell *People*, February 18, March 25, 1909; James F. Byrnes, "All in One Lifetime," (rough draft), Folder 956, James F. Byrnes Papers, Clemson University Library, South Carolina (henceforth, Byrnes Papers).

6. Aiken *Journal and Review*, August 13, October 12, 1909; Alsop and Kinter, "Sly and Able," p. 44.

7. Barnwell *People*, December 3, 10, 1908; March 25, April 1, 1909; "Biographical Sketch of James F. Byrnes," James F. Byrnes Papers, University of South Carolina Archives, Columbia, South Carolina; Edgar Brown to Byrnes, October 6, 1941, Folder 109 (4), Byrnes Papers; Aiken *Journal and Review*, August 3, 1909.

8. Beaufort *Gazette*, June 28, July 5, August 22, 1912; Barnwell *People*, July 11, August 22, 1912; Aiken *Journal and Review*, August 16, 20, 1912.

9. "Speech at Rivers Bridge Memorial," May 4, 1916, in "Speeches 1935 and Prior, Brynes Papers; Aiken *Journal and Review*, April 8, 15, 22, August 5, 1913, May 2, 1916; Beaufort *Gazette*, April 11, 1913; Barnwell *People*, April 10, 17, August 13, 1913; *Congressional Record*, 63rd Congress, 1st Session, pp. 5571–72 (henceforth *CR*).

10. *CR*, 63rd Congress, 1st Session, pp. 42711–12; 64th Congress, 1st Session, pp. 1576–78, 1602–05; 65th Congress, 1st Session, pp. 1098–1102.

11. Idus A. Newby, *Black Carolinians: A History of Blacks in South Carolina from 1895–1968* (Columbia, 1973), pp. 157–60, 189–93; *CR*, 66th Congress, 1st Session, pp. 4303–5.

12. *CR*, 66th Congress, 1st Session, pp. 4303–5.

13. Ibid.

14. Ibid.

15. Elliot Rudwick, *W. E. B. DuBois: A Study in Minority Group Leadership* (Philadelphia, 1960), pp. 238–41; Barnwell *People*, October 16, 1919; Aiken *Standard*, October 10, 1919; Columbia *State*, October 6, 7, 1919; Aiken *Journal and Review*, October 22, 1919; *CR*, 66th Congress, 2nd Session, pp. 980–81.

16. Byrnes to W. W. Ball, January 18, 1920, William Watts Ball Papers, Perkins Library, Duke University, North Carolina (henceforth, Ball Papers).

17. *CR*, 67th Congress, 2nd Session, pp. 543–45.

18. *CR*, 68th Congress, 1st Session, pp. 1659–61; James F. Byrnes, *All in One Lifetime* (New York, 1958), pp. 38–39. In his autobiography, Byrnes claimed that he objected to the appropriation only as a favor to a northern congressman who wanted to stop it but was afraid to speak against it for fear of angering his black constituents. A political favor may have been involved, but if so, Byrnes pursued it with uncommon zeal.

19. Aiken *Journal and Review*, September 15, 1920, June 27, 1923; Greenville *News*, July 22, 1923; *Charleston News and Courier*, August 5, 1923.

20. Daniel W. Hollis, "Cole L. Blease and the Senatorial Campaign of 1924," *Proceedings of the South Carolina Historical Association* (1978): 60; Greenville *News*, August 10, 1924; Columbia *State*, August 29, 31, 1924.

21. Columbia *State*, September 3, 7, 9, 1924; Byrnes to Frank Hogan, October

13, 1937, Folder 14, Byrnes Papers; Jordan, *Primary State*, p. 69; Thomas W. Waring to W. W. Ball, September 15, 1924, Ball Papers. Blease defeated Byrnes by about 1 percent of the votes cast. On the eve of the election, a flyer was printed reminding voters that Byrnes, an Episcopalian, had been raised a Catholic before converting at the time of his marriage in 1906. Circulated by Klansmen, the flyer was "deadly poison in the Klaverns up the State" and "amazingly effective" among the broader population, said a shrewd reporter of the *Charleston News and Courier*, T. R. Waring. At the time many people thought it was a deciding factor.

22. Columbia *State*, July 8, 1930; Interview with Judge Donald Russell, October 13, 1982; "Campaign Circular," July, 1930; Byrnes to William Berguson, July 9, 1930; "Misc. 1930," Byrnes Papers.

23. Eliot Janeway, "Jimmy Byrnes," *Life* 14 (January 4, 1943): 68; Columbia *State*, June 21, July 6, 9, 10, 1930; "Radio Speech," September 8, 1930; "Speeches 1935," Byrnes Papers; Jordan, *Primary State*, p. 71; Greenville *News*, September 16, 1930. In 1930, Byrnes defeated Blease by about the same margin he had lost to him in 1924.

24. Moore, "New South Statesman," pp. 97–216, 270–89; *Washington Post*, January 3, 1934; Franklin D. Roosevelt to John G. Winant, September 8, 1934, Official File 716-B, Franklin Delano Roosevelt Papers, Roosevelt Library, Hyde Park, New York, (henceforth FDR Papers); *Sphere* (March 1934), in Byrnes Papers; George E. Mowry, *Another Look at the Twentieth Century South* (Baton Rouge, 1973), p. 55.

25. CR 74th Congress, 1st Session, pp. 6534–46; Byrnes to K. G. Finley, March 23, 1936, "Legislation 1933–1941," Byrnes Papers.

26. Columbia *State*, June 11, July 7, 8, 1936; Yorkville *Enquirer*, July 9, 1936; Byrnes to W. P. Law, July 3, 1936, "Misc. 1936," Byrnes Papers; *Charleston News and Courier*, July 1, 3, 4, 5, 6, 1936; *Time* 27 (August 24, 1936): 22.

27. "Press Release," July, 1936, "Misc. 1936," Byrnes Papers.

28. Byrnes to Frank Lever, August 3, 1936, to W. P. Law, July 3, 1936, to J. A. Bolton, March 3, 1936, "Misc. 1936," Byrnes Papers.

29. Columbia *State*, June 11, July 7, 8, 1936; Yorkville *Enquirer*, July 9, 1936; Greenville *News*, July 12, 1936; "Charleston Speech," n.d. 1936, "Misc. 1936," Byrnes Papers; Jordan, *Primary State*, pp. 73–74.

30. Byrnes to B. M. Baruch, December 12, 1936, Bernard M. Baruch Papers, Princeton University Library, New Jersey; A. G. Kennedy to Byrnes, June 5, 1937, Harry M. Arthur to Byrnes, June 26, 1937, "Misc. 1937," Byrnes to L. C. Wilson, October 19, 1936, Folder 1112(2), Byrnes Papers. For his state's adverse reaction to the domestic policies of Roosevelt's second administration, see Jack I. Hayes, Jr., "South Carolina and the New Deal, 1932–1938," (Ph.D. diss., University of South Carolina, 1973).

31. Byrnes to C. L. Cobb, August 4, 1938, "Misc. 1938," Byrnes to "Sir," August 3, 1937, Folder 26, Byrnes to Wilton E. Hall, December 13, 1938, "Misc. 1938," Byrnes papers.

32. Sidney Baldwin, *Poverty and Politics: The Rise and Decline of the Farm Security Administration* (Chapel Hill, 1968), pp. 305–7; Byrnes to Will Alexander, October 9, 27, 1937, "Misc. 1937," Byrnes Papers; Will Alexander, *Columbia Oral History Collection*, Columbia University Library, New York, pp. 606–7.

33. *Time* 30 (November 29, 1937): 10–12, (December 6, 1937): 15, (December

27, 1937): 9–10; Byrnes to George Warren, August 23, 1943, Folder 136 (1), Byrnes Papers; Harvard Sitkoff, *A New Deal for Blacks* (New York, 1978), p. 296.

34. *Time* 31 (January 24, 1938): 8–9; *CR*, 75th Congress, 2nd Session, pp. 305–10.

35. Ibid.

36. Allen Michie and Frank Rhylick, *Dixie Demagogues* (New York, 1949), pp. 82, 68; William O. Douglass, *Go East Young Man* (New York, 1974), p. 414.

37. Harold L. Ickes, *The Secret Diary of Harold L. Ickes*, 3 vols., *The Gathering Clouds, 1939–1941* (New York, 1954), 3: 417; New York *Herald-Tribune*, February 4, 1941; Walter White to Eleanor Roosevelt, April 17, 1941, to Franklin Roosevelt, June 12, 1941, OF 41-A, Roosevelt Papers; Byrnes, *Lifetime*, pp. 129–31.

38. Byrnes to Brantley Harvey, April 29, 1942; Harvey to Byrnes, May 5, 1942, Folder 1261; Byrnes to James H. Price, January 5, 1942, Folder 1279, Byrnes Papers; *New York Times*, January 13, 1942; *Taylor v. Georgia*, 315 U.S. 25 (1942); *Ward v. Texas*, 316 U.S. 547, 555 (1942); "The Lawyer in Wartime," June 4, 1942, "Speeches," Byrnes Papers. For an excellent, brief analysis of Byrnes's service on the Court, see Walter F. Murphy, "James F. Byrnes," in *The Justices of the United States Supreme Court, 1789–1969: Their Lives and Opinions*, 4 vols., ed. Leon Friedman and Fred L. Israel (New York, 1969), 4:2517–40.

39. *New York Times*, October 6, 1942. For a good discussion of Byrnes's performance at OES and OWM, see John W. Partin, "Assistant President for the Home Front: James F. Byrnes and World War II," (Ph.D. diss., University of Florida, 1977).

40. John W. Partin, "Roosevelt, Byrnes, and the 1944 Vice-Presidential Nomination," *Historian* 42 (November 1979): 85–100; Walter Brown, unpublished diary, July 11, 1944, Folder 74 (1), Byrnes Papers; Byrnes, *Lifetime*, pp. 219–20; *Washington Post*, July 18, 1944.

41. Byrnes to J. C. Derieux, August 2, 1940, to J. H. Johnson, May 14, 1940, Folder 72 (1), Transcript of Byrnes's telephone conversation with Roosevelt, July 14, 1944, Brown Diary, July 12, 15, 16, 1944, Folder 74 (1), Byrnes Papers.

42. Robert A. Garson, *The Democratic Party and the Politics of Sectionalism, 1941–1948* (Baton Rouge, 1974), pp. 94–130; Anthony Barry Miller, "Palmetto Politician: The Early Political Career of Olin D. Johnston, 1896–1945," (Ph.D. diss., University of North Carolina, 1976), pp. 418–47; Columbia *State*, June 4, July 20, 1944; Walter White, *A Man Called White* (New York, 1948), pp. 266–67; Walter Brown, Diary, July 11, 1944, Folder 74 (1), Byrnes Papers.

43. Leon Harris to Byrnes, May 15, 1944, Byrnes to Jesse Boyd, May 15, 1944, Folder 140 (2), Walter Brown, Diary, July 12, 1944, Folder 74 (1), Byrnes Papers.

44. Brown, Diary, July 12–19, 1944, Transcript of Byrnes's conversation with Roosevelt, July 14, 18, 1944, Folder 74 (1), Byrnes Papers.

45. Ibid. Partin, "Roosevelt, Byrnes and the 1944 Vice-Presidential Nomination," pp. 85–100. All the byzantine maneuvers behind the vice-presidential race are too complicated to be retold here in any great detail. Briefly, FDR made many conflicting statements boosting many different candidates, especially Wallace, the darling of the northern liberals, and Byrnes, the hero of the southern conservatives. While stroking their respective constituencies and perhaps wanting to give them some time to prove him wrong, however, the president probably thought all along that it would be both politically desirable and necessary to have a moderate, compromise choice like Tru-

man on the ticket. Although the president's reasoning was understandable, the way he pursued it was unnecessarily confusing for the party and unnecessarily cruel to the other candidates involved. Certainly it was for Byrnes who, before the president's intervention, was commonly thought to have lined up seven to eight hundred delegates behind his nomination and who knew Hannegan had already had "Roosevelt-Byrnes" placards printed in anticipation of that event. For a detailed analysis, see the Partin article.

46. Byrnes, *Lifetime*, p. 230; Byrnes to Clint Graydon, July 29, 1944, Brown, Diary, July 12, 1944, Folder 74 (1), Byrnes Papers; Harold Ickes, Diary, July 16, August 11, 1944, Harold L. Ickes Papers, Library of Congress; Henry Wallace, Diary, July 10, 13, 1944, Henry A. Wallace Papers, Columbia University Library, New York; Samuel I. Roseman, *Working with Roosevelt* (New York, 1952), pp. 448–51; *Charleston News and Courier*, July 25, 1944.

47. On Byrnes as secretary of state, see George Curry, "James F. Byrnes," in *The American Secretaries of State and their Diplomacy*, 20 vols., ed. Robert Ferrell and Samuel F. Bemis (New York, 1965), 14: 87–317; Patricia D. Ward, *Threat of Peace: James F. Byrnes and the Council of Foreign Ministers, 1945–1946* (Kent, Ohio, 1979); and especially Robert L. Messer's well written and highly perceptive *The End of An Alliance: James F. Byrnes, Roosevelt, Truman and the Origins of the Cold War* (Chapel Hill, 1982). Unfortunately, the best available treatment of Byrnes's later years is still his inadequate autobiography. "Embittered apostate" is the oft-quoted characterization made by Adlai Stevenson in 1952. In presidential races from 1952 through 1968, Byrnes endorsed, respectively, Dwight Eisenhower, Harry Byrd, Richard Nixon, Barry Goldwater, and, again, Nixon.

48. White, *A Man Called White*, p. 267.

49. Chester Bowles, *Columbia Oral History Collection*, Columbia University Library, New York, pp. 79–80.

50. Byrnes, *Lifetime*, p. 105; James McNaughton to James McConaugh, January 2, 1943, to Don Birmingham, September 6, 1945, James McNaughton Papers, Harry Truman Library, Independence, Missouri.

51. Murphy, "Byrnes," p. 2533.

52. Ralph McGill, *The South and the Southerner* (Boston, 1959), pp. 220–21.

A Last Gasp: Clyde R. Hoey and the Twilight of Racial Segregation, 1945–1954

SUSAN TUCKER HATCHER

"A high-souled gentleman, deep-eyed in the most noble traditions of the South." So a fellow North Carolinian described Clyde Roark Hoey on the eve of his election to the United States Senate in 1944. Wearing a swallowtail coat adorned with a red flower, striped trousers, winged collar, high-topped shoes, and a gray fedora atop long white hair, this sixty-seven-year-old, near physical prototype of the Civil War era arrived in the Washington of the atomic age. Along with his antique appearance, courtly manners, and flowery oratory, Hoey brought the climate of the antebellum South: its philosophy, its passion, and its anxieties. For his constituents this gentleman of the old southern school represented the familiar, though dying order and seemed to buffer them from confusion. Hoey's was a world, however, which failed to speak to the upheaval and change of post World War II America. This chapter will examine Hoey's attempt to sustain the southern myth throughout his political career. The focus of the myth that informed his life centered on questions of race and rights—in his view much the most ominous of all the postwar issues he faced in the Senate.

In view of his personal history, Hoey seems destined to have perpetuated white supremacy and the southern way of life. A first generation North Carolinian, he was born in Shelby, a pleasant small town in the foothills of North Carolina, on December 11, 1877. His paternal ancestors, originally O'Hugheys, had immigrated from Ireland probably in the 1700s and had changed their surname to Hoey (pronounced Hooey). His grandfather was a South Carolina planter with large slave holdings, his father was a Confederate captain, and two uncles died for the Rebel Cause, all of which intensified Hoey's reverence for the "brave soldiery of the Sixties" and his attachment to the paternalism of the Old South.[1]

Family not only helped to shape Hoey's social philosophy but his political career as well. The "Shelby Dynasty," essentially a family alliance, included, in addition to Hoey, his brother-in-law former governor O. Max Gardner, and also Gardner's father-in-law Judge James L. Webb and James's brother Judge E. Yates Webb. These men shared an interest in state and local politics, and they assisted one another in their political ambitions. It was Gardner's sister, Bess, whom Hoey married. Born in the same town, Bess and Clyde went to school together, and according to his account he became seriously interested in her when he was only twelve. But they waited nine years to marry. He did not propose until he had passed the bar examination and explained, "I began practicing law by persuading my intended wife to marry me." They had three children: Clyde Roark, Jr., Charles Aycock, and Isabel Young.[2]

In addition to family, religion and oratory were great forces in Hoey's life. Besides strongly contributing to his demeanor and molding his character, they were instruments through which he exerted his greatest influence on others. Deeply religious, but not sanctimonious, Hoey had something of the Methodist backwoods preacher about him. The old-time religion, rather than the social gospel, appealed to him. His mother had guided him to his early interest in the church, which Hoey joined at the age of nine. After teaching a young couples class when he was nineteen and serving as Superintendent of Sunday School, he helped organize a men's Bible class and to teach it for thirty-one years. As governor and as senator, Hoey regularly attended church and frequently taught Sunday School in Shelby, Raleigh, or Washington. When a black constituent impunged his Christianity because of his racial stand, Hoey seemed to see no connection.[3]

Widely known as the "silver-tongued orator," Hoey could hold an audience spellbound. One friend commented, "when he got through you weren't sure what he had said, but it was beautiful." (No doubt this same gift of eloquence helped earn him his reputation as a ladies' man.) He spoke usually without notes, and often extemporaneously, ready at all times to begin and end a speech to the timed second. His speeches nearly always included verses from the Bible, the book that influenced him the most, and his rendition of the Twenty-third Psalm, his favorite, caused a listener to pronounce it "sublime." He admired the language and diction of the Bible, and at least one admirer said, "He spoke with a rhythm that was biblical in its beauty and . . . closely akin to music." His favorite ending to a speech was the last stanza of "My Country 'Tis of Thee." Besides evoking God and country, Hoey's ability to turn phrases, twit opponents, and tell funny stories put him in demand as a public speaker. Once when asked what he had told a group, he replied with a smile, "Nothing that I . . . haven't said a thousand times before. But they were happy."[4]

Hoey, like many of his generation, was largely self-educated. The family's uncertain economic situation forced him to leave school at the end of the fifth grade. His only other formal schooling, three months at the University of North Carolina where he completed a two-year law course, occurred during the summer of 1899. But before that, at age sixteen, he had purchased the county newspaper, made it a thriving concern, and used it to expound his beliefs in righteousness, the glory of the past, and the Democratic party.

Journalism led him into politics. In 1899 he ran for the legislature to help recapture it from a coalition of Republicans and Populists. The fact that he first ran for political office in the days when, in his words, the "Negro element was unrestrained," reinforced his commitment to separation of the races. "The whole state was ablaze" with the campaign for white supremacy, as he was later to recall. He was elected before reaching his majority to become the youngest member of the House. In the 1899 session he spoke in favor of "disfranchising all the Negroes possible."[5]

Hoey won reelection in 1900 in a campaign of support for a constitutional amendment providing for a literacy test and a poll-tax requirement for voting. Two years later he noted in an editorial that the Democrats had made substantial gains as a result of the poll tax which kept many black Republicans from the polls. After two terms in the North Carolina House, Hoey moved on to the state Senate where he served a single term.[6]

Fifteen years were to elapse before Hoey again held elective office. In the interim, he built a considerable reputation as a trial lawyer. In 1919 when the Ninth District seat in Congress became available in the midst of a term, Hoey ran and won. During his brief incumbency, he voted the southern party line. He cast his first vote in 1920 along with a bloc of southern members who were solidly against a bill to increase the pensions of Union soldiers and their widows. When Congressman George Tinkham of Massachusetts introduced a resolution to reduce the representation of the South (in accordance with the Fourteenth Amendment) because of Negro disfranchisement, Hoey ridiculed its sponsor, suggesting that Tinkham's very name revealed the flawed character of one "ambitious to tinker with so vital a matter as suffrage in the South." He called Tinkham a "South-hating Republican" and pointed out that representation to Congress "had always been based on population and not on voting strength." Hoey was not sorry to leave Washington. As a Democratic newcomer in a Republican-controlled House, he had been able to accomplish little or nothing. Out of office he remained a party leader and active state politician, one who campaigned faithfully in every election for the Democratic slate.[7]

In 1936 Hoey won the governorship in what was to be remembered as one of the bitterest primary fights in state politics. His opponent accused him of being the machine candidate, lukewarm on Roosevelt's New Deal, and against repeal of the state sales tax. All this was true. Afterwards, there was some question that Hoey owed his victory to abuse in the use of absentee ballots, though this was never proved. This is not to say that Hoey personally participated (he did not have to), but many honorable men were the beneficiaries of very corrupt political practices.[8]

As governor, Hoey faced the difficult task of uniting the democratic factions in a program to "dig out of the Depression." In truth, he mostly put into operation in the state, programs mandated and paid for by the federal government. No matter, he went out of office four years later, according to an editorial in the *Greensboro Daily News*, the most popular governor within memory demonstrating what was surely his greatest talent—astuteness in dealing with people. More than any of his predecessors, Hoey made state government accessible to the people, either by traveling to them or by receiving them in his office. To state Democrats of a more moderate stripe, Governor Hoey with his outmoded views had set back for many years the progressive cause in North Carolina. To the state's Negroes, Hoey seemed to be "in their corner," while continuing to foster a "climate" that encouraged North Carolinians to preserve segregation. He supported Negroes in the field of education but only so long as they conformed to the status quo. Except for lynchings, Negro life in North Carolina, as one reminisced, was not much better than in Mississippi, Alabama, and Georgia.[9]

Long before Hoey reached the governorship, his political philosophy was firmly established. Ever mindful of the South's agrarian roots, Hoey defended the political, economic, and social philosophy as well as the specific issue of segregation which was the southern position. Southern senators, he asserted, were particularly qualified as guardians of the American way of life. To him, their region had always been "typically American" and "its rarefied democratic atmosphere" did not breed communism or other subversive ideas.[10]

He claimed to be a "Democrat after the traditions of Jefferson, Jackson, and Cleveland, and Wilson," but he was far from believing in the "leveling" ideas of Jefferson. Hoey also saw the South as a bulwark against another potential danger—the growth of federal power—which could "threaten the very existence of the Republic and our free institutions." The government, he thought, ought not to attempt what private enterprise was willing and able to do, and it could not be run different from private business with any hope of permanent success.[11]

Hoey became most impassioned, however, when he expounded on the peculiarly southern interpretation of civil rights and its corollary, the doctrine of states' rights. He warned against the possible destruction of "our civilization" by radicals in pursuit of their concepts of race relations. Whites outside the South might not understand the need for segregation, he conceded, but southerners knew that the separation of the races was essential for social peace and harmony. He was equally convinced that the North Carolina constitutional amendment disfranchising Negroes (on which he had campaigned for the State House) had brought "good results" for the state.

Segregation of Negroes, he contended, was not discrimination against them; it did not "in any way interfere with their success." On the contrary, it was advantageous to both races, since separate facilities provided an equal chance for both to pursue their goals separately. Both races, Hoey insisted, felt freer, happier, and more at home and better satisfied mingling with their own kind than they would feel associating with one another in the same schools and churches and in society at large. Furthermore, he was convinced that any attempt by the federal government to change the southern racial arrangement would encroach upon states' rights and would amount to "punishing the Southern States because of the customs of our people." Such an attempt would also violate a basic human right: "The highest right of man is the right of association."[12]

This was the philosophy Clyde R. Hoey took to the Senate in January 1945. World War II was approaching its end, and the Senate along with the nation was about to turn its attention from winning the war to winning the peace. On the part of Americans and their allies, World War II was presumably a war against racism, at least as manifested in Nazi Germany. Inevitably the war gave a stimulus to the movement against racism in the United States as well. That, along with an expanding black middle class with raised expectations who lived in a consumer culture coalesced to fuel the civil rights revolution in the decade following the war.

Democratic and Republican politicians took up the cause, and both major parties included antidiscrimination planks in their platforms of 1944, 1948, and 1952. In 1945 and later, President Truman urged action upon Congress, which eventually responded with a series of bills. The federal courts also handed down antidiscrimination rulings, culminating in the historic *Brown v. Topeka* decision of 1954.

Hoey vehemently opposed any efforts by the president, Congress, and the courts to secure more rights for blacks. "We are going to battle with this crowd . . . to the finish," he vowed, and regardless of the outcome, "they will certainly know they have been in a fight. . . . " Hoey had reason to feel at ease with his views in the Senate, since it was under the control of fellow southerners. Of the ninety-six senators, fifty-six were Democrats, and among these the southern Democrats provided most of the leadership. Not only did the chairmen of the more important committees come from the South, but so did the Senate's president pro tempore (Kenneth McKellar of Tennessee) and its majority leader (Alben Barkley of Kentucky). During Hoey's tenure in the Senate (1945–1954), its party composition was not to remain always so favorable to him and his fellow Democrats. The Republicans dominated for three and one-half years (1947–1949 and 1953–1954). Even so, given the political alliance between southern Democrats and conservative Republicans, especially on matters of race, Hoey and his cohorts were still able to exert power even during their periods of minority status.[13]

Throughout his life, Hoey never apologized for the South—its past or its present. On the contrary, to show that "we do not spend all our time down South suppressing the colored man," Hoey in a single year inserted in the *Congressional Record* at least three articles depicting achievements of Negroes in North Carolina. This state, he said, employed more Negro teachers in proportion to Negro pupil enrollment in its segregated schools than Pennsylvania, New York, Ohio, or Michigan in their integrated systems. North Carolina Negroes were not "held down." They could, and did, he contended, become doctors, lawyers, teachers, bankers, landowners, and insurance executives. How many achieved these positions, however, he neglected to say. The state's amicable race relations were due to a belief in "race integrity" and not "amalgamation," in "race pride" and not "prejudice," in "race development" and not "association." We in the South, Hoey insisted, "understand each other," and North Carolina has "about the best Negroes in the world."[14]

At least one Negro constituent concurred, and a Senate colleague said (facetiously, no doubt) that he regretted not being a North Carolina Negro. There were also other skeptics. A Negro newspaper deplored Hoey's "damnable half-truths" and declared: "North Carolina is no Negro heaven." Hoey retorted that the editorial was "incendiary" and "damaging" to good race relations.[15]

To Hoey, federal civil rights legislation of any kind was not only unnecessary but futile and even dangerous as well as unconstitutional. The South was progressing in race relations and would make still more progress if only the outside "agitators" would stop interfering in its internal affairs. In any case, he insisted, it was impossible to legislate prejudice out of people. "Repressive" legislation might lead to "dire"consequences.

On the one hand, it might encourage and strengthen the Ku Klux Klan, and on the other hand it might cause an increase in Negro assaults on white women. Hoey once summarized his constitutional argument in a hasty letter to a constituent:

I am definitely in favor of granting to the Negro every right provided for under the Constitution and [willing] to see that those rights are fully enforced [sic]. We have all of the law that is necessary. There is no law and no provision of the Constitution which denies to an individual [the right] to choose his own associates and there is no provision which makes it either necessary or essential [,] to preserve the rights of any other citizen [,] that people shall be forced to go to the same hotels, the same restaurants, the same schools, the same churches or the same public gatherings.

I believe in maintaining the broader respect [for constitutional provisions] and the ones of more vital importance which guarantees [sic] to the Negro, as well as the white person, the right to obtain an education, the right to work, the right to be protected in his home and wherever he may go to the end that he may develop and improve himself and make the largest possible contribution to the common good. I stood for all of these things while I was Governor. I am still standing for them, but I do not believe that you can bring about goodwill and good relationship between the races by passing laws and permitting agitators to stir-up strife and disorder among the races [on account] of supposed rights and privileges.[16]

Hoey identified four different groups demanding civil rights legislation: "do-gooders," "professional uplifters and downsitters," "hell-raisers," and just plain politicians. According to his definition, the do-gooders enlisted the support of women's organizations and church people "by playing up civil rights as a moral reform." The up-lifters and downsitters, including the National Association for the Advancement of Colored People (NAACP) and the Congress of Industrial Organizations, believed that breaking down all racial barriers in the South would bring the "perfect utopia" for everyone. The hell-raisers, the socialists and communists, encouraged the NAACP, and "unquestionably" were "at the bottom" of much of the civil rights agitation, for by removing racial barriers they could foment strife that would benefit their own cause.[17]

Democratic and Republican politicians were, in Hoey's view, guilty as any of the agitating groups. When both parties included civil rights planks in their party platforms, he said they were "haywire on the race business"— willing to throw the South "to the wolves" to capture the Negro vote in the North. When Republicans introduced and Democrats supported civil rights legislation, he accused his own party of having betrayed the South. The northern and western Democratic "crowd" were "whooping-it-up" to gain political advantage. As Hoey saw it, the only motive of the politicians was expediency, not principle. He considered it "most unfortunate" that the Democratic president should have given in to the agitators and called upon Congress to convert their demands into law.[18]

At the National Democratic Convention in 1948, some southerners, but not Hoey, angered by the adoption of a strong civil rights plank, walked out of the convention and formed a Dixiecrat party. Loyalty and realism kept Hoey in the party. He saw himself as a Democrat whose duty was to save the party from socialism. Walking out would not accomplish that, and it would contribute to the election of Dewey, who on civil rights was even more adverse to the South than Truman. As for Dixiecratic candidate Governor J. Strom Thurmond of South Carolina, he "of course" had no chance of winning. A vote for him would be wasted and would not help the South.[19]

When Truman nevertheless emerged victorious in November, a Hoey constituent suggested that the results indicated popular support for civil rights legislation. The senator disagreed. The president, he countered, had won election for a combination of reasons, not for just one. Furthermore, a number of state legislatures outside the South had been unwilling to take positive civil rights action. Though Californians had gone for Truman, they had defeated what Hoey considered a civil rights measure (but what was actually a proposition for the construction of low-rent housing). All of which,

Hoey said, demonstrated that people in other parts of the country, too, opposed these programs.[20]

When, in 1945, Truman appointed a committee on civil rights, Hoey denounced it as a "very extreme body," though he praised one of its members, Frank P. Graham, president of the University of North Carolina, for dissenting from its most radical proposal—to end segregation. Hoey condemned the committee's 1947 report, *To Secure These Rights*, as "so extreme that it nullified itself." Its recommendations, besides being "ill-considered," "far-afield," and mere "propaganda," magnified the bad, minimized the good, and, it followed, would damage the Negro race and destroy the existing racial harmony.[21]

Of the ten recommendations on civil rights that Truman presented to Congress on February 12, 1948, even so bitter a critic as Hoey objected to only five: those having to do with the District of Columbia, the poll tax, lynching, employment, and segregation. Truman proposed home rule for the District of Columbia, he said, so "they themselves can deal with the inequalities arising from segregation." This, of course, was not how Hoey saw it. As a member of the Committee on the District during his first year in the Senate, frequently acting as its chairman, Hoey was already on record as unequivocally opposing suffrage for the inhabitants. Besides his fear that self-government would result in the federal conduct of elections, Hoey approved heartily both the fact that Congress directed the District's affairs and the methods that Congress used. The size of the Negro population in the District of Columbia and the number and status of their jobs no doubt influenced him. Negroes already regarded Washington as a "Negro heaven," he declared. They were favored when it came to government employment, constituting 42 percent of all employees in the Washington, D.C. post office. The Eightieth, Eighty-first, and Eighty-second Congresses refused to approve home-rule bills. When, in 1952, North Carolina's junior senator, Willis Smith, moved to give Washington back to Maryland and let Washingtonians vote as Marylanders, Hoey voted with a minority (35–41) in favor of the Smith motion.[22]

Hoey opposed Truman's proposal on the poll tax, not because he feared repeal but because he feared federal control over states' rights. He had supported repeal of the poll tax as a prerequisite to voting in North Carolina long before he had become a United States senator. He had hoped other states would follow North Carolina's example in abolishing the requirement. But he opposed, as both unnecessary and dangerous, a federal law to accomplish the same end when such a bill came before the Senate in 1946. He then said that three of seven states retaining the requirement were preparing to get rid of it. It would soon disappear without federal action, and the proposal before the Senate was nothing but a "smokescreen" for federal control of the ballot box and for congressional interference in state affairs. He cooperated in a filibuster that defeated the measure when it came up in a special session in 1948. Most North Carolinians seemed to approve his stand, but the Greensboro *Daily News* editorialized that, in filibustering, he was participating in a "sit-down" strike against the public interest. In a major Senate speech of 1949 he said that talk about the poll tax disfranchising citizens was a "great bugaboo about nothing." How could the tax be an "onerous" burden when it exempted women, required only four hours of labor to pay a mere dollar or two per year, and went into the school fund to help educate the voters' own children. By 1953, having exhausted his arguments and wearied of the subject, Hoey suggested a constitutional amendment giving Congress the power to abolish the tax as the only constitutional way to resolve the question.[23]

Hoey's position on the antilynching bill was one of unequivocal opposition. He declared in 1949 that he could not "conceive of a more useless measure." All forty-eight of the states already had "drastic" laws against lynching, he argued, and these were among the best enforced of any criminal statutes. In 1947 there had been only one lynching as compared with thirteen thousand murders and twelve thousand rapes. "Why pass a law to stop a crime already extinct?" In any case, Hoey maintained, a federal law against lynching, like one against the poll tax, would violate the rights of the states. Lynching, after all, was neither an interstate act nor connected with interstate commerce. So Hoey refused to heed the urgings of a minister and member of the NAACP from his native Cleveland County who urged him to support the bill that would end "mob violence." In a radio address in 1949 Hoey said that only local officials could stop lynchings. These officials would naturally resent federal interference, and Hoey liked to quote Dr. Harry Emerson Fosdick as having said federal interference would supplant "cooperative good will by coercive ill will." He failed to add that Fosdick actually favored a federal antilynching law. To Hoey, such a law would make it more difficult than ever to obtain arrests and convictions. He was among the group who introduced in the committee an amendment to the antilynching bill to make it apply to "labor rioting and other unlawful demonstrations by picket lines" (one of his pet peeves). His purposes, he explained, was "to call attention to the absurdity of trying to legislate about mobs and the failure to include mobs involved in labor disputes.[24]

The issue of discrimination in employment had emerged during the war. As a result of great pressure President Roosevelt, on his own authority, had set up a temporary Fair Employment Practices Commission (FEPC), to prevent racial discrimination in hiring for war industries. Afterwards, congressional action would be necessary if the agency were to have a regular and lasting basis. Each time President Truman requested legislation to create a permanent Fair Employment Practices Commission in 1945, 1946, 1947, 1948, and 1950, Hoey did all he could to prevent passage. When, in 1946, the Senate Committee on Education and Labor reported favorably a bill to establish a permanent Fair Employment Practices Commission, he denounced it as "un-democratic, un-American," and "unconstitutional." In a Senate speech, his first one of any length, he predicted that the bill would create an "army of snoopers" who would go "trailing" about the country and "dragging" innocent men into court for exercising their free choice in hiring. He begged his colleagues not to "crucify America upon a cross of bureaucracy." Proponents of FEPC, angered by Hoey's stand, picketed the hotel in Washington where he stayed.[25]

In private correspondence, Hoey elaborated upon his objections to the FEPC bill. There was "no employment" and "no fairness" in it, only "discrimination against the white race." He would "vigorously oppose any law that required any person to work for another against his will, for that would be slavery." If adopted, the pending measure, rather than appeasing "this pressure crowd"—"activated by political expediency and communistic conception"—would be "feeding their appetites." It would be the forerunner of others to remove all segregation in schools, churches, hotels, and private and public assemblies. It "would set back the hands of the clock on the wheel of progress for at least twenty years."[26]

It was clear that Hoey and his southern colleagues in the Senate would use the filibuster to prevent a bill authorizing a FEPC from being adopted. Thus another perennial issue, the acceptability of the filibuster, became a part of the civil rights struggle. Hoey defended the filibuster as the only way for the minority to delay such "venal" legislation until the majority could be awakened to its dangers. When, in 1949, the House passed a set of civil rights bills, Hoey and other southern senators sponsored a filibuster in the Senate that prevented any of the measures from becoming law.[27]

In 1949 Truman and liberal Democrats in the Senate tried to eliminate the filibuster threat. The administration measure would have amended the rule relating to cloture, or limitation of debate, so as to require the approval of what Hoey called a "bare" majority—a majority of the senators present—instead of a two-thirds majority. A bitter floor fight ensued.[28]

Hoey did his part in this filibuster. Indeed, a caucus of Dixie forces scheduled him to speak early in the struggle, since they thought that his type of oratory "would have a good effect." He did not disappoint them. After reviewing at length the kinds of questions that had come before the Senate in the past for which the Founding Fathers had required the approval of two-thirds of the Senate, he challenged his colleagues to name a single important measure that would have been in the best interest of the American people and that had been defeated because of the existing cloture rule. He denied that the proposed rule change would increase the efficiency of the Senate or expedite its business. "Numerous discussions over trivial matters," not filibusters, waste the time of the Senate. Colleagues on both sides of the aisle warmly praised Hoey's speech. Democrat Spessard Holland of Florida pronounced it "an inspiration."[29]

Others were not so pleased. North Carolina NAACP leader Kelly M.

Alexander criticized Hoey for his stand and warned that southern filibusterers and their Republican supporters would lose Negro support (if, indeed, they ever had any). Hoey maintained, however, that the "best element" of Negroes realized that passage of the civil rights program would be "more detrimental than beneficial" to them. He scoffed at charges of collusion between northern Republicans and southern Democrats and contended it was simply a matter of the two groups having the same concern for preserving the integrity of the Senate and its open forum. To charges that southern Senators were delaying all legislation, he replied that Truman's civil rights proposals were the "four horseman of politics," and he blamed those "projecting this fight," that is, those advocating a change in rules. Its opponents had offered and were still willing to lay the issue aside and take up other matters. Congress, Hoey asserted, could work out a moderate civil rights program "most any time" the administration was willing to be "fair and reasonable." The administration, he observed, was irritated because we "enlisted" more Republican votes than it did. When the senator proposed setting up an FEPC similar to the World War II commission to investigate complaints of discrimination and publicize any unfavorable findings, an editor of the Raleigh *News and Observer* praised him for positive southern suggestions," not "mere negation." Mobilizing public opinion rather than legislating against discrimination in employment was "the kind of Southern thinking" deserving of "the respect of thoughtful men everywhere."[30] In an earlier editorial, however, the state's major daily newspaper had reprimanded Hoey for distorting President Truman's Civil Rights proposals in a speech before the Democratic Club of Washington.

Political observers and senators themselves widely acknowledged that a senator's position on the rules-change proposal indicated his civil rights position. The NAACP cautioned its members not to be deceived by "legalistic mumbo-jumbo": a vote against the rules change was a vote against civil rights. Hoey tried, but could not separate the two. The question of cloture, he told a constituent, was "a great deal broader than the race question." To limit debate would mean to adopt "Hitler tactics," and endanger the free enterprise system, thereby giving the "utmost satisfaction" to "subversive elements." To another correspondent he said that talk was considered obstructionist only when southern Senators tried to prevent "vicious," "punitive" and "sectional" legislation that was desired by "ultra liberals." He commented that those wishing to stop the filibuster spoke for hours at a time but never admitted that they were filibustering. He accused Republican Senator Wayne Morse of Oregon of killing more time "than all the Senate filibusters combined." Eventually Hoey admitted that the majority in Congress were in favor of doing away with all segregation, and the minority had been able to prevent that only because they had been able to filibuster.[31]

In 1949 Hoey voted with the majority—twenty-three Republicans and an equal number of Democrats from southern and border states—to overrule

Vice-President Alben W. Barkley's attempt to invoke cloture by a ruling of the chair. The vote was a "splendid" victory, Hoey claimed, but he admitted that it represented "genuine concessions" on both sides. Debate on the proposal to amend the rules ended with partisan approval of a somewhat stricter cloture provision than the 1917 rule then in force. The resulting amendment, which Senate administration leaders called "worse than useless," allowed the imposition of cloture by a vote of two-thirds of the total Senate membership: the requirement had previously been two-thirds of the membership present and voting. Twenty-nine Democrats (nineteen of them southern) joined with thirty-four Republicans to support Republican Kenneth Wherry's compromise. The record vote of sixty-three to twenty-three proved a definite setback for the administration.[32]

Hoey resisted all federal attempts at integration, whether they involved the District of Columbia fire department, veterans' hospitals, public housing, the armed forces, or the public schools. He warned his constituents that integration of the District of Columbia fire department would lower efficiency and morale of the firefighters. He filed, with the proper government agencies, a complaint regarding integration of patients at the federal hospital at Oteen, North Carolina. But he supported increased state funding for separate hospitals for the Negro race. After all, ill health among Negroes could threaten the well-being of whites throughout the nation as well as the state.

In 1949 Truman announced that the federal government would not give mortgage loan guarantees for buildings with segregation restrictions. Hoey thought this was a "vicious" policy, but he assured a constituent that it was not to be taken seriously, for enforcement in the South was certain to be lax, if not lacking. Even so, he reprimanded the president for meddling in housing and loan policy after Congress had defeated a proposal to prohibit segregation in public housing programs.[33]

As had the First World War, the advent of World War II spotlighted black problems in employment, the treatment of soldiers, and black-white tensions in the cities and at military bases. As early as 1941, Negro leader and strategist A. Philip Randolph had included integration of the armed services among his original demands when he threatened a mass march on Washington unless Roosevelt halted discrimination in defense plants. In response, Roosevelt established the Fair Employment Practices Commission. In 1948 Randolph told a Senate committee that he would advise Negroes to refuse military induction unless Truman ended segregation in the military. Truman soon issued a directive to that effect. That same year, some lawmakers tried unsuccessfully to amend the draft bill to prohibit segregation. Hoey, greatly relieved at their failure, nonetheless worried that they might try again later. In 1949 Secretary of Defense Louis Johnson aided their causes, ordering the Army, Navy, and Air Force to integrate.[34]

According to Hoey, most Negroes were as strongly opposed as he was to the social and physical association of the races. They were not agitating for integration. Hoey insisted that blacks actually preferred being put in separate companies to being "scattered out through some white group." "Not a single Negro soldier" had ever complained to Hoey about the "established custom" of segregating troops. Negroes were "more at home" with each other, had a better chance for advancement, and "took pride" in their own units. "The mere fact of all of one race in a company," if the food, clothing, and facilities were the same or equal, was hardly discrimination. "'Putting the White boys and Negro boys to sleep and eat" and socialize together could have "disastrous" results. In Hoey's scheme of things, the ultimate result might be "mongrelization of our civilization."[35]

In 1950, the Senate debated extension of the 1948 Selective Service Act. The controversy at this time centered primarily on identical Democratic and Republican amendments designed to eliminate a provision which the Armed Services Committee had approved at the insistence of Georgia's Richard Russell to allow inductees and volunteers to choose assignment to a racially "pure" rather than a mixed unit. In the Senate as a whole, however, southerners twice failed to secure the necessary votes for passage. Hoey attributed the failure to the determination of the "anti-segregation crowd." But the Korean War played an important part. Integration seemed the best way to combat the increasing waste of manpower in the overflowing all-Negro units.[36]

The Eisenhower administration continued the program of eliminating segregation in the armed forces. Though he temporized on civil rights in his State of the Union message in 1953, Eisenhower firmly declared one year later that segregation in the military and elsewhere in government was "on the way out." Republican Eisenhower, Hoey maintained, was going even further than had Democrat Truman in issuing orders to integrate—a case of Republicans trying to "out-Herod Herod for the Negro vote." The President must be depending on the "sorry" advice of his aides, Hoey charged, since he himself was ignorant of the workings of government. In any case, the Defense Department reported that, as of August 31, 1954, there were no longer any all-Negro units.[37]

Federal aid to education was one measure of the Truman Fair Deal that both Hoey and the NAACP endorsed. They parted company, however, when the NAACP urged inclusion of an antisegregation clause in any federal aid law. The fundamental purpose of all federal aid bills was to provide a minimum of schooling for all children. Hoey faced the issue for the first time when an administration-backed bill was debated in the Senate in 1945. Hoey gave the bill his enthusiastic support because he thought that the South and especially North Carolina, where the average income was lower and the per capita wealth smaller, would be the chief beneficiaries. Many southerners opposed such a measure, however, fearing that federal aid meant federal control. Hoey, however, insisted that each state controlled its share of the money. Otherwise, the federal government, as he saw it, could, and probably would, deny aid to states that operated segregated schools. To reassure constituents who feared that the government might try to take control, he reminded them that North Carolina State College at Raleigh, under the federal aid program, had been receiving federal funds for forty years without government interference. In May 1949, while taking up a bipartisan bill with specific prohibitions of federal control, Republican Senator Henry Cabot Lodge, Jr., of Massachusetts, had introduced an antisegregation amendment on behalf of the NAACP. Hoey expressed relief when only sixteen senators (all of them Republican) voted (16–65) for the measure. Two days later the Senate passed the federal aid to education bill itself by a bipartisan vote of 58 to 15 (Republicans 22–12; Democrats 36–2). But the measure bogged down, as an earlier one had done, in the House Committee on Education and Labor, largely because of the efforts of a fellow North Carolinian, Congressman Graham A. Barden, chairman of the Subcommittee on Education, who was willing "to go along with federal aid" to education but not to private or church schools.[38]

Since the early 1950s the NAACP had been instituting suits in the federal courts with the object of eliminating racial discrimination in public schools. At first, NAACP lawyers used an indirect method, attacking the most obvious inequities, such as lack of graduate and professional schools for Negroes and the low salaries of Negro teachers. Hoey took exception to the charge of discrimination against Negro teachers in the matter of salaries. He cited a comparison of Negro and white teachers' salaries in the 1947 *North Carolina Public School Bulletin*, which reported that, on the average, Negroes received $51.00 a year more than whites. Hoey failed to mention, however, that according to that article the average training of Negro teachers was higher than that of white teachers. By 1948, however, he had adjusted these salary figures downward: Negro and white teachers received equal pay, he said. In fact, in North Carolina the Negro teacher salary "caught up with the white teacher salary and passed it in 1945. . . ."[39]

The Supreme Court, however, had only begun. In 1950, in *Sweatt v. Painter*, it refrained from a final decision on the constitutionality of the "separate but equal" principle, but did indicate that clearly separate facilities would be unacceptable. The "Trumanized Supreme Court," as Hoey called it, and Attorney General Howard McGrath seemed willing to "go very much further" than before to maintain the rights of Negroes to enter state professional schools (*Sweatt v. Painter* and *McLaurin v. Oklahoma State Regents*) and to have the same facilities as whites in interstate travel (*Henderson v. United States, 1950*). The Eisenhower administration continued the trend, successfully urging, in a brief filed in 1954 with the Interstate Commerce Commission, an end to segregation on public transportation.[40]

The year 1953 saw the legal battle about segregated schools coming to a climax. In November the Department of Justice under Attorney General

Herbert Brownell filed a brief with the Supreme Court responding to questions asked of the department by the Court regarding the school-segregation cases. The brief, while seemingly supporting the position of the NAACP, did not come out "foursquare" against racial segregation in public schools, according to Hoey. Still, this action incensed him. He issued a statement denouncing Eisenhower and Brownell for exceeding their authority. "Under the Constitution," he declared, "the executive and judicial branch[es] are separate and neither should encroach upon the prerogative of the other." To North Carolina's Attorney General he voiced his concern over the prospect that the Supreme Court might "outlaw" segregation. "Certainly," he predicted, "it will impose greater problems than we have had to face heretofore."[41]

On May 12, 1954, in his seventy-seventh year, Clyde Roark Hoey died in his Senate office facing a picture of Robert E. Lee on the wall. Then Democratic Senator Lyndon B. Johnson of Texas, in his eulogy, linked these two men from different centuries who shared the same ideals. Hoey had earned the association. Not only had he spent his entire political career of five decades demonstrating his loyalty to their native region, he had devoted his life to trying to preserve Lee's South—that society of polished ways and understood relationships, especially between the races.[42]

During his decade as United States senator, Hoey had remained essentially the same person he had always been—flamboyant in dress, conventional in character, conservative in belief. He never altered his racial philosophy, sincerely believing that segregation was vital to the South, advantageous to blacks as well as whites, and preferred by both races. Nor did he modify his objective—preservation of the racial status quo. His only concession to changing times was tactical. Opposition, he cautioned, should be kept on the "high ground" of constitutional rights and states' rights free from "rancor."[43]

Superficially, Hoey seems to have been essentially the same kind of conservative as the majority of his constituents and fellow politicians. But Mayne Albright, a Raleigh attorney and self-styled "progressive" Democrat, considered Hoey even more conservative than the conservatives. "The things he stood for," Albright said in 1982, "were the things of the past, not of the future and not even of the present."[44] In that case, did the fact that the voters made Hoey the only North Carolinian ever to be state representative, state senator, governor, congressman and United States senator mean that they, like him, were more reactionary than conventional? Most white North Carolinians were probably not as zealous as Hoey in their commitment to the Old South, but they knew what they had when they voted for him time after time. They saw Clyde Hoey as a man of noble character and great personal charm who supported their familiar world of agricultural interests, fiscal conservatism, anti-unionism and, above all, racial segregation. Most southern politicians took the same position as Hoey, especially on issues of race, but what separated him from the majority of his colleagues was his great capacity to stay the course even to the point of self-deception. It not only allowed him to use the Constitution, patriotism, and religion to justify the South's racial position to others (which many of them did, too) but to convince himself it was a righteous cause.

The style was the man. Even his claw-hammer coat of the traditional southern "statesman," seen by many as an effective political prop, more accurately reflected a naiveté consistent with his principles. With his dress he provoked an image of what he sought to hold in place. As former Senate colleague, Claude Pepper of Florida, saw it, "Hoey dressed like he thought; Conservative to the point of being old-fashioned." Although Hoey possessed some characteristics of a southern demagogue of the Right—the distinctive wearing apparel, hypnotizing oratory, and folksy charm—he never fell into that category. His rhetoric, while mesmerizing—"He took the Bible and wrapped the American flag right around it"—was not inflammatory. Most of all, he lacked the aggressive personality and intent to be one. Hoey was an honest man conservative in nature and genuine in that he embodied his own region's fantasies, the region that preferred as southern writer John Crowe Ransom said "to look backwards and not forwards."[45]

Hoey *was* the southern myth. He lived it and believed it. What had been seen by his family as stubbornness and sincerity a half a century earlier became the courage of his convictions, and finally directed his life. The reality of the postwar period was upheaval and change. In Hoey's life myth obliterated the present reality, and the two became one. The fight to keep racial segregation was a battle to preserve southern civilization. Attempts to the contrary he considered threats to his section. Hoey represented the last gasp of an order about to disappear. Above a photograph of the throng at Hoey's funeral, the local paper ran, with unintended irony, a headline reporting the Supreme Court decision declaring unconstitutional his lifelong principle—compulsory segregation of the races in public schools. Hoey and his cause were fading together. Not altogether unfitting for a man whose reality had become a myth.

NOTES

1. Hoey to Mrs. Frank C. Benjamin, February 26, 1954, Clyde R. Hoey Papers, Duke University Library, Durham, North Carolina (henceforth Hoey Papers); *Heritage of Cleveland County* (Winston Salem, 1982).

2. Hoey to Mrs. Frank C. Benjamin, February 26, 1954, to Larston D. Farrar, January 17, 1948, Hoey Papers.

3. Hoey to H. M. Taylor, February 22, 1950, to Dr. Gus Turbeville, February 15, 1954, to L. E. Kirkley, March 7, 1952, Hoey Papers; *Raleigh News and Observer* (North Carolina), February 3, 1950; Otis Hairston letter to the editor.

4. Bishop Paul Hardin, interview, Lake Junaluska, North Carolina, September 28, 1980; Senator Sam Ervin, interview, Morgantown, North Carolina, October 9,

1979; Frank Jeter, "The Governor Just Kept on Talking," *The State*, November, 1978, p. 11, May 1, 1970, p. 12; Leona Young to Hoey, October 15, 1949; Hoey to Mrs. S. Brown Shepher, April 6, 1949, Hoey Papers; Edwin Gill in his presentation of Hoey portrait to North Carolina General Assembly, May 23, 1957, North Carolina Collection, University of North Carolina Library, Chapel Hill, North Carolina.

5. Hoey to P. D. Buie, June 19, 1950, to Louis T. Moore, November 14, 1952, Hoey Papers; *Raleigh News and Observer*, August 4, 1898, January 13, 1899, p. 3.

6. *Shelby Daily Star*, May 12, 1902, editorial.

7. *Raleigh News and Observer*, January 6, 1920, December 11, 1920, January 15, 1921, January 19, 1921, March 3, 1921; *Congressional Record*, January 14, 1921, p. 1434, January 18, 1921, pp. 1630–32, 1648 (hereafter referred to as *CR*).

8. John R. Hughes, interview, Greensboro, North Carolina, September 10, 1980; *Raleigh News and Observer*, February 17, 1936, June 12, 1936; Secretary of State Thad Eure, interview, Raleigh, North Carolina, October 13, 1980.

9. Eure interview; *Raleigh News and Observer*, January 10, 1941, editorial; *Greensboro Daily News*, January 9, 1941, p. 4; Capus Waynick, interview, High Point, North Carolina, October 21, 1980; Robert L. Thompson, "First of the Gad-about Governors," *The State*, May, 1970, p. 11; Mayne Albright, interview, Raleigh, North Carolina, December 2, 1982; Rev. Otis L. Hairston, Sr., interview, Greensboro, North Carolina, August 26, 1983; *The Negro Almanac* (New York, 1983), p. 347. The table shows lynchings from 1882–1962: North Carolina, 85; Mississippi, 538; Alabama, 299; Georgia, 491.

10. Children, UDC State Convention, August 27, 1953, Hoey Papers.

11. Hoey to Carol Conley, November 25, 1952, to Joyce L. Craig, May 14, 1952, to Hoyt McAfee, June 14, 1950, Hoey Papers.

12. Hoey to W. T. Skinner, Sr., February 4, 1954, to Wilbur D. Hiatt, June 24, 1952, to P. D. Buie, June 19, 1950, to Dr. H. Shelton Smith, August 2, 1948, to B. G. Hardison, July 3, 1948, to Brenizer L. Price, August 3, 1948, Hoey Papers.

13. Hoey to W. L. Totten, Sr., March 1, 1949, Hoey Papers; *Congressional Digest*, Vol. 24, 1945.

Senate Leadership, Seventy-ninth Congress, January 1945

President Protempore: Kenneth McKellar (D-Tenn.)
Majority Leader: Alben Barkley (D-Ky.)

Committee Chairmen

Agriculture: Elmer Thomas (D-Okla.)
Appropriations: Carter Glass (D-Va.)
Finance: Walter George (D-Ga.)
Foreign Relations: Tom Connolly (D-Tex.)

14. *CR*, 80th Congress, 1st Session, Part 10, p. 551, Part 11, p. 2688, Part 12, p. 3222; Hoey to C. P. Wall, February 21, 1948, to C. A. Irvin, July 27, 1944, Hoey Papers; *CR*, January 23, 1946, p. 236, March 2, 1949, p. 1729.

15. Howard Boswell to Hoey, July 10, 1945, Hoey Papers; *CR*, January 23, 1946, p. 235; *The Carolina Times*, February 15, 1947; Hoey to Ralph A. Rochelle, February 10, 1947, Hoey Papers.

16. Hoey to B. G. Gentry, February 19, 1948, to Anna Jean Walker, March 10, 1948, to Fred C. Wilson, February 25, 1948, to Katie B. Prigeon, February 25,

1948, to Raymond D. Christman, March 10, 1948, to Rev. James H. Overton, Jr., August 3, 1948, Hoey Papers.

17. *CR*, January 17, 1946, p. 237; Hoey to Dr. Henry T. Graham, June 24, 1947, to Mrs. S. W. Wilkinson, March 22, 1949, to Hudson DePriest, May 28, 1952, to John W. Hester, June 15, 1951, to J. F. Glass, August 6, 1948, to W. J. Olive, June 16, 1947, Hoey Papers.

18. Hoey to John W. Hester, June 15, 1951, to John DuBose, June 9, 1950, to Rev. S. A. Steward, February 27, 1948, to Anna Jean Walker, March 10, 1948, to Hudson DePriest, July 15, 1948, to William N. Jefferies, February 6, 1950, to Ernest L. Culbreth, February 17, 1948, Hoey Papers.

19. Hoey to James R. O'Daniel, July 21, 1948, to H. T. Davis, June 19, 1950, to Dr. W. E. Murphy, July 19, 1948, to Henry Benoit, July 20, 1948, to Bobby Pace, September 13, 1948, Hoey Papers; Gary Clifford Ness, "The States' Rights Democratic Movement of 1948," (Ph.D. diss., Duke University, 1972), p. 115, 129; *The State*, July, 1948.

20. Hoey to Charles A. Crews, March 10, 1949, Hoey Papers; "Local Election Highlights," *American City* 63 (December 1948): 120.

21. Barton J. Bernstein, *Politics and Policies of the Truman Administration* (Chicago, 1972); Hoey to Bruce F. Heafner, November 7, 1947, to Clyde W. Scott, February 17, 1948, to Ada M. Field, February 25, 1948, to Dorothy Ledford, April 30, 1952, Hoey Papers.

22. Editorial, *Raleigh News and Observer*, March 22, 1948; Hoey to Dr. D. Aitchison, June 20, 1947; to Paul Richman, December 20, 1948, to Eleanor Case, April 4, 1952, Hoey Papers.

23. Hoey to Mrs. J. B. Rhine, August 9, 1946, Hoey Papers; Greensboro *Daily News*, August 5, 1948, August 6, 1947; *CR*, March 2, 1949, pp. 1725–26; Hoey to Reed Sarratt, February 5, 1953, Hoey Papers.

24. *CR*, March 2, 1949, pp. 1726–27; Hoey to Thelma Graham, January 9, 1948, to Mrs. Elmore Day, Jr., August 5, 1948, to Rev. J. H. Lightsey, August 15, 1946, Hoey Papers; *CR*, March 24, 1949, pp. 1865–66; Hoey to W. G. Smart, April 5, 1948, to Louis Sutton, March 12, 1948, Hoey Papers; Telephone conversation with Dr. Robert Moats Miller, August 8, 1984.

25. *CR*, January 17, 1946, p. 233–40; *Oxford Public Ledger*, September 3, 1946; *Congressional Quarterly Almanac*, 1946, pp. 78, 79.

26. Hoey to G. L. Johnson, December 14, 1949, to Vina Ruggero, February 26, 1952, to H. E. Moody, February 23, 1950, to Weimar Jones, February 16, 1950, Hoey Papers.

27. *CR*, January 27, 1947, pp. 279–82.

28. Hoey to Rev. I. B. Butler, January 25, 1949, Hoey Papers.

29. *New York Times*, March 3, 1949, p. 22; Hoey to W. Tom Bost, March 11, 1949, Hoey Papers; *Raleigh News and Observer*, March 4, March 3, 1949; *CR*, March 2, 1949, pp. 1724–25.

30. AP Files, Raleigh, North Carolina March 14, 1949; Hoey to Lucie Whitehead, December 5, 1949, to Mrs. Jessie Daniel Ames, March 21, 1949, to Charles A. Crews, March 10, 1949, Hoey Papers; *Raleigh News and Observer*, March 20, 1949; Editorial, March 22, 1949; Editorial, March 22, 1948.

31. NAACP *Bulletin* (Spring, 1949): 1, 4; Hoey to J. W. McCorkle, March 21, 1949, to J. V. Moffitt, Jr., March 10, 1949, to Russell S. Walcott, March 9, 1949,

to R. B. Chandler, August 5, 1952, to Rev. Leslie Conrad, Jr., February 10, 1949, to H. R. Callahan, April 26, 1949, Hoey Papers.

32. Hoey to Mrs. George E. Bisnar, March 16, 1949, Hoey Papers; *Congressional Quarterly Almanac*, 1959, pp. 583–91. Hoey again sprang into opposition when the Senate considered FEPC and/or anticloture bills in 1950, 1952, and 1953. In May 1950 he helped to defeat a motion to take up the FEPC bill, realizing anew that if its proponents were ever able to apply cloture, they could pass any kind of bill they desired. Senate committee approval of an FEPC bill and a resolution relaxing the requirements for cloture (neither was debated on the floor) constituted the only congressional action on civil rights in 1952. At that time Hoey blocked consideration of the Humphrey-sponsored FEPC bill when he objected under a rule requiring unanimous consent. Against a 1953 FEPC bill, he reiterated his argument that present laws were sufficient to protect any people against discrimination on account of race, color, creed, or national origin.

33. Hoey to John Russell Young, April 16, 1948, to Clement Murphy, April 5, 1948, to Dr. Watson O. Goode, April 3, 1948, to Governor Gregg Cherry, November 11, 1946, to W. H. Marley, December 6, 1949, Hoey Papers.

34. August Meier and Elliot Rudwick, *From Plantation to Ghetto* (New York, 1970), Hoey to Col. Philip S. Finn, Jr., June 21, 1948, Hoey Papers.

35. Hoey to Roman V. Ceglowski, June 10, 1948, to Mrs. W. H. Brittain, April 12, 1948, to J. W. Wilson, April 20, 1948, to Dr. Sheldon Smith, August 2, 1948, to Mary Livermore, February 20, 1951, to J. A. Hilliard, June 13, 1949, Hoey Papers.

36. Hoey to R. L. Prince, June 29, 1951, to Mrs. R. I. Edney, June 11, 1951, Hoey Papers; *Congressional Quarterly Almanac* VI, 1950, p. 296–98; Richard Dalfiume, *Desegregation of the U.S. Armed Forces* (Columbia, Mo., 1969), p. 207.

37. *Congressional Quarterly Almanac*, XII, 1956, p. 458; Hoey to Mrs. R. S. Moore, December 1, 1953, Hoey Papers.

38. *Raleigh News and Observer*, February 3, 1945, p. 4; Hoey to Mrs. Joe W. Lemmond, April 11, 1947, to Charles Norfleet, April 20, 1948, to Thomas E. Street, February 25, 1950, to Nellie M. Powell, May 6, 1949, to Rev. R. C. Smathers, January 13, 1950, to J. Clyde Auman, January 17, 1950, to Richard G. Stockton, April 1, 1949, to Ethel P. Edwards, May 16, 1949, Hoey Papers; *Congressional Quarterly Almanac*, 1949, pp. 326, 327; Elmer L. Puryear, *Graham A. Barden* (Buies Creek, N.C., 1979), p. 81, 92.

39. Hoey to Kathleen Lindsay, April 16, 1951; *North Carolina Public School Bulletin* (October 1947): 4; Hoey to John H. Ingle, November 7, 1947, to Elmore Day, August 3, 1948, Hoey Papers; James C. N. Paul, *Law and Government: The School Desegregation Decision* (Chapel Hill, 1954), p. 19.

40. Hoey to John V. Idol, June 22, 1950, to W. L. Tetten, Sr., April 11, 1950, Hoey Papers; *CR*, April, 1950, pp. 2743–44; Benjamin Munn Zeigler, ed., *Desegregation and the Supreme Court* (Boston, 1958).

41. Hoey to A. F. Barker, Jr., December 11, 1953, to Mrs. R. S. Moore, December 1, 1953, to R. M. Hitt, Jr., November 4, 1953, Hoey Papers; AP Files, Raleigh, North Carolina, November 26, 1953; Hoey to Harry McMullen, December 2, 1953, to Phil Joiner, February 26, 1954, Hoey Papers; Richard Kluger, *Simple Justice* (New York, 1976), p. 651. When, in 1953, Eisenhower nominated Earl Warren for Chief Justice of the United States, a constituent suggested to Hoey that he hold up confirmation until the Supreme Court had decided the pending segregation

cases. Hoey replied that this would not be practical and, besides, that other members of the Court posed "just as much danger" as Warren.

42. *Memorial Addresses Delivered in Congress for Clyde Roark*, Hoey, U.S. 83d Cong. 2d sess., 1954. (Washington, U.S. Govt. Print. Off., 1954), p. 71.

43. Hoey to J. Melville Broughton, August 17, 1948, to Delta Sigma Theta Sorority, Greensboro, North Carolina, March 15, 1948, Hoey Papers.

44. Interview with Mayne Albright, October 8, 1982.

45. Interview with Congressman Claude Pepper, September 16, 1980; Interview with Senator Sam Ervin, October 9, 1979; Reinhard H. Luthin, *American Demagogues* (Boston, 1954); Thomas Young, Floyd Watkins, Richard Beatty, *The Literature of the South* (Glenview, 1968).

Southern Senators and Reform Issues in the 1920s: A Paradox Unravelled

ERIK N. OLSSEN

It has often seemed paradoxical that the congressmen from the most conservative region, the South, afforded such support to the two great outbursts of reform in the first half of this century, the New Freedom and the New Deal. When progressivism has been defined as a cultural mood, the South has been ignored.[1] But when historians have looked at specific reforms—such as regulation of railways or the open primary—they have discovered that the reform wind which swept the nation also swept the South. True, in some instances the southern variant of certain reforms, such as the primary, embodied a reactionary purpose, and perhaps alerted historians to this possibility elsewhere. But this was not generally the case.[2] The South contained relatively clear social divisions, uncomplicated by the new immigration, which sometimes resulted in the emergence of politicians variously described as demagogues or reformers. James K. Vardaman of Mississippi, one of the most radical senators in the wartime Congresses, is a good example.[3] Yet men like Vardaman never controlled the southern delegation and historians, in confronting the paradox, have usually concluded that the interrelated hunger for national power, together with loyalty to party, suffice to explain why congressional delegations from Dixie provided the two great reforming presidents, Woodrow Wilson and Franklin Roosevelt, with their most reliable support.[4]

By looking at the behavior of the southern Democrats during a period of Republican ascendancy it is possible to disentangle the commitment to reform from the need to support a powerful Democratic president. Not that the task is simple. The nature of the two-party system meant that the Democrats tended to oppose the Republicans, but the war Congresses themselves show that this opposition to Republican conservatism was not based solely on political opportunism. The congressional southerners, as is well known, divided on several major war issues and provided the leadership for some major drives to push Wilson in more radical directions. On taxation, for instance, men like Claude Kitchin of North Carolina and Thomas Hardwick of Georgia bowed to none in their resolve to make the rich pay, and pay dearly.[5] During the downturn in prices which followed the Armistice, despite the president and his cabinet, almost the entire southern delegation demanded that the War Finance Corporation be revived in order to aid hard-pressed cotton producers. The more radical launched a vehement attack upon the policies of the Federal Reserve Board. Like Grover Cleveland, Wilson endangered his control of the southerners when he refused to offer even symbolic assistance during an economic crisis.[6]

This aside, the followers of Robert La Follette (R-Wis.) and George Norris (R-Nebr.) would have had little success in the 1920s had it not been for Democratic and southern support. Some midwestern Democrats, like Montana's Burton Wheeler and Clarence Dill (Wash.), regularly voted with Norris, but so too did several southern senators. More striking still, however, is the fact that when Norris voted with a majority of the Senate most southerners voted with him. Without support of southern Democrats, in short, almost no reform legislation would have been enacted during the 1920s. This was most marked between 1919 and 1924, for the triumph of Calvin Coolidge persuaded several leading southern Democrats to reconsider their political strategy. But before Coolidge's election, most southern senators supported the Water Power Act and the Shipping Act of 1920, women's suffrage, Prohibition, the Maternity and Infancy Welfare Act, the various measures favored by the so-called Farm Bloc, and in 1921 and 1924 they helped to formulate and enact fairly radical taxation laws. Although split over strategy after Coolidge's victory in 1924, most southerners supported Norris on Muscle Shoals; a majority of them backed the Boulder Dam legislation wanted by the Norris group. They also supported the Howell-Barkley Labor Bill which sought to establish collective bargaining and the position of the railroad unions within that industry. On more obviously partisan issues, such as the investigations of corruption in 1924 and the rejection of Coolidge's nomination for attorney general in 1925, southerners voted almost unanimously with Norris.[7]

Only on taxation did the southerners clearly part company with the Norris group after 1924, but the anger of progressive Democrats ensured that no further tax legislation was submitted to Congress before 1932. Although often described as a victory for Andrew Mellon, the secretary of the treasury from 1921 until 1933, the 1926 Act retained the special rates of the 1921 Act on all but the surtax, and followed the 1924 Act on normal rates, exemptions, and indirect taxes. If we assume that Mellon wanted in 1926 what he asked for in 1921, then he did not have much success. Mellon admittedly repealed the 1924 clauses on publicity, gifts, and inheritance, but Congress retained the 1921 rate on inheritance despite Mellon, who wanted it repealed, and again despite Mellon, Congress removed almost all federal indirect taxes. Under the 1926 Act, indeed, indirect taxes constituted a smaller proportion of total tax revenues than at any other time in the history of the United States. And only in 1932, in the midst of an extraordinary economic crisis, did he try again to reinstate a sales tax.[8]

Historians who have noted the persistence of the reform impulse into the 1920s have either not attempted to explain the role of the Democrats, have dismissed it as negligible, or have used the old Republican saw, accusing them of playing politics. David Burner remarked that "Many Democrats were chiefly interested in embarrassing the President" after 1924, although, in fact, the leaders had resolved to do the opposite.[9] Yet Burner's argument, although not original to him, commands continuing support because it explains the paradox generated by conflicting stereotypes that southerners are conservative and that Wilson and Roosevelt were reformers. The apparent accuracy of this interpretation is strengthened by the obscurity of most Democratic congressmen. After all, the famous reformers—La Follette, Norris, and William E. Borah—were midwestern Republicans. There were no Democrats, let alone southerners of equal importance. Yet many southern Democrats believed, as Robert Owen (Okla.) told Cordell Hull, that "All true Democrats are liberal in their sympathies"—although some, he hastened to add, were more liberal than others.[10]

An analysis of voting patterns in the 1920s confirms Owen's claim. The Senate Democrats certainly had a conservative fringe, yet throughout the decade, on all issues, most southerners voted with men like Norris over 65 percent of the time. The following table reveals the true state of affairs. The table is based on percentage scores achieved by Senators on three indices developed by contemporaries in order to decide whom to support and whom to oppose for reelection. The first column gives the scores of selected Senators on twenty-six roll-call votes selected by the American Federation of Labor; the second gives the scores on thirty-three roll-call votes chosen to measure support for the Farm Bloc between 1920 and 1923; and the third is based on seventy-five roll-call votes chosen by the Conference for Progressive Political Action between the vote on the antistrike clause in the Esch-Cummins Transportation Bill 1919 and the passage of the Child Labor constitutional amendment in 1924.[11] The scores achieved by well-known progressive Republicans confirm the validity of this method, yet the main interest on the table is the clarification of the behavior of less famous Senators.

Of the twenty-four senators who scored more than 90 percent on each test, seventeen were Democrats and four were southerners (seven were southerners if we include Texas in the South).[12] Of the twelve senators whose lowest score fell between 80 and 90 percent on one of the tests, six were southerners and all but one of them scored almost 100 percent on the CPPA index. The lowest scores by Democrats were obtained by nine men, of whom only four were southerners, two of them from Louisiana. Two of the lowest scoring Democrats, Oscar Underwood (Ala.) and William King (Utah), have been included in the table to demonstrate the range of voting behavior within the Democratic caucus.[13] The lowest Republican performances, registered by George McLean (Conn.) and Walter Edge (N.J.), have also been included to throw into relief the fact that Republicans from New England and the Mid-Atlantic states provided the basis for opposition to reform (thirty-eight of them failed to score 50 percent on any index and twenty-seven had a maximum no higher than 29 percent, Underwood's lowest score). Southerners did not define the extremes of Senate politics unless, as with the antilynching bill of 1922, the issue directly threatened white supremacy or was thought to do so.

By analyzing in more detail Oscar Underwood's Senate career further light can be thrown on the paradox. His father had been an antisecessionist Whig who joined the Union Army but returned to the South during Reconstruction. Underwood studied in Minnesota and graduated in law from the University of Virginia in 1884. He settled in Birmingham, Alabama, and his wealth grew with the town. In the 1890s he supported Grover Cleveland and opposed William Jennings Bryan, for whom he always had a low regard.[14] This alone distinguished him from almost every other southern Senator in the 1920s. Yet he was an out-and-out Jeffersonian, opposing concentrations of economic and political power. "Special privileges for none and equal opportunities for all [whites]" constituted his creed. In Alabama he was a died-in-the-wool reactionary, allied to the middlemen steel interests. In the 1920 election organized labor, the Prohibitionists, Tom Watson, and Bryan all opposed him but he slipped back with a small majority. Labor, he believed, intended to take over the Republic.[15] Underwood's conservatism probably was less important than his support for Republican foreign policy in costing him the post of minority leader, yet although he served as floor leader for Coolidge in 1925 on the Muscle Shoals issue, he also sustained surprising support for issues of importance to the AFL. On issues of morality in government, on the tariff, and on the principles of Jeffersonian democracy Underwood stood firm.[16]

Underwood was an isolated figure in the Senate's Democratic caucus during the 1920s, for only on the tariff did he wholeheartedly agree with most of his colleagues.[17] But the Democratic senators in general contained no voting bloc as cohesive as that led by La Follette in the Sixty-eighth Congress and Norris thereafter. Yet two sizeable if loose clusters of southerners existed throughout the twenties and more often than not voted with the well-known reformers. Factional cohesion may well have been less, however, because the entire caucus, with one or two exceptions, shared a broad commitment to the Wilsonian tradition and had their own commit-

Table 1
The Scores of Selected Senators on Indices of the American Federation of Labor, the Farming Bloc, and the Conference for Progressive Political Action*

Name	AFL	Farm	CPPA
R. La Follette (R-Wis.)	100	100	100
S. Brookhart (R-Ia.)	100	100	100
R. Owen (D-Okla.)		100	100
G. Norris (R-Nebr.)	100	100	94
M. Sheppard (D-Tex.)	100	94	99
C. Dill (D-Wash.)	100		
H. Ashurst (D-Ariz.)	95	100	95
T. Caraway (D-Ark.)	95	100	95
W. Harris (D-Ga.)	95	97	94
C. Swanson (D-Va.)	95	93	95
A. Jones (D-N.Mex.)	93	96	97
E. Mayfield (D-Tex.)	93		93
D. Walsh (D-Mass.)	93	93	91
T. Heflin (D-Ala.)	90	90	93
E. Ladd (R-N.D.)		95	94
P. Trammell (D-Fla.)	89	100	91
K. McKellar (D-Tenn.)	95	95	88
H. Johnson (R-Calif.)	100	86	93
P. Harrison (D-Mass.)	95	87	97
K. Pitman (D-Nev.)	88	87	97
J. Kendrick (D-Wyo.)	85	87	98
F. Simmons (D-N.C.)	85	93	92
L. Overman (D-N.C.)	80	81	90
D. Fletcher (D-Fla.)	72	96	81
C. Glass (D-Va.)	84	61	88
E. Smith (D-S.C.)	73	87	82
J. Robinson (D-Ark.)	80	64	74
P. Gerry	60	55	91
P. Norbeck (R-S.D.)	89	77	86
W. Borah (R-Idaho)	81	87	73
A. Capper (R-Kans.)	61	78	71
O. Underwood (R-Ala.)	70	28	54

Table 1 (*cont.*)

Name	AFL	Farm	CPPA
W. King (D-Utah)	58	22	69
G. McLean (R-Conn.)	0	8	7
W. Edge (R-N.J.)	11	0	8

*If there is no entry the senator failed to vote on at least 30 percent of the roll-call votes. For a full listing of the votes used see Erik N. Olssen, "Dissent from Normalcy: Congressional Progressives in Congress, 1918–1925," Ph.D. diss., Duke University, 1970, Appendix A, pp. 361–68.

ments to "progressive" legislation. One of these loose voting-blocs was never particularly large or powerful. It consisted of senators who voted most often with the Norris group and even, at times, attended meetings of that group.[18] Only four senators behaved this way in the Sixty-eighth, Sixty-ninth, and Seventieth Congresses, others voting with them closely in one Congress and then moving away in another. The most cohesive four men were the two senators from Texas, Morris Sheppard and Earle Mayfield, Kenneth McKellar of Tennessee, and William Harris of Georgia. McKellar probably spoke for all of them when he told La Follette, in declining an invitation to attend a meeting called by the Conference for Progressive Political Action in 1922, that the Democrats generally supported progressive legislation. Although not as cohesive as the La Follette or Norris groups, these men sustained similar voting records and often cooperated with the midwestern progressives, most of whom were at least nominally Republican.[19]

Sheppard, like Henry Ashurst (D-Ariz.), attended the 1922 conference organized by the Conference for Progressive Political Action, but thereafter maintained only informal links. If we exclude Texas from the South, for the senators from that state have more in common with the delegation from the Southwest (Oklahoma, Arizona, and New Mexico) than with the other southerners, then between 1922 and 1928 only two southerners regularly voted with the Norris group in support of reform at least 70 percent of the time on all issues. This may be considered unimpressive. However, although Norris is the archetypal progressive it is, as several historians have noted, impossible to disentangle regional and reform issues. In the Sixty-eighth Congress, for instance, Norris and La Follette supported the Norbeck-Burtness Bill, a measure to aid midwestern wheat farmers, and opposed southern attempts to include within the bill provision for the southern staples. Not all disagreements between La Follette and Norris and their most sympathetic southern colleagues can be explained so simply, but it points to the fact that interests and ideals were intimately interrelated.[20] Those who voted most often with La Follette and Norris were from west of the Mississippi and north of the border states. Even recognized urban liberal Democrats, such as David Walsh (Mass.) and Robert Wagner (N.Y.), often voted no more frequently with Norris. And when it came to elections, the railroad unions strongly supported the most progressive southerners.[21]

On the broad range of economic issues, from regulation to subsidies, the southwestern Democrats, and as many as half the southern delegation, easily accepted the proposals favored by men like La Follette and Norris. Their Jefferson heritage made them just as committed on issues such as the direct primary and corruption. Southern xenophobia rather than sympathy for unions persuaded them to support immigration restriction in 1921 and 1924, but their conservatism on many social issues must not obscure their ready commitment to other forms of reform. Although most of them supported Prohibition and at least two (Mayfield and Black) belonged to the Ku Klux Klan, there were few roll-call votes relating to either measure.[22] In the broadest sense the poverty of these states resolves the paradox posed earlier. Even indisputably "conservative" southerners, such as Underwood, sustained much more "progressive" voting records than their Republican colleagues from New England and the Mid-Atlantic states.

The sectional dimension to reform at the federal level reflects the brute fact that some regions, conspicuously the South, exported primary products and imported capital, technology, and manufactured goods. On economic measures, most of which involved some regional redistribution of income, politicians from such states, even when allied to the economic elites within their states, could speak and vote like reformers. Even the most conservative southerners, those who bitterly opposed any alliance with the progressive Republicans, voted regularly for Farm Bloc legislation in 1921–1922.[23] Faced with similar threats to those interests within their states they behaved predictably, yet the more progressive Democrats within the Senate tended to represent the poorest white people in the South even though, for the most part, they accepted the policies associated with the "New South."[24]

The paradox of southern support for federal reform is thrown into sharper relief by looking at the second loose voting group that frequently voted with La Follette and Norris. Although they were not a cohesive voting bloc these men—F. M. Simmons and L. Overman (N.C.), D. U. Fletcher (Fla.), C. Swanson (Va.), "Cotton Ed" Smith (S.C.), T. Caraway (Ark.), C. Culbertson (Tex.), and even Thomas Heflin (Ala.)—often voted for reform. Quite self-consciously most of them occupied a sort of "middle-ground," seeing themselves as flexible conservatives. Contemporaries sometimes tied themselves in knots over how the members of this cluster could best be classified. *Labor*, the official weekly of the railroad unions and a major voice for reform in the 1920s, annoyed McKellar in 1926 by describing one of this cluster, "Cotton Ed" Smith, as a progressive. McKellar wrote to *Labor*'s editor, the ex-Democratic congressman Edward Keating, complaining that Smith was a conservative. Keating replied that Smith's voting record, even on labor bills, had been "decidedly above average." Smith had opposed the Mellon taxation bills in 1921, 1924, and 1926, and "stood by Norris and yourself in your fight to save Muscle Shoals, opposed the confirmation of Warren . . . and backed Thomas J. Walsh (D-Mont.) in his effort to investigate the aluminum trust."[25] South Carolina's railway workers may not have worked for Smith, but *Labor* endorsed him and continued to do so until 1938. And as can be seen from Table 1, his voting record in the early twenties was no worse than that of William E. Borah (R-Idaho), Arthur Capper (R-Kans.), or Peter Norbeck (R-S.C.).[26]

There is no simple explanation for the voting records of these men but it cannot be argued that only a Democratic president could force them to support reform. Although they loyally backed Wilson's program in the Sixty-fifth Congress, they broke ranks with the administration in the Sixty-sixth Congress (1919–1921) over the question of reviving the War Finance Corporation to aid hard-pressed southern farmers. Table 1 reveals that they persistently voted for reforms favored by La Follette and Norris until the 1924 elections.

This strategy of cooperating with the progressive Republicans was admittedly strongly supported by their favored candidate for the Democratic nomination, William Gibbs McAdoo.[27] Not all members of the Democratic caucus were happy with this and, after Calvin Coolidge trounced the compromise Democratic candidate for president, those who had grumbled in private became outspoken. Nathaniel Dial (S.C.), Walter Bruce (Md.), Thomas Bayard (Del.), Carter Glass (Va.), and Underwood denounced the old strategy and attributed their party's rout to the "unhappy identification with the La Follette crowd of radicals."[28] Although the party leaders, Joseph Robinson (Ark.) and Pat Harrison (Miss.), veered right, in part because the middle ground had shifted, a majority of this cluster continued to give most of their votes to Norris on the major issues of the late 1920s. On Muscle Shoals, for instance, although Underwood and Robinson cooperated with the Coolidge Republicans, a majority of the Democrats and the southerners supported the Norris bill.[29] On the Howell-Barkley bill, which would have imposed collective bargaining on the railroads and given federal recognition to the standard unions, all progressive southerners and most of this group indicated their support.[30]

Any explanation of the voting behavior of these men must start with southern poverty. Yet the scores of these men on the three indices and their continued support for certain reforms cannot be explained only in these terms. Others from the South were both more conservative and more progressive. Few have attracted biographers and those that have, like Duncan Fletcher (D-Fla.), have been described as "reluctant" or even "conservative" progressives.[31] As a group, however, these men shared some distinguishing characteristics. They had been born between 1850 and 1865 and established their careers in the midst of the great social upheavals that rent the South. During the 1880s and 1890s all members of this cluster had been actively involved in politics in states where agrarian protest enjoyed great strength.

True, they fought the Populists in their home states but they learned to temper their conservatism, to bend with radical winds, for only in this way could they ensure the continued power of those interests with which they allied. Although they all became adept at exploiting racism and sectional pride, at blurring prospective social divisions, they also became remarkably flexible in devising reforms designed to weaken Populist appeals. It is almost a cliche, now, that southern Populism was more radical than its Midwestern variant. When Grover Cleveland opted for a policy of high-minded inaction and fanned the flames of political unrest in the South, all of these men deserted him and threw their support to William Jennings Bryan. Cleveland's inaction threatened local Democratic control. These men became proficient with populist rhetoric and were often condemned for using it as an octopus uses ink, but over long political lives their behavior suggests that having been scorched once by the angry radicalism of the "rednecks" and "poor whites" they had learned to tack close to the wind. When the storms of radicalism had spent themselves they still moved, almost like sleep-walkers, to deflect the assault. Even after the one-party system had been established, somewhere in the South there was some leader to remind them how easily the flames of protest might be fanned again.[32]

The career of Furnifold Simmons of North Carolina illustrates well these general comments. Simmons was born in 1854. His father was a plantation owner, the plantation having been in the family for two hundred years and boasting about one hundred slaves. His father—and the same is true of all but one in this cluster—was also a Whig. He opposed secession but sat in the North Carolina legislature during the Civil War. Simmons attended private schools, Wake Forest, and then Trinity College, where he met his future colleague, Lee Overman, as well as Walter Hines Page. It is interesting, and possibly significant, that the major intellectual influences on this future senator were not the transcendentalists and the Founding Fathers, but the English traditions of common law and Whiggery—Sir Edward Coke, William Blackstone, Thomas Macaulay, and Benjamin Disraeli. The rigidity of certain forms of Jeffersonianism was alien to Simmons. Education quickened the political heritage of his family, the acute sense of an organic and developing political order whose health depended upon the "auspicious union of order and freedom".[33] His early political experience only strengthened the view, for when he first sought office he lost to a black Republican. In his next campaign a split in enemy ranks enabled him to win, but in the next election he lost to a spokesman for the Southern Farmers' Alliance. Like others in this cluster Simmons never fashioned a strategy for eroding support for the black Republicans but in the 1890s he became the architect of disfranchising all blacks. The decade's racism also helped block and then destroy the local Populists, but not before the North Carolina Populists, under Marion Butler's leadership, almost defeated the Democrats.[34]

Like many well-to-do young men Simmons believed in a limited range of reforms long before he met the Populist challenge. He believed that politics ought to be conducted according to moral principles and like so many southerners he convinced himself that blacks were the source of most political corruption. He favored increases in the education vote; and Prohibition also commanded his support. In the 1890s the Populists, helped by Cleveland's high-minded inaction, threatened Democratic rule within the state. Racism was not sufficient to dispel the threat, and so he learned the art of offering just enough reform to head off the champions of change and to retain the loyalty of men more radical than himself, such as Claude Kitchin and Josephus Daniels. As a politician Simmons had few peers, for he mastered the skills of manipulation and administration. Yet he retained—and rightly—his reputation as a "conservative." Between 1901 and 1912 Simmons had to face progressive challenges. In 1913 progressive Democrats in the Senate, which Simmons entered in 1901, tried to deny him the chairmanship of the Finance Committee. President Wilson discussed the tariff with him, declared himself satisfied, and Simmons retained the post.[35] By 1918 Democratic Progressives had learned to trust the slight and industrious senator from North Carolina and by 1926 the Republican progressives knew they could rely on him.[36]

In 1922 Simmons contested the minority leader's position with Arkansas's Joseph Robinson. Although there was no clear ideological dimension to this contest, Simmons commanded the support of most of the better-known progressive Democrats. Claude Kitchin, fast ailing but still a staunch progressive, strongly urged the selection of his fellow Tarheel because of his skill in cooperating with the progressive Republicans. On two occasions during the Sixty-seventh Congress, in the lengthy struggles to defeat Mellon's taxation bill and enact an intermediate credits bill, Simmons had successfully led a coalition of progressive Democrats and progressive Republicans, the latter, it should be said, almost incapable of working together.[37] Of the twelve highest scoring Democrats on the three indices, ten supported Simmons. Caraway voted for his fellow Arkansan, and T. J. Walsh (Mont.), not yet a very committed progressive, supported and organized Robinson's successful campaign on the basis of the party's need for a leader from west of the Mississippi.[38] Yet in 1924 Simmons masterminded the coalition which, tacking far to the left of the House Democrats led by John Nance Garner (Tex.), routed Mellon's proposal to reform the taxation system. *Labor* invariably gave him an enthusiastic endorsement. In 1930–1931, in his last term, he led the same alliance in a long, finally unsuccessful, attempt to defeat the Smoot-Hawley tariff.[39]

Although the biographical details vary, the others in this cluster shared similar experiences and had also learned in the turmoil of the 1890s than an inflexibly conservative position was self-destructive—a lesson they never forgot. Fletcher (Fla.), Charles Culbertson (Tex.), Lee Overman (N.C.), Claude Swanson (Va.), "Cotton Ed" Smith (S.C.), and even Hoke Smith (Ga.), joined Simmons in rejecting Wilson's authority when he refused to make even a symbolic gesture to southern farmers in 1919. Although unlike midwestern progressives, none of them was given to reflecting on their political behavior, it is hard to believe that they did not remember how Cleveland's inaction, twenty years earlier, had threatened Democratic control of the South. Nor did they reflect on their behavior in private correspondence. Most of them, indeed, left no papers behind, and when they did they are singularly unrevealing.

Within this loose cluster of southerners were some men born in the 1870s rather than the 1850s. They were not in their thirties when the Populists emerged but they became politically conscious in 1896, and in some cases cast their first ballot in that election. Without exception they were supporters of Bryan and, once Wilson won the nomination in 1912, they were loyal Wilsonians. Early in their careers these men—Byron Patton Harrison (Miss.), Joseph Robinson (Ark.), and Walter George (Ga.)—faced rivals capable of mobilizing a coalition of rednecks behind a program of reform. The loose and factional structure of southern politics made this a constant prospect. Even in the twenties, although no outstanding southern radical sat in the Senate, men like Thomas ("Tom Tom") Heflin (Ala.) and Thaddeus Caraway (Ark.) represented at times the violence and anger that often characterized the most radical southern movements. Too little is known of Arkansas politics to understand clearly the context in which Robinson and Caraway established their careers (although they voted in different ways), but Harrison and George had backgrounds not unlike that of Simmons and his cohorts. Arthur Link may be correct in stating that these men had no clear political philosophy, but their instinctive willingness to support so many reforms was rooted less in opportunism or partisan loyalty than in their knowledge that only by espousing reform could they retain power. If they represented the dominant economic elites of their states, then those elites, besides their hostility toward the dominant national elites, recognized the importance of reform as an antidote to more dangerous movements.

Harrison and his colleague from Mississippi during most of the 1920s, Hubert Stephens, illustrate the point. Stephens only stood for the Senate in 1922 to keep the aging and ailing Vardaman out, and in this he succeeded. Previously, Harrison had removed Vardaman from the Senate in 1918. Yet both Harrison and Stephens established their political careers by supporting Vardaman when he attacked the "secret caucus" and achieved dominance in Mississippi. Vardaman led a movement dominated by poor whites and rednecks and, as governor and then senator, he supported many reforms. Whether Vardaman effectively helped his supporters may be debated, but President Wilson detested his "disloyalty" on war issues and Harrison, seeing his chance, contested the senator's seat. In a torrid primary, which saw Harrison defeat the champion of the rednecks, he did not wrap himself in the mantle of conservatism. Moreover, Vardaman's credentials as a racist were impeccable, which meant that the sort of attack launched against the

Populists could not be used. Harrison downplayed all difference on domestic economic issues, sticking determinedly to loyalty to President Wilson and the Republic. Yet Vardaman continued to pose a threat and "The Man," Bilbo, was emerging. Harrison never forgot the nature of the major challenge that could be launched against him.[40]

Harrison's biographer has described him as a "Quintessential Conservative" and, like his friend Joseph Robinson, Harrison's unhappiness with the New Deal after 1935 has frozen his ideological image. Yet to describe him simply as a conservative is inadequate, for it leaves no way of distinguishing between different forms of conservative experience and behavior. Harrison undoubtedly thought of himself, especially after the Court packing plan of 1937, as a conservative, but his understanding of conservatism differed dramatically from that entertained by Underwood, John Davis (the party's presidential candidate in 1924), or conservative Republicans such as Reed Smoot of Utah. So long as this one word is forced to serve so many purposes and describe such diverse voting behavior, our understanding of the political process must be confused. Men like Simmons, Harrison, Fletcher, and Robinson tempered their conservative instincts and convictions in a distinctly southern way. In this period, where almost all southerners accepted segregation and the one-party system, the defining characteristic of the dominant form of political conservatism was flexibility. They were like men on a political tightrope, cautiously stepping backwards into an uncertain future. And the uncertainties they feared had been defined by their lifelong political experience. This experience, together with the South's poverty, persuaded them to use political power to redress regional inequalities, to denounce Wall Street, and to promote what George Tindall called "business progressivism." They may have shared "no fundamental political principles" as Link said, but they had a fairly clear sense of direction.[41]

There is one further consideration. The unique character of southern politics has long been recognized but it is not often admitted that in some respects that tradition was more radical than the midwestern tradition. But on those policy areas related to agriculture, southerners inhabited a radical subculture. Theodore Saloutos, in his study of farmer politics, has documented the radicalism of the southern agenda—the demand for acreage controls, parity, a sub-treasury, state-owned warehouses, more liberal credit and monetary help, and subsidized marketing. In a context where the radical position was so extreme, it became possible for conservatives to make demands that would have been radical in another context. Thus these southern conservatives quite easily expounded the need for thorough regulation of railroads, corporations, and middlemen, especially at the federal level where few southern economic interests were affected.[42] Not that men like Simmons and Harrison usually took the initiative; far from it. But when issues of this sort emerged in the Senate they sided with better-known progressives and during the postwar depression voted for an array of measures that, but ten years before, would have been considered revolutionary. Had they not done so, or so their political experience had taught them, they might well have surrendered political power in their own states to more radical leaders. Nor, it should be added, did they have any difficulty in understanding the larger aims of the two Democratic presidents. They acted on different stages for different audiences, but they all recognized that a conservatism unable to move with the times would be suicide.

Although the more radical southerners—men like Harris, McKellar, Sheppard, and Black—helped to define the agenda for reform in their region they were not, in general, involved in defining the national agenda. The other cluster, the reforming conservatives, never helped to define the agenda of reform in the South, the Senate, or the nation. Yet they occupied a position of great power, for they were the brokers of the Senate even when they did not control the committees. They did not always carry out this role capably. During the presidency of Herbert Hoover, and especially in 1932, they tried to steer a middle course only to find themselves outflanked by Louisiana's flamboyant Democrat, Huey Long.[43] But in the twenties, and from 1933 until 1936, they played the role fairly successfully. As the brokers of the Senate they decided when to transform the pleas of Norris into resolutions and laws, and when to isolate him as a solitary voice.

Although it has long been recognized that the congressional progressives achieved much in the 1920s, they were never numerous enough to triumph. It deserves to be known that the men who provided the votes that allowed such successes as were accomplished—on Muscle Shoals, taxation, investigations, farm legislation, and collective bargaining on the railroads, for instance—were southerners. Their experience, and even their conservatism, was distinctively southern and fitted them for the role they wanted and often played with great skill, that of helping to define the direction and speed of change. Just as they helped shape and enact so much of what we call the New Deal, so, in 1937–1939, they called a halt. At no time, however, did they succumb to ideological rigidity. The same cannot be said of the Republicans from the Northeast.

NOTES

1. Henry May, *The End of American Innocence: A Study of the First Years of our own Time, 1912–1917* (New York, 1959) and Robert Crunden, *Ministers of Reform: The Progressives' Achievement in American Civilization, 1889–1920*, (New York, 1982).

2. C. Vann Woodward, *The Origins of the New South, 1877–1913*, (Baton Rouge, 1951); Arthur Link, "The Progressive Movement in the South, 1870–1914," *North Carolina Historical Review* 22 (April 1946): 172–95; Anne Firor Scott, "A Progressive Wind from the South, 1906–1913," *Journal of Southern History* 24 (February 1963): 53–70; J. Morgan Kousser, *The Shaping of Southern Politics: Suffrage Restriction and the Establishment of the One-Party South, 1880–1920* (New Haven, 1974).

3. William F. Holmes, *The White Chief: James Kimble Vardaman* (Baton Rouge, 1970).

4. Arthur Link, "The South and the 'New Freedom': An Interpretation," *American Scholar* 20 (Summer 1951): 316; Richard M. Abrams, "Woodrow Wilson and the Southern Congressmen, 1913–1916," *Journal of Southern History* 22 (November 1956): 437; George B. Tindall, *The Emergence of the New South, 1913–1945* (Baton Rouge, 1967), pp. 4–32, 238–41.

5. Alex M. Arnett, *Claude Kitchin and the Wilson War Policies* (Boston, 1937); Seward T. Livermore, *Politics is Adjourned: Woodrow Wilson and the War Congress, 1916–1918* (Middleton, 1966); Arthur Link, *Wilson: Campaigns for Progressivism and Peace, 1916–1917* (Princeton, 1965).

6. Arthur Link, "The Federal Reserve Policy and the Agricultural Depression of 1920–1921," *Agricultural History* 20 (July 1946): 166–75; Burl Noggle, *Into the Twenties: The United States from Armistice to Normalcy* (Urbana, 1974). For a conventional account of the major senatorial critic of Federal Reserve policy see Ralph M. Tanner, "James Thomas Heflin: United States Senator, 1920–1931" (Ph.D. diss., University of Alabama, 1967).

7. Erik N. Olssen, "Dissent from Normalcy: Progressives in Congress, 1918–1925" (Ph.D. diss., Duke University, 1970); Charles M. Dollar, "Southern Senators and the Senate Farm Bloc, 1921–1925" (Master's thesis, University of Kentucky, 1963) and "The Senate Progressive Movement, 1921–1933: A Roll Call Analysis" (Ph.D. diss., University of Kentucky, 1966). Dollar was as interested in exploring the statistical techniques as he was in the historical issues and his techniques were more elaborate than mine (although mine were adequate to the questions), but we both came to similar conclusions about the cohesion of the La Follette and then the Norris groups and the importance of the southern Democrats; see Erik Olssen, "The Progressive Group in Congress, 1922–1929," *The Historian* 42 (February 1980): 243–63 and Patrick O'Brien, "A Reexamination of the Senate Farm Bloc, 1921–1933," *Agricultural History* 47 (July 1973): 248–73. David Burner, *The Politics of Provincialism: The Democratic Party in Transition, 1918–1932* (New York, 1968), provides a lively synthesis.

8. Burner, *Politics of Provincialism*, pp. 162–67. See also Sydney Ratner, *American Taxation: Its History as a Social Force in Democracy* (New York, 1942) and Benjamin G. Rader, "Federal Taxation in the 1920s: A Re-Examination," *The Historian* 33 (May 1971): 415–35. See also *Labor Fact Book* (New York, 1938), pp. 56–57 and *Historical Statistics*, Series Y 264–79, p. 713 and Table IX, p. 703. For the 1932 bill, Jordan A. Schwarz, "John Nance Garner and the Sales Tax Rebellion of 1932," *Journal of Southern History* 30 (May 1964): 162–80.

9. Burner, *Politics of Provincialism*, p. 171. In 1925 the party's leaders, Underwood, Robinson, and Harrison, tried to cooperate with President Coolidge on Muscle Shoals while most of the more conservative Democrats publicly attacked previous "alliance" with the progressive Republicans; see Olssen, "Dissent from Normalcy," pp. 265–74 and Preston J. Hubbard, *Origins of the TVA: The Muscle Shoals Controversy, 1920–1932* (New York, 1968), chapter 6.

10. Owen to Hull, May 1923, copy in Carter Glass Papers, Alderman Library, University of Virginia (henceforth Glass Papers).

11. The AFL's roll-call votes are in the Henrik Shipstead Manuscripts, Minnesota State Historical Society; the CPPA index is in the Mercer G. Johnston Papers, Library

of Congress (henceforth Johnston Papers); and the Farm Bloc's measures were a matter of common knowledge, for which see James Shideler. *Farm Crisis, 1919–1923* (Berkeley and Los Angeles, 1957), chapter 6.

12. The three senators from Texas were Charles Culberson, Morris Sheppard, and Earle Mayfield. For Texas politics see Lewis L. Gould, *Progressives and Prohibitionists: Texas Democrats in the Wilson Era* (New York, 1949), chapter 12. The Texans, together with other senators from the Southwest, sustained among the most "progressive" voting records of any Democrats. They were Henry Ashurst (Ariz.), A. A. Jones (N. Mex.), Robert Owen (Okla.), and Thomas Gore (Okla.), although the Republicans captured one of Oklahoma's Senate seats in 1922.

13. The others were J. Shields (Tenn.), E. Broussard (La.), J. Ransdell (La.), T. Bayard (Del.), W. C. Bruce (Md.), N. Dial (S.C.), and H. Myers (Mont.). Dial and Bruce led the revolt against the alliance with the La Follette group; see Burner, *Politics of Provincialism*, pp. 160–61.

14. Underwood to S. P. McDonald, June 2, 1920, Oscar P. Underwood Papers, Alabama Department of Archives and History, Montgomery, Alabama (henceforth Underwood Papers).

15. Underwood to Frank J. Nizell, March 18, 1920, to Fred I. Thompson, March 19, 1920, and to Frank Nelson, May 13, 1920, Underwood Papers.

16. Oscar P. Underwood, *The Shifting Sands of Party Politics* (New York, 1928).

17. Charles M. Dollar, "The South and the Fordney-McCumber Tariff of 1922: A Study in Regional Politics," *Journal of Southern History* 39 (February 1973): 45–66.

18. *Labor*, December 9, 1922, pp. 1–2. Sheppard (Tex.), Ashurst (Ariz.), and Owen (Okla.) from the Southwest attended.

19. McKellar to La Follette, Sr., November 25, 1922. Kenneth D. McKellar Papers, Memphis Public Library, Memphis, Tennessee (henceforth McKellar Papers). This cluster also included P. Trammell (Fla.) in the Sixty-eighth and Sixty-ninth Congresses and, throughout the decade, A. A. Jones (N. Mex.), H. Ashurst (Ariz.), and the four westerners, J. Kendrick (Wyo.), C. Dill (Wash.), and the senators from Montana, T. J. Walsh and B. K. Wheeler.

20. Charles M. Dollar, "Southern Senators and the Senate Farm Bloc, 1921–1925: An Illustration of Roll-Call Analysis," unpublished paper presented to Southern Historical Association, Richmond, 1966, pp. 8–9. See also John D. Hicks and Theodore Saloutos, *Twentieth Century Populism: Agricultural Discontent in the Middle West, 1900–1939* (Madison, 1951), chapter 11.

21. The railroad unions strongly supported all of these men; Erik Olssen, "The Making of a Political Machine: The Railroad Unions Enter Politics," *Labor History* 19 (Summer 1978): 389, 391–92. Alben Barkley, Hugo Black and West Virginia's Matthew Neely have long been recognized as staunch New Dealers.

22. The new reform agenda which was fashioned late in the 1920s ignored these issues, for they also divided the members of the Norris group. See Olssen, "Progressive Group," 258–60.

23. The sectional dimension to reform was first noted by Samuel T. Hays, *The Response to Industrialism, 1885–1914* (Chicago, 1963) and C. Vann Woodward, *Origins of the New South*. For the congressional expression of this phenomenon see Howard W. Allen, "Geography and Voting on Reform Issues in the United States Senate, 1911–1916," *Journal of Southern History* 27 (May 1961): 216–28 and Jerome

Clubb, "Progressive Reform and the Political System," *Pacific North West Quarterly* 65 (July 1974): 130–145. Per capita income was lower in the South than in any other region and few southerners had to pay income tax. Maurice Leven, Harold Moulton, and Clark Warburton, *America's Capacity to Consume*... (New York, 1934), p. 173. Leven, *The Income Structure of the United States* (Washington, 1938) and George H. Borts, "The Estimation of Produced Income by State and Region," in *The Behavior of Income Shares: Selected Theoretical and Empirical Issues, Studies in Income and Wealth* (Princeton, 1964), pp. 317–81.

Unfortunately only McKellar among the more "progressive" Democrats left a large collection of private papers. See also George F. Sparks, ed., *A Many Colored Toga: The Diary of Henry Fountain Ashurst* (Tuscon, 1962) which throws no light on his political views; Tanner, "James Thomas Heflin"; Escal Duke, "The Political Career of Morris Sheppard, 1875–1941" (Ph.D. diss., University of Texas, 1958); and Polly Ann David, "A. W. Barkley: Senate Majority Leader and Vice President", (Ph.D. diss., University of Kentucky, 1963). There is little in Tindall, *Emergence of the New South*, to explain the persistence of this political tradition, but for the Southwest see Gould, *Progressives and Prohibitionists*; Gilbert Fite, "Oklahoma's Reconstruction League: An Experiment in Farmer-Labor Politics," *Journal of Southern History* 21 (November 1947): 535–55; and James R. Green, *Grass-Roots Socialism: Radical Movements in the Southwest, 1895–1943* (Baton Rouge, 1978).

25. Edward Keating to McKellar, June 22, 1926, McKellar Papers. Smith finally broke with the New Deal because of the "death sentence" provision in the public utility holding company bill of 1935. Before then he voted for most New Deal measures, even when unhappy; James T. Patterson, *Congressional Conservatism and the New Deal: The Growth of the Conservative Coalition in Congress, 1933–1939* (Lexington, 1967), pp. 42–43.

26. Nobody has ever doubted the "progressivism" of these three Republicans; see Gilbert Fite, *Peter Norbeck: Prairie Statesman*, (Columbia, 1948); Homer E. Socolofsky, *Arthur Capper: Publisher, Politician and Philanthropist* (Lawrence, 1962); and LeRoy Ashby, *The Spearless Leader: Senator Borah and the Progressive Movement in the 1920s* (Urbana, 1972). The three biographers do, however, take their subjects at face value.

27. McAdoo hoped to capitalize on the great "radical" upsurge of 1922; see McAdoo to Edward Keating, November 24, 1922; Claude Kitchin to McAdoo, December 2, 1922; and McAdoo's letters to John Nance Garner and F. M. Simmons, December 2, 1922. William Gibbs McAdoo Papers, Library of Congress, (henceforth McAdoo Papers).

28. Glass to Frank Roberts, March 19, 1925, Glass Papers; for Bruce, *Congressional Record*, 68th Congress, 2nd Session (December 29, 1924), pp. 911–16; for Dial, *New York Times*, January 4, 1925, p. 18 (and Nathanial Dial Papers, Perkins Library, Duke University); for Bayard, *Congressional Record*, 68th Congress, 2nd Session (January 28, 1925), pp. 2575–27. With James Broussard (La.) and Owsley Stanley (Ky.) they formed a short-lived Thomas Jefferson League, the advertisements for which are in the Royal Copeland Papers, University of Michigan Library.

29. Olssen, "Dissent from Normalcy," pp. 267–73 and Hubbard, *Origins of TVA*, pp. 153, 156–57.

30. Olssen, "Dissent from Normalcy," pp. 274–80; "Memorandum on Howell-

Barkley Bill Progress, February 1–20, 1925," Donald Richberg Papers, Chicago Historical Society.

31. Wayne Flint, *Duncan Upshaw Fletcher: Dixie's Reluctant Progressive* (Talahassee, 1971).

32. These generalizations have been shaped by the careers of the following senators: F. M. Simmons (N.C.), D. U. Fletcher (Fla.), Lee Overman (N.C.), W. George (Ga.), C. Swanson (Va.), C. Culberson (Tex.), T. Caraway (Ark.), and T. Heflin (Ala.). See Flint, *Fletcher*; Tanner, "Heflin"; Henry C. Fernell, "Claude A. Swanson of Virginia" (Ph.D. diss., University of Virginia, 1964). For Simmons, see n. 34, infra, and for more general analysis V. O. Key, Jr, *Southern Politics* (New York, 1949); Woodward, *Origins of the New South*; and Kousser, *Shaping of Southern Politics*.

33. The quotation is from T. B. Macaulay, *History of England from the Accession of James the Second*, 6 vols. (London, 1913), I: 1–2.

34. J. Fred Rippy, ed., *F. M. Simmons: Statesman of the New South: Memoirs and Addresses* (Durham, N.C., 1936); Richard L. Watson, Jr., "A Southern Democratic Primary: Simmons vs. Bailey in 1930," *North Carolina Historical Review* 42 (Winter 1965): 21–46; and the Furnifold M. Simmons Papers, Perkins Library, Duke University (henceforth Simmons Papers). I am indebted to Dr. Richard L. Watson for help in understanding Simmons but he is in no way responsible for this interpretation. On Butler and the North Carolina Populists see Robert F. Durden, *The Climax of Populism: The Election of 1896* (Lexington, 1966).

35. For North Carolina politics in this period see Key, *Southern Politics*, pp. 212–13, and for Simmons and Wilson see Arthur Link, *Wilson: The New Freedom* (Princeton, 1956), p. 183. See also Dewey Grantham Jr., *Hoke Smith and the Politics of the New South*, (Baton Rouge, 1958), pp. 240–41, 247–48.

36. Interview with Senator Burton Wheeler, 1968. The relationship was somewhat strained in 1926, however, when Simmons led most Democrats on a more moderate tack, see Burner, *Politics of Provincialism*, pp. 162–63, 165–67.

37. Claude Kitchin to Lee Overman, November 20, 1922, Simmons Papers. Other relevant letters are in Claude Kitchin Papers, Wilson Library, University of North Carolina. See also, Olssen, "Dissent," pp. 124–26, 128–29, 139–50.

38. Walsh to C. Dill, September 19, 1922, T. J. Walsh Papers, Library of Congress and Interview with Senator Burton Wheeler, 1968.

39. Olssen, "Dissent," pp. 249–59. The fullest archival source on the course of the tariff struggle is the W. T. Rawleigh Tariff Manuscripts in the files of the People's Legislative Service, Johnston Papers.

40. See Holmes, *White Chief*, pp. 342–58, 375–79 and Albert D. Kirwan, *Revolt of the Rednecks: Mississippi Politics, 1876–1925* (New York, 1951), pp. 284–91, 299–303. Key Pittman (Nev.), a southerner by birth and a close friend of Harrison and Joseph Robinson, began his senatorial career in a similar political environment, only just defeating a socialist.

41. Tindall, *Emergence of the New South*, p. 224.

42. Patterson, *Congressional Conservatism*, p. 3, in locating the basis of opposition to the New Deal in the southern delegation (and ignoring the Republicans), remarked that "In the Senate nearly half the twenty-two southerners often voted against the New Deal on non-agricultural economic issues." By his own account, however, this was in the period from 1937 to 1939 (p. 330), and the qualification is striking. The

most cogent exposition of this point is Theodore Saloutos, *Farmer Movements in the South, 1865–1933*, (Lincoln, 1960) and especially his "Conclusion."

43. Jordan A. Schwarz, *Interregnum of Despair: Hoover, Congress and the Depression* (Urbana, 1970).

# PART II

The World of Work

Sectional Influences on National Policy: The South, the Labor Department, and the Wartime Labor Mobilization, 1917–1918

WILLIAM J. BREEN

Major wars have had profound, if sometimes muffled, effects on modern societies. Arthur Marwick, the British historian, has argued that in England the Great War promoted the development of a whole new code of social mores which demonstrated "that British society was becoming increasingly homogeneous, both as between men and women and as between social classes." George B. Tindall has argued that what was true of individuals and classes in Great Britain was also true of distinctive regions within the United States. In the South, the effect of the war was to act as a powerful solvent of narrow, parochial attitudes. "Sectional loyalty receded at least temporarily before the universal cry for unity." In various ways, the war "altered and enlarged" southern perspectives and, as a result, sectionalism "retreated before nationalism."[1] The wartime mobilization was a fillip to the morale of the advocates of the New South: the region was being forced to adopt a more national and less sectional outlook. However, like most historical generalizations, Tindall's proposition can be faulted in some of its specifics. Southern attitudes toward the efforts of the federal government to develop and implement a national labor policy remained distinctly parochial. In this critical area the South remained untouched by the nationalizing currents unleashed by the wartime mobilization.

The national government was slow to develop a wartime policy. President Wilson himself had been reluctant to encourage any real preparedness activities in the regular departments and when America entered the war there was no consensus on an appropriate labor policy. Even an appreciation of the importance of developing such a policy did not exist. Individual government departments and agencies went their own way in dealing with labor matters: special labor adjustment boards were created to deal with particular problems or industries with no attempt at coordination on such key issues as wages, hours, or working conditions. It was not until January 1918 that Wilson took the first steps toward developing a unified labor administration by appointing Secretary of Labor, William B. Wilson, as wartime Labor Administrator. Under Secretary Wilson's supervision, a rudimentary administrative apparatus emerged which began to take some steps toward developing a coherent national labor policy.[2] As a key part of his wartime labor administration, Secretary Wilson, in January 1918, created the U. S. Employment Service (USES) as a separate and independent division within the Labor Department.[3]

Prior to American entry in the war, the Department of Labor had operated a small employment service primarily designed to assist immigrants arriving in the major eastern seaports. This service was located within the Bureau of Immigration, which the Department of Labor had inherited when it was created in 1913. During 1917, the Department of Labor sought to expand this machinery into a genuinely national employment service but Congress initially refused to pass the necessary appropriations. It was not until late 1917 that Congress finally appropriated a niggardly $250,000 for employment work: the Department had requested $750,000. In December 1917, however, President Wilson agreed on the need for such a national service and allocated an additional $825,000 from his special Emergency Fund. In January 1918, when Secretary Wilson severed the link with the Bureau of Immigration, the USES was free to develop as one of the key agencies in the wartime administrative machinery associated with the industrial mobilization.

However, the Department of Labor had a difficult struggle to secure widespread acceptance of the critical role of its expanded employment service in the wartime labor market. Even by the spring of 1918, when it was clear that a serious labor shortage existed which would have to be met by shifting labor from different sections of the country, there was no consensus on the appropriate role for the USES in the crisis. Individual states were suspicious of any federal initiatives in this area, fearing that their labor force would be shipped outside state boundaries. Different government departments were reluctant to concede a preeminent role to the Department of Labor in this field. The War Department, for example, with its enormous construction program, became the largest single factor in the wartime labor market but it remained profoundly suspicious of the Department of Labor's efforts to establish a national employment service, fearing both the department's prounion ideological bent and its general administrative ineptitude and paucity of experience in the employment field. John B. Densmore, the director-general of the USES complained bitterly about the uncooperative attitude of the War Department, particularly as the USES tended to be blamed for the activities of all labor agents recruiting for the federal government.[4]

The actions of the War Department's labor recruiters had serious repercussions on the South's economy. Densmore himself believed that the injury done to southern agriculture by labor agents recruiting for the War Department was so great that he did not know "how it will be repaired." Other southern industries were also seriously affected. The Florida lumber industry, operating at capacity supplying the southern shipyards, complained about the labor "pirating" done by the War Department. In April 1918 Densmore arranged a conference with the entire congressional delegation from Florida, a delegation from the lumber industry, and representatives from the U. S. Shipping Board. The conference urged that immediate action be taken to prevent contractors working for the War Department at the huge Muscle Shoals site in northern Alabama "... from stripping these [Florida] mills of labor that are getting out the wood for the ships."[5] In May 1918 the Chamber of Commerce of Selma, Alabama, sent a formal letter to the War Department complaining that the labor agents from the nitrate plants at Muscle Shoals and Sheffield, and the government contractors on the Warrior River were "playing havoc with the labor situation in that State." The Chamber argued that the labor supply in the Selma area was needed to harvest the crops already planted. Because of an exodus of farmhands following the floods in 1916, there was a shortage of labor in the section. The labor agents of the War Department contractors were "making extravagant promises, carrying away considerable numbers of laborers, and completely demoralizing those who were left."[6]

Well before American entry in April 1917 the European war had begun to affect the southern economy. Northern industry, experiencing boom conditions because of European war orders, found itself short of common labor. European immigration, the traditional source of industrial unskilled labor, had ceased with the outbreak of hostilities. This left the southern black population as the largest pool of available unskilled labor in the country. Most of this labor was concentrated in agriculture although a small proportion had moved into "Negro job" industries such as lumbering, naval stores, unskilled work in blast furnaces and rolling mills, and railroad construction and maintenance. From late 1915, labor recruiters were active throughout the Southeast and, by 1916, the Pennsylvania and Erie railroads were regularly transporting trainloads of Negroes north from that region and several railroads and large corporations had established regular camps as distribution points by the end of the year. Large numbers of blacks were willing to move. "The cotton crisis of 1914–1915, the ravages of the boll weevil, floods over much of the Deep South in 1915 and 1916 unsettled large areas and contributed to the migratory urge."[7] By 1916 the Great Migration was well under way.

American entry into the war brought about not only a greatly increased demand for common labor in the North, but vastly increased the demand for labor in the South. In Virginia, the Hampton Roads area was developed by the federal government as one of the major port facilities in the country. The population of Norfolk, 67,452 in 1910, increased to over 100,000 by 1917. Other southern ports experienced rapid expansion and absorbed large numbers of unskilled laborers. Shipbuilding, particularly wooden shipbuilding, expanded rapidly in southern yards especially along the Gulf Coast. By early 1918, the government had let contracts for 150 ships in southern shipyards. Because of the heavy demand for timber to construct wooden ships and Army cantonments in the region, the southern lumber industry experienced a tremendous boom. The construction of a number of very large government explosives and chemicals plants in various southern states also produced a surging demand for construction labor. Alabama, with the nitrate plant and the Wilson Dam at Muscle Shoals, and Tennessee, with the giant Old Hickory powder plant near Nashville and three other large government-sponsored plants built during the war, were major beneficiaries of government programs. The effect of this was to upset dramatically the labor market throughout the entire South, and to threaten its traditional reliance on a large pool of unskilled black labor. "The most significant immediate effect of the war on the South," noted George Tindall, "was to create situations of dynamic change in an essentially static society."[8]

Even before America entered the war, the Department of Labor attempted to allay the complaints and fears of southern employers and politicians concerning the exodus of black labor. Because some of this migration had used the rather limited facilities of the Department's embryonic employment service, the Department's immediate response was to withdraw "its facilities from group migration" by southern blacks. In the summer and fall of 1916, it sent two black investigators, both on loan from the Department of Commerce, to tour the South and investigate the problem. Their report suggested that there was no need for immediate alarm although they recommended that a detailed investigation be made and the situation be closely monitored. A more elaborate investigation, conducted in the summer and fall of 1917, and directed by James H. Dillard, formerly a professor and dean at Tulane University, and the president of the Jeanes and Slater Funds for Negro education in the South, was begun less than a month after America entered the war. This was a direct response to the ". . . great response from many sources . . . expressed over the probable loss to the Nation of southern crops through the departure from that section of Negro workers in appalling numbers."[9]

Responding to southern complaints about a growing shortage of labor, the secretary of labor was even prepared to risk the wrath of the unions by approving a relaxation of the restrictions on the temporary admission of Mexican agricultural labor. The possibility of such an action had induced a predictable response. In early August 1917, responding to rumors of such proposed relaxation of the immigration regulations, Samuel Gompers had written bitterly to Secretary Wilson to protest any such alteration and to point to the long battle waged by organized labor to eliminate that source of "unfair competition." Gompers argued that there was no shortage of labor and that the hysteria being whipped up over the issue was directly related to "the desire of employers to profit through exploitation of illiterate workers. . . . " In the opinion of the Executive Council of the American Federation of Labor it was "unwise" of the government "to yield to this clamor rather than maintain standards of human welfare and protect the rights of citizens in accord with the purpose and intent of the laws of the land."[10] The secretary of labor, however, was prepared to override union opposition in order to pacify southern demands.

The Department's first response was to encourage the importation of American citizens from Puerto Rico and the Virgin Islands. Plans were laid to transport 50,000 of these islanders in the winter of 1917–1918. Louis F. Post, the assistant secretary of labor, announced in February 1918 that the U. S. Employment Service intended to bring in these laborers to work in the South and Southwest on railroad maintenance "during the slack agricultural season and released for farm work during the height of that season. . . . "[11] The following month, Secretary Wilson granted permission to east coast Florida truck farmers to import Bahamans. The shortage of available shipping put limits on this source of unskilled labor, however. By the time of the Armistice, approximately 13,000 Puerto Ricans and 2,500 Bahamans had been brought to the mainland. In April, the secretary suspended the clauses in the immigration law relating to the literacy test, the head tax, and the contract-labor prohibition to allow admission of farm laborers from Mexico, the West Indies, and Canada for periods of not more than six months. In June the rulings were extended to cover Mexicans hired for railroad track maintenance, all forms of mining, and construction work for the federal government. Approximately 17,600 Mexicans entered the United States during 1918 under the relaxed provisions.[12]

A further response to southern pressure demanding special consideration for sectional interests was the establishment of a Division of Negro Economics within the Department of Labor. Pressure for the appointment of a special advisor on black labor problems had come from the black community itself, a petition from leading blacks on the matter having prompted the action. These included James H. Dillard; R. R. Moton, principal of Tuskegee Institute; Eugene Kinckle Jones, executive secretary of the National League on Urban Conditions among Negroes; John R. Shillady, secretary of the NAACP; and Thomas Jesse Jones, educational director of the Phelps-Stokes Fund. A special conference was held at the Department of Labor in February 1918 when representatives of the petitioners appeared before Assistant Secretary of Labor Louis F. Post to press their case.[13] In May, George Edmond Haynes, a professor of economics and sociology at Fisk University, became the first Director of Negro Economics within the department. Haynes was one of the executives of the National League on Urban Conditions among

Negroes and had wide support among both blacks and whites. The first black to receive a Ph.D. from Columbia University, a cofounder of the National Urban League, his research and published work had focused on black migration patterns, which fitted him well for the task. Sympathetic to Booker T. Washington's "accommodationist" philosophy, Haynes encountered some early criticism from more radical blacks.[14]

The aim of the new Division of Negro Economics was to attempt to open industrial opportunities for black labor and then to maintain interracial harmony on jobs where blacks were hired. Haynes set about appointing representatives in each state and establishing integrated citizens' councils at the state and local levels to monitor race relations in each district, to promote job opportunities for blacks, and to attempt to promote racial harmony especially in the workplace. Haynes also instituted a national publicity campaign designed to promote interracial harmony and to awaken the black community to the government's labor needs. In order to assist the fledgling Division, Secretary Wilson ordered the U. S. Employment Service, which had established a national organization covering all the states, to provide assistance to the Division of Negro Economics. With the help of local USES offices, the Division had established fifteen state branches, in both the North and South, by the end of the war.[15]

The USES itself had also responded to southern pressures. In an effort to allay fears of an impending agricultural labor shortage, the service instituted its own special investigation of the southern labor situation. Two black examiners, both attached to the Washington office of the USES, were dispatched in March 1918 to make an investigation of the "colored farm situation in the South." Beginning in Virginia, the examiners were to investigate allegations of shortages of farm labor within different sections of each state and to try to even out any imbalances by recruiting surplus labor from other sections of the state. It was an attempt to meet the problem of farm labor shortage without raising the bogey of "stripping" any individual state of its labor.[16]

The establishment of a separate Negro Division within the U. S. Employment Service was another example of the effort made by the Department of Labor to placate the South. The pressure to establish some kind of special Negro division within the department had come largely from Giles B. Jackson, a black lawyer and politician in Richmond, Virginia. Jackson was also president of the Richmond-based National Civic Improvement Association and had been lobbying for the establishment of some special federal "colored labor advisory position" since 1916. He had proposed a three-pronged, self-help program for black workers consisting of surveys of farming conditions among farmers, publicity campaigns aimed to convince blacks to remain in the South, and the establishment of advisory councils of local businessmen and others to discuss the best ways to utilize black labor. His program called for a $700,000 congressional appropriation which he would administer under the auspices of the Department of Labor. He had considerable political support and had secured the approval of presidential advisor Joseph P. Tumulty, and the endorsement of Senator Thomas Martin of Virginia and the Richmond Chamber of Commerce. However, influential segments of the black community were very opposed to Jackson. W. E. B. DuBois regarded him as "one of the most disreputable scoundrels the Negro race has produced . . . " and Emmett Scott, special assistant to Secretary of War Baker on Negro matters, concurred.[17]

Jackson and three other blacks had approached Samuel Gompers in the summer of 1917 with a proposal to establish a "Bureau of Negro Economics" with the aid of some government funds. Gompers, who applauded the scheme which was clearly designed to keep blacks in the South, wrote to Secretary Wilson supporting the proposal and asking him to consider Jackson's plan and "perhaps to have a personal conference with him."[18] Jackson did not wait to hear from Wilson. Securing a letter of introduction from Senator Thomas Martin of Virginia, he had an interview, in mid-February, with John B. Densmore, the director-general of the Employment Service, who endorsed the proposal of a "Bureau of Negro Economics." Unable to see the secretary, Jackson again wrote to Gompers asking him to transmit the letter to Wilson, and to take the matter up in person with the secretary.[19] At the same time that he appointed Haynes to head the Division of Negro Economics, Secretary Wilson created the Negro Division of the USES and appointed Jackson as its director. The secretary had thus established two separate but clearly overlapping agencies concerned with black labor within his Department.[20]

Jackson's plans for his Division were ambitious. He stressed the need to get Negro labor out of the big cities and to counteract "German propaganda" which, he believed, was creating dissatisfaction among rural blacks and causing them "to leave farms and to go to the large cities where they are now living in idleness." Jackson wanted authority to appoint an assistant-chief, a secretary, and an assistant-secretary, three to five other assistants for clerical work, a publicity agent, twenty-five field agents, and funds to purchase "a strong road automobile, plus allowance for upkeep, garage, chauffeur. . . . "[21] The only thing that Assistant-Secretary of Labor Louis F. Post would approve was Jackson's request for a stenographic secretary.

On June 7, 1918, Jackson submitted a revised "Sketch for the Plans of Operation of the Negro Division of the U. S. Employment Service." It outlined a program of aggressive propaganda aimed at Negro church meetings and various types of conventions together with the establishment of both a special Woman's Division and a Boy's Division within the Negro Division. Jackson also proposed to use the connections he had established in 1915 when he was president of the Negro Exposition Company which organized the Exposition in Richmond, Virginia. Although three years old, the directory of that exposition, he believed, would be "of great value for reaching the colored people in all districts in several states...."[22] The proposal was given to Haynes who pointed out the possibility of confusion and friction with the organization that he had established in twelve states, eight of them in the South, designed "to arouse the rank and file of Negro workers." He also commented that it would be unwise to authorize the proposed publicity campaign among the blacks before there was greater understanding of the purposes of the program among the whites. Haynes urged that Jackson be instructed to curb his proposed publicity campaign and to insure that it was in harmony with the larger program of the Labor Department.[23] Post approved the thrust of Haynes' memorandum and recommended it to Secretary Wilson. On July 9, the secretary sent a formal memorandum to the director-general of the USES which basically disapproved all of Jackson's proposals. Even contact with the various Negro religious and fraternal organizations for publicity purposes had to have the approval of the Department in advance.[24] In effect, the Negro Division of the USES was not permitted to do anything. Jackson's appointment was merely a piece of patronage designed to appease southern political pressure.

After complaining of the high cost of living in Washington on his salary of $2,750, Jackson was permitted to move back to his home in Richmond in late 1918 and to operate from there, working under the supervision of the USES state-federal director for Virginia. For political reasons, Secretary Wilson was eager to appear to retain the services of Jackson. In early March 1919 Hugh Rein, Louis F. Post's private secretary, told John Densmore that "The Secretary wants to keep him if it is at all possible."[25] Nevertheless, the Negro Division together with a large part of the expanded USES, was phased out at the end of June 1919 when Congress refused further appropriations.

The director of the USES was, himself, willing to go to considerable lengths to appease southerners. The shortage of black labor in traditional southern occupations was, of course, directly related to the high wage rate prevailing in the war industries. In the hearings before the congressional committee on the Sundry Civil Bill in 1919 Densmore stated that this problem had been discussed at length in the conference he had with the Florida sawmill industry representatives. One of the sawmill operators stated that the labor agent for Muscle Shoals was "offering my niggers . . . $3.80 and $4.00 a day, while I am paying them $2." Densmore agreed that one could not blame the sawmill laborers for seizing the opportunity presented by the labor agent. His solution to the Florida labor situation was simple: the USES would simply not inform black labor of opportunities elsewhere. "But we will benefit them [sawmill operators] this much, that if the $2 fellow in the sawmill down there is satisfied with his $2—and he is or he would not be working there—we, as a part of the Government, are not going to represent to him and lay before him newspapers showing what they do at Muscle Shoals to get him to move away from there. We will let him alone...."[26]

Controlling the flow of information about job opportunities was one way to try to control the movement of labor. The basic policy of the USES was to standardize wages on government contract work (and thus minimize the practice of different government contractors enticing labor from each other) and to centralize all labor demand through the USES. Standardization of wages would not necessarily help private industry although the centralization of demand through the services could indirectly help southern workers.

Further, the USES was prepared to tolerate some rather questionable initiatives on the part of its southern district supervisor, Cliff Williams of Meridian, Mississippi, a large-scale manufacturer of portable saw mills, and reputedly interested in improving social conditions.[27] In August 1918 Williams outlined a plan for a "Labor Registration and Card System," designed "for the stimulation of labor power." It suggested a General Registration Day where all able-bodied men and women would sign a Blue Pledge card agreeing to work six days a week. This would then be followed by a general canvass of all workers "forcing all to show Blue card." The pledge card system was designed to be used in conjunction with the passage of city ordinances making idling a punishable offense. The aim was to prevent "continual or part-time loafing." The scheme also called for the establishment of an inspection system maintained and paid for by the employers of the locality.[28] Post was deeply suspicious of the whole plan and felt that this was just a form of labor conscription for private purposes; this was "especially true of the States in which wage earners are for the most part Negroes. The 'work or fight' order is referred to nominally without discrimination of race or social condition, but in fact it is felt by the working class to be directed at them." Referring specifically to the interracial meetings being held in New Orleans and in Montgomery, Alabama, which were largely the work of Williams, he commented that the work cards "are so framed and so used as to be regarded as operating to coerce the Negro wage earner and his dependents into private service while employers and their dependents are undisturbed. . . . "[29]

In spite of Post's reservations, Williams's plan was put into operation. Williams eventually addressed approximately 150 mass meetings composed of both blacks and whites where Loyalty Leagues were organized. "These organizations effectively got behind local authorities for the enforcement of antiloafing laws and the prevention of indiscriminate labor recruiting. . . . In Montgomery, Alabama where the league introduced a card system, 40,000 people were signed up in the first forty-eight hours, and eventually about 80,000 in Montgomery County became Loyalty League members." A similar success story was reported from Mobile where, in less than a month after establishing a league, "the city had been cleaned up and loafing abolished." It was alleged that over 3,000 idlers were put to work in that city: "Some of these, gamblers and touts, confessed that they had not performed an honest day's labor in 25 or 30 years."[30]

A number of southern communities, panicked by the exodus of black labor, reacted with blatant efforts to control the outflow of black population. In Macon, Georgia, in an effort to keep out labor agents, the city council passed an ordinance setting "the license fee for agents at the laughably high figure of $25,000, and compounded the impossible by requiring that agents be recommended by ten local ministers, ten manufacturers, and twenty-five businessmen."[31] Other cities and states were equally draconian. In May 1918 the director-general of the USES complained to the secretary of labor that the attitude of the southern states promised to "result in grave curtailing of production and construction . . ." needed for the war effort.

Florida has arrested numerous of these labor agents and now has in jail at Gainesville two officers of our Service who have been recruiting common labor for the Army projects at Norfolk. The telegram from our officer reads: "Florida absolutely forbids recruiting labor from the state." The Chamber of Commerce of Atlanta, Georgia, and Congressman Howard of Georgia have telegraphed this office protesting against recruitings in Georgia, the Chamber of Commerce stating that "the feeling is running high and they don't know if they can restrain action by the local people."

Recruiting in Tennessee has met with similar experiences. This situation seems confined to the southern states where we are now obliged to turn for common labor, and if officers of this government service are not permitted to recruit labor for the war industries by the action of these states, or semi-official bodies therein, we shall be subjected to a severe handicap in supplying this much-needed labor.

Densmore went on to point out that private employment agents were successful because they operated secretly and tended to take labor indiscriminately, often from essential war industries.[32] Despite his complaints, the practice continued. At the time of the Armistice, for example, local authorities in Wiggins, Mississippi, had arrested the local representatives of the USES for attempting to remove workers.[33]

By 1919, six southern states had imposed taxes up to $2,000 on the shipment of labor interstate. Most southern states had laws which made it an offense even to invite someone to quit employment. Florida, Georgia, Mississippi, and Virginia required a license tax of $500 in each county where an agent operated for purpose of securing labor to be sent interstate. North Carolina required both an annual state tax and a tax of $100 in each county where business was transacted. South Carolina was even more severe—the law imposed a tax of $2,000 per year for each county in which the labor agent worked.[34]

Southern pressure helped to dismantle the USES immediately after the war. The inability of southern politicians and economic groups to rise above sectional interests in labor matters was clearly shown in the vicious debate in 1919 over future funding for the employment service. Governor Sidney J. Catts of Florida led the attack on the service and on the Division of Negro Economics, stating that in his state both offices were staffed with "carpetbag, negro federal officers . . ." who were promoting racial amalgamation.[35] At congressional hearings in mid-1919, southern lumbermen made clear their opposition to any continuance of this federal activity. Resolutions which bitterly opposed any continuation of the USES were submitted by the Georgia-Florida Saw Mill Association and from the North Carolina Pine Association. A statement from John H. Kirkby, president of the National Lumber Manufacturers' Association, assailed the right of the federal government to maintain such an agency. "The sooner Washington gets it out of its head that the people of this Republic want to change the Constitution and create in Washington a strongly centralized power for the control of local affairs of the people, the sooner will tranquility and order result." The prepared statement also assailed the USES as "a mere proselytising [sic] agency for the American Federation of Labor, which discriminates every day against the great agricultural masses of the country." H. H. Snell, the representative of the lumbermen of the entire southern pine industry, made the clearest and bluntest statement concerning race. The bulk of the labor in the southern lumber industry was black and employers "feel that those who employ this labor are better positioned to understand the problem than those who may come from the outside." Snell did not want any interference "by men who have no knowledge of the subject and who would interfere with the progress of the negro element much more than they can possibly forward it." Even worse, the black laborers might come to feel that the federal government was "their special champion, and a wedge will be driven between the employer and his employee."[36]

The wartime experience called into question many cherished southern political traditions. One historian has pointed out that southern congressmen during the war "gave overwhelming support to policies which continued and even accelerated the trend toward centralization of governmental authority and activity in the executive."[37] In a particularly telling illustration of the change wrought by the war, Richard L. Watson, Jr., has perceptively elaborated on this theme, citing the Lincoln's Birthday speech of Representative Edward Pou of North Carolina who "called on Congress to thank 'an all-wise God' for Lincoln, who 'kept us one Nation, sovereign and free.'" George Tindall has suggested that the wartime experience "altered and enlarged" southerners' perceptions: "Southern politicians had moved into the orbit of national politics. Sectionalism had retreated before nationalism. . . . Parochialism had diminished. . . ."[38] However, if it is true that the South was swept along by the tide of nationalism in 1917–1918, there were limits to this wartime fervor. The southern outlook on labor matters, for example, remained narrow and parochial. In many ways, the South had more to lose in terms of its economy than any other region. Wartime mobilization directly threatened the low-cost wage structure which was one of its important regional advantages. The wartime experience exposed the vulnerability of the South when faced with the nationalizing demands of the war economy. In their efforts to control the wartime migration of black labor and in their efforts to use the Department of Labor to achieve this objective, southerners consistently placed regional interests before national interests. In spite of the extraordinary efforts of the USES and the Department of Labor to alleviate southern fears and resentments, vocal interests in the South felt that the war experience had been detrimental to the long-term economic interests of the region. The mobilization had also indicated the way in which increased federal authority, particularly in relation to manpower policy, could, in less sympathetic hands, be used to undercut discriminatory racial practices in the region. Consequently, in the reconstruction period, states' rights and race, always closely linked in southern history, dominated southern reactions to the proposal to make the United States Employment Service a permanent part of the federal administrative machinery. In the area of labor policy, the wartime mobilization had little effect on the southern outlook. In that field, in fact, the war had reinforced southern sectionalism.

NOTES

1. For the quotation see Arthur Marwick, *Britain in the Century of Total War: War, Peace and Social Change, 1900–1967* (London, 1971), p. 124; George B. Tindall, *The Emergence of the New South, 1913–1945* (Baton Rouge, 1967), pp. 63, 69.

2. For an early study of the general development of federal government labor policy see Gordon S. Watkins, "Labor Problems and Labor Administration in the United States During the World War," University of Illinois, *Studies in the Social Sciences* 8 (September 1919). See also the more recent studies by Robert D. Cuff, "The Politics of Labor Administration During World War 1," *Labor History* 21 (Fall, 1980): 546–69; Valerie Jean Connor, *The National War Labor Board: Stability, Social Justice, and the Voluntary State in World War 1* (Chapel Hill, 1983), esp. chapters 1–3; Bruce I. Bustard, "The Human Factor: Labor Administration and Industrial Manpower Mobilization during the First World War," (Ph.D. diss., University of Iowa, 1984).

3. On the history of the U. S. Employment Service see Darrell H. Smith, *The United States Employment Service: Its History, Activities and Organization* (Baltimore, 1923), chapter 1; Ruth M. Kellogg, *The United States Employment Service* (Chicago, 1933), chapters 1 and 11.

4. U. S. Congress, House, Committee on Appropriations, *Sundry Civil Bill, 1919, Hearings*, before a subcommittee of the Committee on Appropriations, House of Representatives, in charge of Sundry Civil Appropriation Bill for 1919, 65th Congress, 2nd Session, 1918, p. 1577.

5. Ibid.

6. U. S. Employment Service *Bulletin* 1 (May 14, 1918): 3. On the attitude of southern management see: James E. Fickle, "Management Looks at the 'Labor Problem': The Southern Pine Industry during World War 1 and the Postwar Era," *Journal of Southern History* 40 (February 1974): 61–76.

7. For the quotation see Tindall, *Emergence of the New South*, pp. 146–47. For the position of blacks in the southern work force see: Tindall, *Emergence of the New*

South, pp. 161–65; Gunnar Myrdal, *An American Dilemma: The Negro Problem and Modern Democracy*, 2 vols. (New York, 1962), 1: 235–37. 296–97.

8. Tindall, *Emergence of the New South*, pp. 53–60. (The quotation is on p. 53).

9. For detail on the two investigations see: U. S. Congress, House, *Fifth Annual Report of the Secretary of Labor; November 10, 1917)*, H. Doc. 927, 65th Congress, 2nd Session, 1917–18, pp. 79–81. (Quotations are on p. 80). See also Henry P. Guzda, "Social Experiment of the Labor Department: The Division of Negro Economics," *The Public Historian* 4 (Fall 1982): 11; John Lombardi, *Labor's Voice in the Cabinet: A History of the Department of Labor from its Origins to 1921* (New York, 1942).

10. Samuel Gompers to Secretary William B. Wilson, August 8, 1917, Library of Congress, Samuel Gompers Papers, Letterbooks, vol. 235, pp. 871–74.

11. USES *Bulletin* 1 (February 4, 1918): 3 (Post is quoted in the article headed "No Need for the Importation of Chinese and Mexican Labor."

12. U. S. Congress, House, *Report of the Director General of the United States Employment Service (August 1, 1918)*, H. Doc. 1449, 65th Congress, 3rd Session, 1918–19, pp. 692–93. See also *The American Year Book: A Record of Events and Progress, 1918*, edited by Francis G. Ware (New York & London, 1919), p. 471. See also *Report of Proceedings of the National War Labor Conference*, Washington, June 13–15, 1918 (Washington, 1918), p. 67. (see esp. address by M. A. Coykendall, Chief of Farm Service Division, USES). H. B. Stafford, "History of the Labor Procurement Section of the Administrative Division, Construction Division of the Army" in "Official History of the Construction Division of the Army" edited by Brig.-Gen. R. C. Marshall, Jr., (Typescript: 17 vols., 1919), vol. 10, Appendix 1, Pt. E. National Archives (Suitland), Record Group 77, Office of the Chief of Engineers, Construction Division, Series 404.

13. USES *Bulletin* 1 (March 4, 1918): p. 3. See also: Guzda, "Social Experiment of the Labor Department," p. 15.

14. USES *Bulletin* 1 (April 30, 1918): 3; Guzda, "Social Experiment of the Labor Department," pp. 17–18.

15. U.S. Congress, House, *Sixth Annual Report of the Secretary of Labor* (October 31, 1918), H. Doc. 1449, 65th Congress, 3rd Session, 1918–19, pp. 111–13. Guzda, "Social Experiment of the Labor Department," pp. 19–20. Note that Guzda indicates that many of the employees of the Division of Negro Economics acted in practice as "Negro" branches within the USES offices where they were located. There was some criticism that they were just "Jim Crow" offices in disguise.

16. The two black examiners were William Jennifer and Harry Arnold. See USES *Bulletin* 1 (March 11, 1918): 4.

17. Guzda, "Social Experiment of the Labor Department," p. 16. Emmett J. Scott in his *Official History of the American Negro in World War 1* (1919: reprinted by Arno Press and the *New York Times*, New York, 1969), does not mention either Giles B. Jackson or the Negro Division of USES. Nor is there any mention in the USES *Bulletin*. For more information on Jackson see Raymond Gavins, "Urbanization and Segregation: Black Leadership Patterns in Richmond, Virginia, 1900–1920," *South Atlantic Quarterly* 79 (Summer 1980): 257–73.

18. Gompers to W. B. Wilson, January 23, 1918. See also Gompers to Giles B. Jackson, January 23, 1918. Samuel Gompers Papers, Library of Congress, Letterbooks, vol. 242 (Reel 230), pp. 822–23.

19. Jackson to Gompers, March 2, 1918; Gompers to W. B. Wilson, March 5,

1918, Samuel Gompers Papers, Letterbooks, col. 244 (Reel 232), pp. 344–46. Jackson mentioned Senator Thomas Martin of Virginia, Congressman W. Schley Howard of Georgia, Governor H. C. Stuart of Virginia, "... and a number of other senators and congressmen who took the matter up with the Secretary..." See Jackson to Lewis [sic] F. Post, March 14, 1919. National Archives (N.A.), Record Group (RG) 174, Department of Labor Records, Chief Clerk's File, Box 133, File 129/14-C.

20. W. B. Wilson to L. F. Post (memo), May 6, 1918, N.A., RG 174, Box 133, File 129/14-C.

21. Jackson to W. B. Wilson, May 6, 1918 (unsigned). See also L. F. Post to C. T. Clayton (memo), May 14, 1918; N.A., RG 174, Box 133, File 129/14-C.

22. Jackson to C. T. Clayton, June 7, 1918 (memo headed: "A Sketch for the Plans of Operation of the Negro Division of the U.S. Employment Service"). Attached to Clayton to Assistant-Secretary, (memo), n.d. See also the supplementary letter: Haynes to Clayton, June 8, 1918, N.A., RG 174, Box 133, File 129/14-C.

23. Haynes to Assistant Secretary Post, (memo), July 1, 1918, N.A., RG 174, Box 133, File 129/14-C. For more detail on Haynes' work see: Guzda, "Social Experiment of the Labor Department." See also Emmett J. Scott, *Scott's Official History of the American Negro in the World War* (1919: republished by Arno Press and the *New York Times*, New York, 1969), chapter 26.

24. W. B. Wilson to Director General of Employment, (memo), July 9, 1918; Post to Jackson, July 24, 1918, N.A., RG 174, Box 133, File 129/14-C. Post's letter spells out clearly the intent of Secretary Wilson's memo of July 9.

25. One page typescript headed: "Telephone Conversation between Mr. Densmore and Mr. Reid, March 19, 1919, 1:45 pm," N.A., RG 174, Box 133, File 129/14-C. See also Jackson to Hon. G. B. Slemp, April 10, 1921, N.A., RG 174, Box 134, File 129/14–1; Jackson to Hon. Lewis [sic] F. Post, March 14, 1919, N.A., RG 174, Box 133, File 129/14C.

26. U. S. Congress, House, Committee on Appropriations, *Sundry Civil Bill, 119, Hearings*... 65th Congress, 2nd Session, 1918, pp. 1577–78.

27. J. B. Densmore to F. Frankfurter, "Memorandum Concerning Personnel and Functions of District Superintendents." (May 29, 1918). N.A., RG 1, War Labor Policies Board Records, Series 2, Box 18, File: "Employment Service, May-June-July:c-i-f-."

28. See unheaded, three-page, carbon typescript (at bottom of p. 3 is typed: "Submitted by James A. Metcalf, Assistant Superintendent, 6th District, U. S. Employment Service, Meredian, Mississippi, August 26, 1918"). Attached to Assistant Secretary Post to Secretary of Labor, October 4, 1918, memo headed: "Labor Card System in Sixth District of U. S. Employment Service," N.A., RG 174, Box 133, File 129/14-D.

29. Post to W. B. Wilson, October 5, 1918, memo headed: "Report of Western Trip," p. 7, N.A., RG 174, Box 89, File 20/746. See also: Assistant Secretary Post to Secretary of Labor, October 4, 1918, memo headed: "Letter of October 17, 1918, from Cliff Williams." William B. Wilson Papers, Historical Society of Pennsylvania, Box marked "1918" (in pencil: "58F"0, File: "1918"; marked in pencil on tab).

30. USES *Bulletin* 1 (January 17, 1919): 7. At each mass meeting a Loyalty League was organized with an executive committee "on which employers, employees, and farmers each had six representatives." There was a deal of sympathy within the black community itself for moves to put idlers to work and to encourage, through the

formation of special Saturday Service Leagues, a full six days' work on the part of all agricultural laborers. See, for example, J. F. Duggar, Director, Cooperative Extension Work in Agriculture and Home Economics, Auburn, Alabama, to Bradford Knapp, Chief, Office of Extension Work in South, U. S. Department of Agriculture, April 5, 1918, N.A., RG 16, Department of Agriculture Records, Office of the Secretary, 1918: Incoming Correspondence: Labor (April), Acc. 234, Drawer 155.

31. David Kennedy, *Over Here: The First World War and American Society* (New York and Oxford, 1980), p. 281.

32. J. B. Densmore to Secretary of Labor, May 21, 1918. N.A., RG 174, Box 133, File 129/14-C.

33. H. W. Weir, Federal Director, Mississippi, to Director-General, USES, November 12, 1918, memo headed: "Soliciting of Labor." Copy attached to: N. A. Smyth, Assistant Director-General, USES, to Hugh Frayne, War Industries Board, November 16, 1918, memo headed: "Recruiting of Labor at Wiggins, Mississippi." N.A., RG 61, War Industries Board Records, Labor Division; 80A.1., General Correspondence; Box 1018, File "210 (Labor Recruiting)." In this particular instance, it was probable that the representative of the USES had actually overstepped his instructions.

34. U.S. Congress, Joint Committees on Labor, *National Employment Service, Hearings* on S.688, S.1442, and HR.4305, 66th Congress, 1st Session, 1919, pp. 170, 272 (see esp. statements by Miss Grace E. Cooke). The southern states were the only ones to pass laws restricting the activities of labor agents or "emigrant agents" as they were called. The reaction had begun well before American entry in the war. In 1915, Alabama passed legislation forcing "emigrant agents" soliciting labor for interstate projects to pay an annual license fee of $500 in every county where they operated. In the same year, North Carolina levied a tax of $100 for a license plus $100 for every county where such agents operated. In 1916, Virginia raised its license fee from $25 to $500 on itinerant labor agents. In 1917, Georgia insisted on a $1,000 bond plus monthly reports to the Commissioner of Commerce and Labor. In March, 1919, North Carolina increased the tax on labor agents procuring labor for work outside the state from $100 per county to $200. See *American Labor Legislation Review* 5 (December 1915): 770 (Alabama and North Carolina); 6 (September 1916): 290 (Virginia); 7 (September 1917): 553 (Georgia); 9 (December 1919): 437 (North Carolina).

35. Guzda, "Social Experiment of the Labor Department," pp. 29–30.

36. U. S. Congress, Joint Committees on Labor, *National Employment Service, Hearings* (1919), pp. 85–87.

37. Idus A. Newby, "States' Rights and Southern Congressmen during World War I," *Phylon* 24 (Spring 1963): 49.

38. Richard L. Watson, Jr., "A Testing Time for Southern Congressional Leadership: The War Crisis of 1917–1918," *Journal of Southern History* 44 (February 1978): 35; Tindall, *Emergence of the New South*, p. 69.

"Big Enough to Tell Weeds from the Beans": The Impact of Industry on Women in the Twentieth-Century South

MARION W. ROYDHOUSE

In July and August of 1928, in the relative cool of the Carolina mountains near Burnsville, cigarette workers, cigar workers, garment workers and cotton spoolers, telephone operators and weavers, gathered at the Southern Summer School for Women Workers in Industry to discuss the industrial development of their region. Southern-born Lois MacDonald, now a lecturer in economics at New York University, taught a group of twenty-five white women from eight southern states. MacDonald made it clear that the process of industrial change was no different here in the South from that of other sections of the country. But, she added, there were some additional factors to consider, "southern people continue to react as individualistic people—as typical agricultural people."[1]

MacDonald's comments suggest the questions that should shape our investigation of the industrialization in the South and its impact upon working people. To what extent did the system of beliefs inherited from the agricultural world carry over into the mill village and the factory town? Moreover, MacDonald was addressing a particular group, women who worked in industry. Such women participated in the shift from rural farm to industrial town. In what ways were the lives of southern women modified by this shift into the industrial order?

In North Carolina, and across the southern piedmont, in the closing years of the nineteenth century, women moved their toil from the fields and cabins of the mountain and piedmont farms to the steamy air and noisy clatter of the textile mill. Others stepped down the road to the tobacco factory. All needed to work to help provide their families with food and shelter. "We begin to work the time we was big enough to tell weeds from the beans," said Vesta Finley, a cotton mill worker from Marion, in the foothills of the

Blue Ridge.[2] It might be paid work or it might be work at home, but it all contributed to the family income and the family survival.

These women combined an agricultural heritage with the new industrial order which was located in the small towns and growing cities of the area known as the Industrial Crescent. Stretching from Greenville and Spartanburg in South Carolina, northwards to include Roanoke and the Dan River mills on the Virginia border, and turning east to Durham and Raleigh, the industrial locus then petered out on the coastal plain which remained a world of planters, tenant farmers, share-croppers, poverty, and rural isolation. It is this region, focusing upon North Carolina, but drawing upon the communities on its borders, that we can use as a valuable case study in the investigation of the lives of women in the industrializing New South in the first forty years of the twentieth century.

The shift from farm to factory was neither sudden nor abrupt. Families moved into town to earn money when illness or death removed males who could run the farm, or when profits were nonexistent and the lure of cash from the factory wage proved too tempting. Women were the most expendable workers on the farm. They were therefore the first to be sent to the mill and factory. Younger men and women often preceded their families in the shift by leaving home and going into town to board with friends or relatives of the family.

Rosa Holland's rural childhood was typical of many of the women who entered the mills in the early years of the twentieth century. "I was born in the sunny hills of North Carolina out in the country on a small farm in a little log cabin. This cabin only had two doors and one window. . . . My father was just a poor farmer and had to work hard. . . . My Mother had to work hard. She did the housework and helped in the field. When I was old enough I had to look after the smaller children as I was the oldest child in the family of four children."[3]

This rural world remained largely unchanged in the years before World War II. Despite the advance of paved roads, the introduction of rural free mail delivery, and (for the select few) electricity, telephones, and automobiles, the majority of rural women, black and white, lived lives restricted to the local county seat and the nearest crossroads hamlet. Housework, fieldwork, children, and work from early dawn to late evening were the horizons of the world of women on the land. One woman in her sixties recalled such a life, saying, "I never knowed much but hard work, borning and caring for children, doing the housework and my part of the farm work."[4]

Crops demanded attention regardless of the needs of children. When tobacco had to be graded for auction women simply could not pick up babies every time they cried. If husbands were ill, the plowing had to be done, although this was the one thing that women rarely did. As a consequence older girls were often given the responsibility for younger siblings. "My mother always went to the field with the ones who were old enough to work. That left most of the housework on me," recalled Grace Elliott.[5]

Once old enough, children were welcome extra hands on the land. "I had to hoe corn and cotton, and help tie and grade tobacco, and after cotton opened I had to pick cotton. If there wasn't work to do at home I would have to help other people."[6] Children could be relied upon to fetch stove wood, to feed hogs, and help weed and pick crops. Young girls washed dishes, made beds, set out cold food for supper, or cooked simple meals.

This toil was undertaken on an inadequate diet. The resultant deficiencies in nutrition led to ill health and disease which sapped the vitality of even the strongest. Pellagra and hookworm were widespread, and in the eastern portions of the state malaria also weakened bodies with its periodic chills and fever.[7]

Life for rural women was often lonely. On rainy days, or at night, men might gather at the local crossroads store, or by the 1930s at the newfangled filling station. But women remained at home. On Saturday the whole family might journey into town to lay in stores and to enjoy a little company. But for women this was a rare outing and the main source of adult companionship came from membership in the local church and from nearby family members.

Indeed the church was the central institution in the community. For black and white alike, whatever the denomination, the church provided a measure of stability in a mobile tenant farming population and welcome respite from the isolation of the farm. A prayer meeting during the week, a monthly church social, and regular Sunday church services provided conversation, local news and gossip, and of course spiritual support.

This rural world remained home for the majority of the state's population before World War II. Yet, despite the continuing overwhelmingly rural nature of the society, by 1920 the impact of the new industrial order could be seen in the rising red brick mills and the bustling growth of the industrial centers of Durham, Winston-Salem, Charlotte, and Greensboro. North Carolina became, for both blacks and whites, a major employer of women in industry. In 1920 more women were employed in North Carolina in the textile and tobacco industries than anywhere else in the South. Moreover, the growth rate for this female labor force was marked. Between 1910 and 1920 the number of women employed in mechanical and manufacturing industries increased by over one-third. In the next decade the increase was nearly 50 percent. In 1870, fifteen out of every one hundred women were working at paid work; in 1930 the figure had grown to twenty-three out of every one hundred.[8]

Although in the overall work force only one worker in every four was female, by 1930 they were nearly half of the cigar and tobacco workers and nearly 40 percent of the textile workers.[9] A few women worked in other industrial occupations. A handful of women became printer's apprentices, engravers, or linotype operators. Others worked in ship building shops, in flour mills, in tinware and enamel factories, and at canning fruit and vegetables.

Even though they were the traditional employers of women, the clothing and garment industries were of lesser importance in the South than in the industrialized North. In the South the concentration was upon the production of yarn, rather than the finished sweater, more on denim and gingham than on the finished products of jeans, overalls, or shirtwaists. In 1930 the clothing factories in North Carolina employed less than 3,000 women. Elderly women, or women who could not find work in industry might sew at home, and every town had its seamstresses, an occupation shared by both black and white women. As manufactured clothes became cheaper, many of these women were forced out of the work force or into other occupations. Black women were hardest hit by this change, as they were excluded from the textile industry almost entirely.[10]

For rural black women the urban shift meant a shift to domestic service and, to a small extent, to jobs in the tobacco industry. A government survey in 1909 found only eighteen black women working in over 152 southern mills. Out of every one hundred black women working in 1920, forty-seven would be on the land, thirty-seven would be in domestic service, and only twelve would be in industrial jobs. In comparison, for every one hundred white women, thirty-three would be farming, and thirty-three would be in industrial occupations.[11]

North Carolina was unusual in the comparatively large numbers of black women employed in the cigar and tobacco industry. By the 1930s half the number of women in the cigarette factories of Durham and Winston-Salem were black; in comparison the figures in Petersburg and Richmond in Virginia were around 20 percent. These black workers were relegated to the leaf departments where the work was the most dirty and the conditions the most difficult. In 1932, according to the Women's Bureau, fully 98 percent of the black cigarette workers in Durham and Winston-Salem were in the leaf departments.[12]

Black women in the industrial work force were, like their rural sisters, more likely to be working in the paid work force, and for a longer period of their lives, than white women. In 1930, 20.7 percent of native-born white women were employed, but 30.6 percent of black women were working.[13] The embedded racism of the society reflected itself in the lower ability of the black community to provide a living wage for a family, and the barriers to "putting something by" to provide for old age or widowhood.

The lives of female industrial workers can be seen as having a distinct number of stages, each of which enables us to analyze the impact of the urban industrial world. First came childhood, whether it be on the farm or in the villages and towns. But these years were brief; childhood was short-lived. By the time that they were fourteen, young women had been in and out of the work force. Some began work during the summers, others had already become full-time members of the work force. This was the second life stage. From this point on until they married, as the majority did in their early twenties, women enjoyed a period of comparative freedom and independence from family responsibilities. They now earned the highest wages of their working lives.

Although there is little hard evidence as to the exact length of time women worked before they married, and the precise number of women who went in and out of the work force for substantial periods in their lives, a careful reading of the available interviews and autobiographies, combined with the census statistics, gives the strong impression that the lives of women who began work in the textile mills and tobacco factories would consist of periods of paid work interspersed with periods of "home work."

In the third stage, married life, could come a withdrawal from the work force. But the lives of married women also revolved around the need to earn a living wage, and that involved the whole family. As a consequence, if there were not enough "hands" in the family to bring home a large enough pay envelope, then wives went back into the work force in their middle years. By the time they were forty, their earning power had begun to drop. The industrial labor force contained few women over fifty and families would have to find other sources of income.

During the years of the greatest growth of industry in the South, many women spent childhoods on farms and moved to town when financial exegencies or the desire for some freedom caused them to move into the industrial work force. When Beulah Parrish's father became blind with pellagra soon after the turn of the century, her family moved into town so that she and her sisters could begin work in a hosiery mill and support the rest of the family.

Like many others, Beulah grew to hate the confines of the mill and the rigid demands of the industrial time clock. "I would often long to be out in the open once again, where I could be among nature," she wrote.[14] One consequence of this reluctance to abandon the rural world was the pattern of shifting back and forth between the factory and the farm. The first generations of factory workers tried to combine the rural and urban world by using income from the mills to support uneconomic farms, or by spending periods in the mills and then returning to the farm.

By the 1930s there were second and third generation families in the mill villages and the situation was similar in the tobacco factories of Durham and Winston-Salem. Children in these families had grown used to store-bought clothes. The family had come to depend on the community of the village and town and had come to prefer it to the loneliness of the rural world. Gradually links with the rural community faded and what remained was a set of feelings and memories.

Those whose families had already made the industrial shift might enter the mills before they could walk. Charlisle Pope was born and reared near a cotton mill, and although her parents took in three or four boarders, both her mother and father worked in the mill, and "us children were too little to leave so we had to go along. We were dumped in the bobbin bin and to stay there till they were through with their work."[15] Young girls could also begin life in the mills by "helping" older sisters or mothers. One woman recalled her first taste of the mill when she carried food to her sisters in the spinning room. "Each day we carried dinner I would help my sisters spool. At first I couldn't do anything but take out the empty quills, later I put in the full bobbins and soon I learned to use the knotters and could tie the ends together."[16]

Some began work during the long summer vacations, although they were sometimes barred from work when the child labor laws were sporadically enforced. Ollie Brown began work in a underwear mill when she was twelve years old. "I did not work the next summer because the [child labor] law was enforced.... The summer I was fourteen I took back the same job with a raise of two dollars a week."[17]

The textile industry took in young people whose eyes and hands were quick and who were easily trained to watch moving machinery. Older men and women were considered too slow and set in their ways to be of use. The machinery usually demanded only a small measure of skill. Training did not take long in the first twenty-five years of the twentieth century when the machinery was run at a relatively slow pace. As the industry grew older the machinery improved in technical quality and was speeded up. In 1910, 66 percent of the women in the textile industry were twenty years of age or younger. Just over 2 percent of the female workers in that same year were over forty-five years of age.[18] Technical changes combined with public pressure in the first two decades of the century to force employers to eliminate most child labor, especially that of children younger than twelve. Campaigns continued in the 1920s to eliminate the labor of children between the ages of twelve and fourteen.

Learners' wages were small, but once the women mastered the needed skills, their wages rose. During the next few years, while their eyesight was sharp and their hands quick, the women reached the peak of their earning power. Young women who had recently begun work in Durham in the midtwenties reported that as long as the work did not "run" too fast, they were satisfied with their jobs.[19] Young, single women had some control over their lives for the first time, and they also had some cash in their hands. Those who did not turn all their wages over to the family were able to buy a few clothes, to splurge on an outing, and perhaps go to the movies. Women in these years were at their most mobile and most independent. These were years that could bring separation from the demands of family responsibilities.

Those who moved into town to board with friends of the family or with relatives could carry on their lives out from under the watchful eye of parents, and they could meet a wider circle of friends and potential spouses in the convivial world of the young workers. It is clear that some women who left home simply stopped contributing to the family wage, and this added to the amount of money to spend on themselves, on clothes, and on entertainment.

The young women also took advantage of whatever social institutions were available to them. Church groups, or groups organized by the social welfare institutions run by the mills, flourished. One young worker who had to look after her siblings was still able to steal time to herself and reported, "I go to the Y.W.C.A. Club on Wednesday night. Sometimes we go to Camp Joy Cliff (a Y.W.C.A. camp) on Saturday afternoons. Sometimes I go to Sunday School and church."[20]

The Young Women's Christian Association (YWCA) provided a welcome place to meet other young women of like mind and interests, but it was also a means of furthering educations cut short by the demands of the work place. In the major industrial centers, and reaching out into some mill communities, the YWCA provided workers' education classes in subjects like etiquette, handicrafts, labor drama, or simply physical recreation. They also ran more demanding classes in economics, English, and mathematics. The YWCA ran summer camps in the mountains where workers could enjoy a brief respite from the factory and with other women workers, college students, and office workers, begin to investigate the economic and industrial structure of the world of which they were a part.[21] In this way some young women became aware of social change and their part in the economic structure.

Yet few women could call their wages or their lives their own for any length of time. Illness, disability, and family responsibilities shaped women's lives. Most had someone to support, if not all the time, at least in moments of family crisis when illness or accidents thrust the family into debt. Women who began to work early in their lives to support a family tended to continue to do so, even if they remained at home for intervals or lived away from the family for periods.

The work experience of Kaola Edwards was in many ways typical. She began work in a hosiery mill, worked for two years, was taken ill with fever, worked in a tobacco factory, then a hosiery mill again, before leaving to nurse a sick sister. She then went back into a cotton mill, nursed her mother, married and worked until she was taken ill again herself. Her husband was killed in 1925 in a work accident and she returned to a tobacco factory in Greensboro.[22]

As the industry grew older so did its work force. Kaola Edwards worked until she married, and returned to work. In 1930 married women made up over one-third of the total female work force. In the cigar and tobacco industry as a whole in 1930 half the women workers were married and an additional 15 percent were either widowed or divorced. The cotton mills also employed large numbers of married women; in 1930 over 44 percent were married and another 8.6 percent were widowed or divorced.[23]

Not surprisingly marriage altered the shape of women's lives. Women who worked until they married usually continued working until they could afford to "leave and go to housekeeping," or until children were born. Some women went back into the labor force soon after their children were born, leaving them in the care of grandmothers or relations, or perhaps working the night shift when their husbands could share the burden of child care. Some returned when their children were older and could be left in the care of the oldest child, usually the oldest girls. Others returned to work when husbands died, or were unable or unwilling to work. Still others were forced back into the work force when spouses deserted them or when they were divorced.

It remained accepted belief that marriage ought to mean acquiring a husband who could support a family. But as Charlisle Pope told an interviewer in the late thirties, "I married when I was sixteen. I thought I wouldn't have to work but I got fooled. I worked all the time except when I was pregnant enough for it to show, as the mill wouldn't permit me to do it then."[24] Bessie Edens, a rayon worker from across the mountains in Tennessee, put the general attitude this way, "most single girls think that they will work just a year or so and get married and then all will be roses for them." Another worker in Roanoke pointed out that this meant that some women did not care about conditions because they believed that marriage would take them out of the mills. "But in most cases they are more closely tied than ever because their husbands don't make enough to keep up a home on his income."[25]

Prevailing social mores were that married women ought not to work in the paid work force and it was a sign of failure when they did. Bessie Edens, while at a workers' school in the Carolina mountains, wrote an impassioned essay which reveals the dilemma of the married woman: "Is a woman supposed to stay at home and do without the things she really needs because she is married?"[26] It seems clear from the evidence that the impact of the traditional beliefs in the separation of the spheres and the place of women in the private sphere of the home and the family continued to have a strong hold on the factory community, and triumphed over reality.

Once married and working, women found themselves with two sets of tasks. Married women simply doubled up; home work and industrial work now occupied their time and were combined to stretch the limits of the day as far as was humanly possible. Given the enormous difficulties, some compromises were worked out. Grandmothers were pressed into service, or older children might do housework and look after children. Some accommodations to the industrial order were made, but they were not in the realms of ideas or changed values. Industrial work replaced field work and the remainder of women's roles stayed the same.

Life for married women in the work force was hard. Grace Elliott, a particularly resourceful and independent worker from Marion, North Carolina, married and took over the care of four children from her husband's previous marriage. She returned to the work force soon after her marriage because she was determined that the children should go to school and be properly fed and clothed.

I would get up at four o'clock in the morning, get breakfast and dinner, milk the cow, get the children's clothes out for them to wear to school and get to the mill 20 minutes til six ready for work. At 12 o'clock I would walk home, eat a cold lunch, and go back to the mill and work till six in the afternoon. After stopping time I would go home, cook supper, iron, sometimes sew after the children had gone to bed.[27]

After four years this determined mother ended up in the hospital, but it was a common enough round for the married woman worker.

As women grew older it became more and more difficult to get jobs in industry, married or not. Some took in boarders, or sent children into the factory. One forty-six year old woman in Burlington in 1908 told government interviewers that she was completely dependent upon the income she got from boarders. Her daughter, aged sixteen, was married and wanted to leave home. She herself was ill with malaria, and the only outside income came from the wages of an eleven-year-old nephew, who worked as a doffer, but who had bronchitis and was sickly. Here seems not to be an unusual position for women who were widows or who were left as the head of a household without younger workers to bring home cash wages.[28]

In broad strokes, this is the outline of the life stages of the women in the industrial work force. We need now to turn to the work place itself and consider the quality of these women's working lives. Whether they went into the mills, and mill villages, or the tobacco stemmeries or manufacturing plants, all of the women workers were affected by the conditions of the work place, the hours worked, and wages paid.

Life in the tobacco factories could be dirty, noisy and dangerous. Women worked at a variety of tasks in the process of producing plug or chewing tobacco, cigars, and cigarettes. Their working hours were long and wages were small. Their health was impaired as a result of dusty, hot, noisy and ill-lighted rooms and tasks that were physically strenuous and monotonous.

Men and women were segregated by racial and occupational divisions of the tasks to be performed. Black and white were kept physically separate, on different floors, or in entirely separate buildings. Black women worked in the most arduous and most unhealthy jobs in the factory. Many black women were employed in the warehouses where the leaf tobacco was prepared for the "sweating process" and where tobacco was left to mature before being taken to the manufacturing plant. Piece rates were paid, and the season was limited. These workers received the lowest wages in the industry.[29]

Other tobacco was sent directly to the plants in Reidsville, Durham, and Winston-Salem. The production of cigarettes and cigars was substantially mechanized by 1920 and as the machine did more and more, male employees were replaced by women. There was no rigid job separation by sex, in that sometimes the segregation was more a function of the type of machine rather than the task. For example, both men and women were employed on machines that rolled and packed cigarettes. Some tasks, such as inspecting, wrapping, and boxing were done only by women. Only men were foremen and mechanics, the most responsible and more powerful jobs in the factory hierarchy. In 1929 a worker summed up the hierarchy that this produced, saying, "men do all the mechanical work and the bossing, women run the machines that turn out the cigars and cigarettes, and negroes do the cleaning and dirty jobs." The lines of power were clear, white men, white women, and then black men and women.[30]

North Carolina had some of the longest working days in the tobacco industry. In 1908 women worked ten hours a day, Monday to Friday, in the cigarette factories and on Saturdays they worked an additional five to nine hours. In the cigar plants the hours were longer still.[31] Wage rates for these long hours varied with the particular task being performed, but women were consistently paid less than men whatever the task.[32]

During the twenties the "speed-up" or the "stretch-out" system increased the number of machines that one worker controlled. The time and motion study expert also descended upon industry. The combination resulted in wage cuts and further mechanization that left women in constant fear of not being able to earn a living wage. If the stretch-out decreased the number of jobs available for women, so too did the Depression. Tobacco stockholders continued to reap a profit because people smoked, whatever their financial woes, but for women working in the tobacco plants it brought hardships. At any time the women might be told to pack up and go home until further notice. As a result they were forced to live on wages even smaller than the already inadequate full-time wage.

But low wages were only a part of the tobacco workers' world. Conditions in the plants contributed to women's daily discomfort and provided a constant health hazard. "It is said that some girls cannot bear it and are obliged to give up work," reported the Labor Bureau agents in 1908. Emma Shields, investigating for the Women's Bureau in 1920 found black women working in buildings where the "air is so heavily laden with fumes and dust that it is nauseating. It is not unusual," she continued, "to see women with hankerchiefs tied over their nostrils to prevent inhaling the stifling, strangling air."[33] The days in the tobacco dust were long, and the breaks short, and some women simply wore out their health in the factory.

If the tobacco factory could be injurious to one's health, the alternatives of work in the mills had the same effect. "Some look old from working when they aren't able to work," wrote one worker, Marian Cochran, about workers in Roanoke. "Most of them complain of being tired all the time. They are slaves of their machines and the foremen don't make life any better for them, either."[34] The same power hierarchy as in the tobacco industry prevailed, and the same complaints about working conditions, wages, and hours were voiced by the workers.

The mills maintained a system of partial sexual segregation and almost total racial segregation. Only a handful of black women worked in the mills, as sweepers and at janitorial work. Generally white women were employed wherever the task was not too heavy and where it was possible, therefore, to save money by employing women a lower rates of pay. Men were employed as mechanics and loom fixers. Only men were considered for positions such as section bosses, foremen, and superintendents. Women were not considered for these overseeing positions, and often the blame was laid upon the women themselves. A mill official of the huge Dan River Mills in Danville, Virginia, told one woman from the North Carolina League of Women Voters that "our work in general is not such as would lend to have women as foremen, and they have never equipped themselves for this leadership."[35]

In other areas, men, women, and children competed for jobs. Both men and women worked at the spinning machines, bending over the work to fix broken threads with a careful twist of the finger or wrist or with a little gadget that fitted over the fingers and was worked with the thumb. Women tended to be in the majority in the yarn-spinning rooms at the end of the spinning process where the spools of thread were lighter and the thread finer. Before 1920 young boys were used as doffers, taking off the full bobbin that carried the thread from the spinning machines, and replacing them with empty ones. But, as the child labor laws were enforced, women replaced children at this task. In the weave room, men and women competed for the highest paying jobs in the mills. Weaving required an acquired skill and a quick eye to detect breaks in the thread; the finer the weaving, the greater the skill demanded.

Wages earned in these factories varied with the sex and skill of the worker. Many women worked on piece rates while others were paid by the hour, and it is difficult to pinpoint the precise amount of money women took home. Moreover, employers were notoriously reluctant to open their payrolls to public scrutiny. Despite these obstacles it is possible to calculate average full-time earnings with some accuracy.[36] Low wages were used to lure textile plants away from the Northeast, and indeed, it has since been shown that this was the major factor in the shift of the textile industry southwards. The value added to the cotton product by wages was at its lowest in the South.

Southern workers were paid less for longer hours and had a lower standard of living than northern workers in the same occupations. Even with fluctuations in wages during the boom years of the cotton industry in the early twenties, the textile workers remained among the lowest paid employees in North Carolina, with the notable exception, to be made everywhere in the South, of those occupations reserved for black men and women.[37]

Between 1900 and 1918 wages rose slowly, but at no time did they keep pace with inflation and the rising cost of living. Income was highly unstable, fluctuating with the vagaries of personal health, the whims of foremen, short time, stretch-outs, and wage cuts. A hosiery worker in Durham who had earned $23.00 a week in 1922 averaged only $15.00 a week two years later. Weavers in the Dan River Mills earned $25.00 to $27.00 a week in the late twenties, but after a series of wage cuts and a stretch-out in 1931 these same women were taking home between $6.00 and $14.00 a week.[38] These women consistently earned less than men, often in jobs where they were performing the same tasks. Women working as weavers in 1929 earned nearly $2.00 a week less than men doing the same job.[39]

These wages were barely sufficient to support one person, and women were often a part of a family wage unit. It was necessary to send every able-bodied member of the family out to work and even then the family income was never secure. Those who worked on piece rates faced lowered incomes as they grew older and could no longer sustain as fast a pace as younger women. Illness and accidents interrupted work and layoffs meant great hardships because few families could accumulate savings to tide them over the hard times.

Compounding low wages were long hours. Southern textile workers, like the tobacco workers, spent some of the longest work days in the nation. In 1900 mills had shifts that lasted an average of ten to twelve and a half hours a day, with a shorter day on Saturday. The pressure of public opinion, the threat of restrictive legislation, and the specter of a glutted market resulting from overproduction induced the manufacturers to reduce these hours a little. By 1920 over half the mills worked a reported fifty-five–hour work week. But some superintendents eager to get more yarn or cloth in production resorted to lengthening the official eleven-hour work day by insisting that the women be at their machines before the whistle blew, and that they continue work until signalled. These rules could lengthen a work day by fifteen to thirty minutes. Other mills simply ignored the official limit. In 1929 the Marion Manufacturing Company was still working a twelve and a half hour shift according to its female employees.[40] Sanctions against such mills were virtually nonexistent, as the state Labor Bureau had few funds to employ inspectors and fines were rarely, if ever, imposed.

During their hours in the mill women were exposed to a number of health hazards. They suffered from a variety of work-related disabilities as well as from illnesses endemic in the mill village populations. Humid air and high temperatures combined with lint and dust to make mill work dangerous to the workers' health. Cotton fibers become full of static electricity and break if the air is too dry; therefore jets of water were sprayed into the air to keep the air humid and the fibers supple. Too often, despite the complaints of workers, the air became saturated and the temperatures soared to above ninety degrees. Women emerged from the mills into the cool night air after working in these conditions drenched in sweat, their clothes sticky and damp.

"You came out of that mill," said Vesta Finley of the Marion mills, "every thread on your body wet.... It was just hot in there. You's just burn to a frizzle."[41]

As a result workers succumbed to a variety of bronchial and respiratory ailments, and their joints became stiff with lumbago. The lint and dust caused what was later diagnosed as "brown lung" disease as breathing passages filled up with particles that floated in the air. The constant noise and vibration of the machinery strained the nervous system and could impair hearing. Long hours in the mill and the lack of fresh air stunted the growth of young girls and boys and made recovery from illness slow. Tubercular men and women continued to work in the factory, exposing other workers and their families to the condition.[42]

Night work was particularly loathed because shifts at night were generally longer than the day shift, and the schedule imposed a further strain on the health, especially for married women. After a night in the mill these women would go home, snatch a few hours sleep, and then get up to do household chores and cook meals. Nolia King, a mill worker in Marion, worked for five months on the night shift in the late twenties. Her description of the experience captures the feelings of many of her fellow workers.

My work began at six o'clock in the afternoon and I stopped work at five in the morning. The mill was hot since there had been no fresh air in it all day.... When I entered the mill the hot air was even at the door and became worse at the center of the mill.... When I first began I had a good appetite and ate my supper regardless of the heat. But after a month's time I didn't want anything.... In the mornings I was so tired I could hardly walk home. In the first four hours I slept very well but after the people began their daily work I would wake up and couldn't get any more sleep that day. In the evening when I went to work I couldn't tell I had had those few hours rest.

All the workers, both men and women, felt the way I did, completely exhausted and old before their time.[43]

Workers, in a form of passive resistance to this work regime, gave vent to their displeasure by moving from mill to mill in search of better conditions and better pay. This was the most common form of workers' control of the work place. Despite the lack of organization in the labor force in the South, there is evidence of discontent and sporadic attempts at worker resistance. Certainly women were aware of their plight and were concerned how the world outside the factory perceived their lives. Lillie Morris Price, who worked all her life in the mills and on a looping machine at home, wrote in 1929 when there were strikes going on all over the state, "I have wondered if the people who wear the socks ever think of the poor, tired girls who make them, working under bad conditions and low wages . . . because they were unorganized and have no power."[44]

Price, and women like her, took part in the wave of strikes; they led the work force out of the rayon mills in Elizabethton, Tennessee, just across the border, and they stood on the picket lines in Gastonia and faced the National Guard units there. Ella May Wiggins became the balladeer of the Gastonia workers and the martyr of the strike when she was shot on the way to a union meeting. Women do not show up in the official records of union officers, or in the obvious positions of leadership, but they were an integral part of the labor movement nonetheless, as recent oral histories of the strikes show.[45]

These hardships of life in the mill and tobacco factory were only a part of the changes brought about by industrialization. The urban shift also brought changes in the institutions that dominated women's lives.

The mill village as a physical and institutional presence overwhelmed its inhabitants. The red brick of the mill rose several stories above the rows of houses that made up the community built to house workers drawn in from the surrounding countryside. "Here we find unpaved streets of red mud and black cinders with no sidewalks. The houses are all alike, and are in long rows up and down the mountainside," wrote one woman describing the East Marion mill village.

> Some of them are painted with very ugly colors while others have no paint at all. ... In the back lot between two houses you would find one toilet, to serve two families. These are open toilets a pit being a few feet deep. They sometimes overflow, then the toilet is moved to a new spot. About every four and six houses you will find an open pump on one side of the street. About four to six families from the opposite side of the street also get water from the same well. Here the cows, chickens and children are all watered together.... On a hill overlooking the village is quite a different scene. Here is a nice little village apart from the workers, nice winding lanes, large shade trees, pretty flower gardens, nice paved streets and sidewalks, paved walks right up to the doors of large nicely painted houses. Here the houses have sleeping porches, heating systems, water systems and lights. These are the bossmen's homes, and this section is known as bossmen's row.[46]

This was the mill village. This was the site of women's daily toil. Visitors, if they ventured beyond the front streets, or bossmen's row, looked askance and concluded that the workers did not care enough to keep their surroundings neat, well watered, and well painted. But as one woman commented angrily, "most prosperous people look down on people that live in a mill village. They think they are better than mill workers. They talk about how ugly the village looks and how dirty the people look and call them 'old mill trash.' But they haven't realized that they hold the money and the mill worker doesn't have enough to make life any better for himself."[47]

For every mill village that had unpaved roads and inadequate sewage and water supplies, the defenders of industrial progress could point to villages where the houses were in a variety of styles and where the picket fences and neat gardens belied the critics' claims. Certainly the newer mills had better housing, and some villages, such as the Cramerton mill villages, were not unpleasant places. But the fact remained that the families in these institutions had to supply workers to the mills or be evicted. Their tenure was linked to the ability to provide "hands."

Men and women alike chafed at the control the mill owners exerted over their lives and they exhibited a resistance toward the welfare programs funded by the mills that welfare workers found galling and described as "contrariness" and which showed the ability of the workers to shape their own lives despite outside pressures. Mill workers resented the condescension that they perceived in the outside society, and tended to withdraw into their own communities. Often there was some antagonism between townspeople and the mill workers, and this reinforced the separation between factory workers and "uptown" people. In the early 1920s one woman told Lois MacDonald that she never went back to her old home because she was ashamed that she now lived on a "mill hill." The general feeling was that you might slave away your life in the mill, but there were few alternatives, "there is nothing else for poor folks to do."[48] Even though women thought that a mill village was a bad place to bring up children, they felt their own children would know nothing else.

Although not all the cotton textile workers lived in mill villages, the villages themselves, with their social isolation, created the image of the "cotton mill trash" and reinforced the low social standing and poor educational opportunities of the families who lived in them. The "lint-head" was an early, stereotypical figure within the society.

Although the mill crusades of the 1880s and 1890s were supposed to give employment to white men and women from the mountains and farms who were to be thus helped to join the modern world of industry and progress, what the mill village succeeded in doing was to create a class of people separate from the rest of the society. They were separate, to an extent, even from the rest of the working class.

Starting in the 1930s, as the mill villages were sold and as mills were surrounded by growing towns and cities, the social divisions began to break down. Mill workers came into contact with those from outside the mill community and had better educations. Some social barriers began to crumble. But before World War II textile workers remained at the bottom of the social heap; held there by low wages, inadequate educations, and prevailing social attitudes. They remained beyond the social pale, regarded as sloppy, lacking in ambition and drive, and in need of education into the mores and habits of the urban society.[49]

Socially separate from the rest of the urban community, and often isolated physically, the mill village particularly relied upon the church as a means of social control as well as a means of providing conviviality in villages bereft of other gathering places. The church provided spiritual succor which made it easier to face the monotony and difficulties of ekeing out a living. Paradoxically the same churches reinforced the economic and social status quo and dampened stirrings of industrial unrest. The focus of the fundamentalist and evangelical churches on spiritual salvation in the next world and acceptance of this one combined with the dominance of the mill owner over the churches to provide for effective social control.

In the company town the mill churches were often subsidized by mill owners, who paid the salaries of the ministers and then exerted pressure on them to refrain from airing opinions contrary to those of the mill management. Even when direct pressure was not applied the mill preachers did in fact reflect the social attitudes of the mill management rather than those of the workers. The mill hierarchy also reproduced itself in the churches. At the Symre Mill in Gastonia the Sunday School was run by the mill superintendent, and the overseers made up the church leadership.[50]

Inside and outside the mill village religious orthodoxy was praised and extended theological debate was frowned upon. Once a year the revival, common to all the mill churches as it was to most evangelical churches in the South, provided a welcome social excitement as well as spiritual uplift. Despite rampant factionalism and interdenominational struggles the southern churches were fairly much agreed on the basic concepts of hell, God, Satan, redemption, and original sin. In their adherence to Protestant fundamentalism preachers concentrated upon a spiritual salvation that held a strong appeal for working men and women. Its roots went back to the origins of the frontier South, when itinerant preachers wandered the trails of the edge of settlement preaching a gospel of hell fire to the isolated settlements. The shift from farm to factory had changed attitudes and values little in this realm and simply reinforced traditional attitudes and emphasized the hierarchical nature of the family relationships and the subordinate role of women.

In sum, industrial growth created cities like Durham and Greensboro, and drew families in from the surrounding farms. Industrial growth also created the mill village and began to reshape the contours of rural lives. Men and boys as well as girls and women now rose with the factory whistles. But some women were already up and working; not in the paid labor forces, but at "home" work. Women of all ages then trooped into the mill yard or trudged down to the factory gate and spent long hours working at the demanding pace of the machine. Despite the monotony, the dirty and often dangerous nature of the work they did, in some places the women were able to enjoy the company of other women, and if the work "ran" well and the machines were not too noisy, work was enlivened by the pleasure of that companionship.

Life outside the factory was also conditioned by the new industrial order. The double day of housework and field work on the farm was now replaced by housework and factory work. The tasks that had traditionally fallen to women remained theirs; women still patched quilts, sewed clothes, cooked and cleaned. But gradually clothes were store-bought and food was no longer canned at home. Links with the farm began to fade. As the physical setting changed, demands upon women in terms of time and the specific nature of the work changed; attitudes changed a good deal less because the values and the conservatism of the rural world remained. The church dominated public life and social attitudes, and the family dominated the private sphere, as they had in the rural communities. Women still expected to marry and bear children, and they expected, regardless of reality, that their husbands would earn enough to support the family. When this did not happen, women went back into the work force. The low wages paid by industrial concerns and the consequent lack of what could be called a living wage meant that the traditional adherence to the separation of spheres and the role of women as nurturer and helpmeet had to give way before the demands of the industrial order. As long as eyes held up, and hands were quick enough, and there were mouths to be fed, women worked in the factory.

Yet everyone struggled to resist change and continued to believe in the strict division of life's tasks by gender. Society's expectations of women changed little with their entry into the industrial work force. In the workplace women earned less than men. They were almost invariably in a position subordinate to them. Women still began to work when they could tell the weeds from the beans, and the experience of "cash money" in their hands meant little difference in overall attitudes toward women's proper place in the worker's world.

NOTES

1. Outline of economics class, Southern Summer School for Women Workers in Industry, American Labor Education Service Records, 1927–1962, Labor Management Documentation Center, Martin P. Catherwood Library, Cornell University, Ithaca, New York (hereafter the S.S.S. Papers). The focus of historians on social and labor history is only now beginning to result in careful studies of the world of southern men and women as workers. See Jacquelyn Dowd Hall, Robert Korstad, and James Leloudis, "Cotton Mill People: Work, Community, and Protest in the Textile South, 1880–1940," *American Historical Review* 91 (April 1986):245–86; Dolores E. Janiewski, "From Field to Factory: Race, Class, Sex and the Woman Worker in Durham, 1880–1940" (Ph.D. diss., Duke University, 1979). For a good general survey of the state of the history of "ordinary people" see James B. Gardner and George Rollie Adams, eds., *Ordinary People and Everyday Life: Perspectives on the New Social History* (Nashville, 1983). Most analysis has focused only on the industrial Northeast, see for example, Leslie W. Tentler, *Wage-Earning Women: Industrial Work and Family Life in the United States, 1900–1930* (New York, 1979) which, despite its title, deals only with large Eastern and Midwestern cities; Milton Cantor and Bruce Laurie, eds., *Class, Sex, and the Woman Worker* (Westport, 1977).

2. Interview with Vesta Finley by Mary Frederickson and Marion Roydhouse, Marion, North Carolina, July 1975 (hereafter Vesta Finley Interview.).

3. Rosa Holland, autobiography, S.S.S. Papers.

4. Interview with "Mrs. Watkins Abernathy," Newton Grove, North Carolina,

Federal Writers' Project Papers, 1936–1940, Papers of the Regional Director, William Terry Couch, Southern Historical Collection, University of North Carolina, Chapel Hill (hereafter FWP Interviews). It is not clear from the manuscripts of the interviews which names were already changed to protect privacy and which were not. Some are pseudonyms. For further evidence of the rural world see Margaret Hagood, *Mothers of the South: Portraiture of the White Tenant Farm Woman* (Chapel Hill, 1939).

5. Grace Elliott, autobiography, S.S.S. Papers.

6. Beulah Parrish, autobiography, S.S.S. Papers.

7. Elizabeth W. Etheridge, "The Strange Hunger: A Social History of Pellagra in the South" (Ph.D. diss., University of Georgia, 1967); Robert W. Twyman, "The Clay Eater: A New Look at an Old Southern Enigma," *Journal of Southern History* 37 (1971): 439–48.

8. U.S. Census, compiled from 1910, 4: 124–37; 1920, 4: 92–109; 1930, 4: 1202–5. It should be noted that the Census category of manufacturing and mechanical industries is regarded as the industrial work force for the purpose of this analysis. Numbers of women employed in other categories which could be considered industrial were minimal. U.S. Department of Labor, Women's Bureau, *Woman's Place in Industry in Ten Southern States*, by Mary Anderson (Washington, D.C.: Government Printing Office, 1931), pp. 10–11; despite the burdensome work women did inside the house, for the sake of clarity I shall follow the Census definitions of "gainfully employed" to mean the number of women over ten years of age (unless noted) in the paid work force at the time of the Census. Note also that the Census concept of gainful employment was a count of occupational status rather than current employment, and so the figures probably underestimate women by not including those who felt that their jobs were temporary, and who considered their primary status that of housewife. See U.S. Bureau of Census, *Historical Statistics of the United States, Colonial Times to 1957* (Washington, D.C.: Government Printing Office, 1960), pp. 36–45. The number of women involved increased from 58,860 to 272,965. U.S. Census, 1930, 4: 1201.

9. U.S. Census, 1910, 4: 1202–5. Note, however, if women included in agriculture are included, between 1910 and 1920 the number of working women decreases, probably because of the changes in the instructions to the census enumerators at the time of the 1910 Census. In 1910 they were instructed that "the occupation ... followed ... by a woman is just as important ... as the occupation followed by a man. Therefore, it must never be taken for granted, without inquiry, that a woman, or child, has no occupation." Furthermore, women who did farm work, but who did not receive wages, were returned as farm laborers in 1910, but not in 1920 or subsequent censuses. See *Thirteenth Census of the United States, 1920: Population*, 4: 26–29; Further figures are from *U.S. Census*, 1910, 4: 124–37; *U.S. Census*, 1920, 4: 92–109; *U.S. Census*, 1930, 4: 1202–5, and compiled from 3: 341.

10. In 1910, 6,241 women listed their occupation as "dressmaker (not in a factory)" and 26.6 percent of these were black. By 1930 the number of dressmakers and seamstresses had been reduced to 2,650. See *U.S. Census*, 1930, 4: 1202 and 1910, 4: 500–1.

11. U.S. Congress, Senate, *Report on Condition of Woman and Child Wage Earners in the United States*, 19 Vols., S.Doc. 645, 61st Congress, 2nd Session, 1909–1910, Vol. 1: *Cotton Textile Industry*, p. 118 (hereafter *Woman and Child*

Wage Earners); Holland Thompson, *From the Cotton Field to the Cotton Mill* (New York, 1906), pp. 249–65; Department of Labor, Women's Bureau, *Women at Work* by Eleanor Nelson (Washington, D.C.: Government Printing Office, 1933); *U.S. Census*, 1920, 4: 987–89; *U.S. Census*, 1930, 4: 374; Interview with Frank T. DeVyver by Marion W. Roydhouse, Durham, N.C., April, 1975; Lorenzo L. Greene and Carter G. Woodson, *The Negro Wage Earner* (Washington, D.C.: Association for the Study of Negro Life and History, 1930), pp. 77–90, 145–151; Elizabeth Ross Haynes, "Two Million Negro Women at Work," *Southern Workman* 51 (February 1922): 64–72; Mary Elizabeth Pidgeon, *Women in the Economy of the United States of America*, reprint ed. (Women's Bureau, Bulletin No. 155, 1937: New York: Da Capo Press, 1975), pp. 48–49.

12. *Woman and Child Wage Earners*, Vol. 18, *Employment of Women and Children in Selected Industries*, 1913, pp. 76–88, 307–22; U.S. Dept. of Labor, Women's Bureau, *The Effects of Changing Conditions in the Cigar and Cigarette Industries* by Caroline Manning and Harriet A. Byrne, Bulletin No. 100 (Washington, D.C.: Government Printing Office, 1932), pp. 109–10, 174–75.

13. Compiled from *U.S. Census*, 1930, 4: 1214.

14. Beulah Parrish, autobiography, S.S.S. Papers.

15. Interview with "Charlisle Pope" by Ethel Deal, Hickory, North Carolina, August, 1939, FWP Papers.

16. Mary Burdette, autobiography, Box 4, Mary O. Cowper Papers, Manuscript Department, William R. Perkins Library, Duke University (hereafter Mary O. Cowper Papers).

17. Ollie Brown, autobiography, S.S.S. Papers; Lois MacDonald, "Another Man With a Hope," *Survey* 15 (January 1927): 522–23.

18. *U.S. Census*, 1910, 4: 500–1; *U.S. Census*, 1920, 4: 781–2; *Woman and Child Wage Earners*, Vol. 18, *Selected Industries*, pp. 77–88.

19. Interviews and research notes for a study of the cotton mill industry, Box 4, Mary O. Cowper Papers.

20. Unidentified mill worker, autobiography, 1929, S.S.S. Papers.

21. See the discussion of the role of the YWCA in Marion W. Roydhouse, " 'The Universal Sisterhood of Women': Women and Labor Reform in North Carolina, 1900–1932" (Ph.D. diss., Duke University, 1980); Lucy P. Carner, "An Educational Opportunity for Industrial Girls," *Journal of Social Forces* 1 (November 1922) 612–15; Mary S. Sims, *The Y.W.C.A.: An Unfolding Purpose* (New York: Woman's Press, 1950). An outgrowth of this work was the workers' education movement, see Mary Frederickson, " 'Bound to be Leaven': The Southern Summer School for Women Workers in Industry" (Ph.D. diss., University of North Carolina, 1980); and for the wider movement see Mary Frederickson and Joyce Kornbluh, eds., *Sisterhood and Solidarity: Education Programs for Women Workers* (Philadelphia, 1984).

22. Kaola Edwards, autobiography, S.S.S. Papers.

23. *U.S. Census*, 1920, 4: 781–82; *U.S. Census*, 1930, 4: 1214.

24. "Charlisle Pope," FWP Papers.

25. Bessie Edens, Southern Summer School Scrapbook, 1929, S.S.S. Papers; Marian Cochran, autobiography, S.S.S. Papers.

26. Bessie Edens, Southern Summer School Scrapbook, 1929, S.S.S. Papers.

27. Grace Elliott, autobiography, S.S.S. Papers.

28. *Woman and Child Wage Earners*, Vol. 16, *Family Budgets*, p. 115.

29. For a description of the manufacturing processes see the following: *Woman and Child Wage Earners*, Vol. 18, *Selected Industries*, pp. 36–111, 307–22; Vol. 9, *History of Women in Industry*, pp. 195–205; *Changing Conditions in the Cigar and Cigarette Industries*, pp. 129–31; Nannie Mae Tilley, *The Bright Tobacco Industry, 1860–1929* (Chapel Hill, 1948); Herbert R. Northrup, *The Negro in the Tobacco Industry* (Philadelphia, 1970).

30. Andrea Taylor Hourwich and Gladys L. Palmer, *I Am A Woman Worker: A Scrapbook of Autobiographies* (New York: Affiliated Schools for Workers, 1936), pp. 45–46; (Ruth Culberson), "What Price Tobacco Profits," Southern Summer School Scrapbook, 1931, S.S.S. Papers; Harry M. Douty, "The North Carolina Industrial Worker, 1880–1930" (Ph.D. diss., University of North Carolina, 1936), pp. 138–39; *Woman and Child Wage Earners*, Vol. 18, *Selected Industries*, pp. 77–88, 307–22.

31. *Woman and Child Wage Earners*, Vol. 18, *Selected Industries*, pp. 77–111. U.S. Department of Labor, Women's Bureau, *Hours and Earnings in Tobacco Stemmeries* by Caroline Manning, Bulletin No. 1 127 (Washington, D.C.: Government Printing Office, 1934), pp. 1–6.

32. U.S. Department of Labor, Women's Bureau, *The Industrial Experience of Women Workers at the Summer Schools, 1928–1930)*, by Gladys L. Palmer, Bulletin No. 89 (Washington, D.C.: Government Printing Office, 1931), p. 50; Southern Summer School Scrapbook, 1929, S.S.S. Papers.

33. Emma L. Shields, "The Tobacco Workers," in *Black Women in White America*, ed. (New York, 1973), pp. 252–55; *Woman and Child Wage Earners*, Vol. 18, *Selected Industries*, pp. 88, 310–11.

34. Ruth Culberson and Marian Cochran, autobiographies, S.S.S. Papers.

35. Secretary to the President of the Dan River Mills, to Mary O. Cowper, January 5, 1925, Box 2, Mary O. Cowper Papers. Interview with Frank T. DeVyver by Marion Roydhouse, Duke University, Durham, N.C., 1975. Description of the processes of cotton yarn and cloth production can be found in Thompson, *Cotton Field to Cotton Mill*, pp. 119–31; Jack Blicksilver, *Cotton Manufacturing in the Southeast: An Historical Analysis* (Atlanta: Georgia State College of Business Administration, 1959); Ben F. Lemert, *The Cotton Textile Industry of the Southern Appalachian Piedmont* (Chapel Hill, 1933).

36. The best available evidence comes from the research of Frank T. DeVyver undertaken for the University of Virginia study in 1928, and the exhaustive compilation of wage rates by Harry M. Douty. The more limited surveys of Jennings J. Rhyne and Liston Pope in Gaston County, Lois MacDonald's investigation in two villages near Charlotte, and the earlier Bureau of Labor investigations of eleven families in Burlington and Greensboro provide further documentation of the general trends. A summary of incomes of Southern Summer School workers can be found in Gladys L. Palmer, *The Industrial Experience of Woman Workers*, which includes both tobacco and textile workers and gives a general indication of wages in the late twenties. Workers at the Southern Summer School also reported wages in the Scrapbooks and autobiographies that were written at the school. Douty, "Industrial Worker"; Abraham Berglund, George T. Starnes, and Frank T. DeVyver, *Labor in the Industrial South* (Charlottesville, 1930); Lois MacDonald, *Southern Mill Hills* (New York, 1928); Jennings J. Rhyne, *Some Southern Cotton Mill Workers and Their Villages* (Chapel Hill, 1930); Liston Pope, *Millhands and Preachers* (New Haven,

1942); *Woman and Child Wage Earners*, Vol. 16, *Family Budgets of Typical Cotton Mill Workers*, 1911; Palmer, *Industrial Experience of Women Workers*.

37. Palmer, *Industrial Experience*, pp. 28–31, 49–55; Liston Pope observed that mill workers were paid at least 50 percent less than other "uptown" people, see Pope, *Millhands and Preachers*, p. 52; DeVyver, *Industrial South*, pp. 152–54.

38. Douty, "Industrial Worker," pp. 98–142, 363–83; DeVyver, *Industrial South*, pp. 69–104; North Carolina Department of Labor and Printing, *Report*, 1919/20, pp. 121–35; MacDonald, *Southern Mill Hills*, pp. 80–85; Hourwich and Palmer, *I Am A Woman Worker*, p. 129; Southern Summer School Scrapbooks, 1927–1931, S.S.S. Papers; Pope, *Millhands and Preachers*, pp. 58–62; Rhyne, *Cotton Mill Workers*, pp. 95–97; Sarah A. Smith, "A Social Study of High Point, North Carolina" (Master's thesis, University of North Carolina, 1933), pp. 40–59.

39. Douty, "Industrial Worker," pp. 107–38; the North Carolina Department of Labor collected wage data, but on comparison with other sources they appear to contain inflated data with regard to earnings over any length of time, see North Carolina Department of Labor and Printing, *Fourteenth Annual Report*, 1910; *Thirty-Second Annual Report*, 1919/20.

40. Vesta Finley Interview.

41. Vesta Finley Interview; Douty, "Industrial Worker," pp. 173–90; Southern Summer School Files, S.S.S. Papers; conditions in the mills did not vary markedly from state to state, and although I have generally quoted examples from North Carolina, conditions depended more upon the age of the mills and the mill management, rather than upon the exact location.

42. Jerry de Murth, "Brown Lung in the Cotton Mills," *America* 18 (March 1978): 206–8; Interview with Frank DeVyver; *Woman and Child Wage Earners*, Vol. 18, *Selected Industries*, pp. 336–39; Vol. 1, *Cotton Textile Industry*, pp. 357–96; Vol. 14, *Causes of Death Among Woman and Child Mill Operatives*, pp. 49–51; Research Notes, Box 4, Mary O. Cowper Papers; MacDonald, *Southern Mill Hills*, pp. 117–19.

43. Nolia King, "Why I Oppose Night Work," Southern Summer School Scrapbook, 1931, S.S.S. Papers; North Carolina Department of Labor reported the night shift as being one or two hours longer than the day shift.

44. Lillie Morris Price, autobiography, S.S.S. Papers.

45. Interviews with Vesta Finley, Rosa Holland, and Lillie Morris Price, Marion, North Carolina; Interview with Bessie Edens by Mary Frederickson, Elizabethton, Tenn., August, 1975; Interview with Lois MacDonald, Stockton, N.J., June, 1975; Southern Summer School Files, 1927–1931, S.S.S. Papers.

46. (Grace Elliott), "The Strike at Marion," in Hourwich and Palmer, *I Am A Woman Worker*, pp. 121–28.

47. Velma Parrish, autobiography, S.S.S. Papers.

48. MacDonald, *Southern Mill Hills*, pp. 74–78.

49. See Jeannette Paddock Nichols, "Does the Mill Village Foster Any Social Types?" *Journal of Social Forces* 2 (March 1924): 350–57; and Rhyne, *Some Southern Cotton Mill Workers* and Pope, *Millhands and Preachers*. For a more sanguine view of the village see M. W. Heiss, "The Southern Textile Social Service Association," *Journal of Social Forces* 3 (March 1925): 513–14; M. W. Heiss, "The Southern Cotton Mill Village: A Viewpoint," *Journal of Social Forces* 2 (November 1924): 345–50;

Marjorie A. Potwin, *Cotton Mill People of the Piedmont: A Study in Social Change* (New York, 1927) and a more moderate view, Harriet L. Herring, *Welfare Work in Mill Villages* (Chapel Hill, 1929). Potwin described the transient work force as "clay eaters, or crackers, or sand-lappers, they dragged themselves to the cotton mills and in mute appeal begged the industry to make what it could of them." (p. 51) In fact people ate clay and soil because of vitamin deficiencies in their diet, hence the sobriquets.

50. Bertha Carl Hipp, "A Gaston County Cotton Mill and Its Community" (Master's thesis, University of North Carolina, 1930), pp. 29–30; Kenneth K. Bailey, *Southern White Protestantism In the Twentieth Century* (New York, 1964).

"Miss Lucy of the CIO": A Southern Life

JOHN A. SALMOND

On a warm Virginia morning in the early fall of 1947, Lucy Randolph Mason, then sixty-five years old, was visiting a small textile town far up the James river in her capacity as southern public relations representative for the Congress of Industrial Organizations (CIO). Her task was to try and persuade the local sheriff that he had a duty to protect organizers from the Textile Workers Union who were attempting to meet with the local mill workers, and not have them removed forcibly from the mill village, as he had done twice before.

Patiently, the grey-haired, little old lady went through her familiar litany. She explained the provisions of the Wagner Act, which clearly made such organizational activities legal. She discussed various recent rulings of the Civil Rights Division of the Department of Justice, which, often as a result of her prodding, had reluctantly begun to take action against obstructive local law enforcement officials—such as the man before her. She finished, as she usually did in such situations, with a general disquisition on basic civil rights.

The sheriff was noticeably unimpressed. Indeed, he could scarcely contain his impatience. "Lady," he said as soon as she had finished, "I would like to ask you some questions. What's back of you? Who sent you here, and what salary do you make? And by what right do you come into the State of Virginia talking all this about civil rights?"

He had asked for it. Miss Mason drew herself up to her full height, which wasn't very great, and proceeded to tell him who she was. It was a crash course in Virginia and southern history. Her great-great-grandfather, for a start, was George Mason, writer of Virginia's first constitution after the Revolution and author of the Virginia Declaration of Rights, much of which became incorporated into the Bill of Rights of the Constitution of the United States; a man whose thought underpins much of the legal foundations of American life. Three of her kinsmen on her father's side signed the Declaration of Independence. On her mother's side, she was closely connected to John Marshall, the first chief justice. Her great-grandfather, James Murray Mason, had been a Confederate envoy to Britain during the war between the states, the Mason of the Mason-Slidell affair, while her own father had ridden with Mosby's raiders. And, as if that were not enough, Robert E. Lee was her father's second cousin. That, she told the sheriff, her lineage, and its place in Virginia's history, gave her the right to talk to him about his duties and responsibilities. The young man was now impressed. "Madam," he said, (it was no longer "lady") "I still don't know what the CIO pays you, but you sure are worth it."[1]

And she certainly was. From the time she joined the CIO in 1937 at the age of fifty-five until her retirement in 1953, Miss Mason confronted many such a man. Her own papers, the CIO files, and the tributes of those organizers who worked with her are dramatic testimony to her success in achieving some measure of justice and protection for those brave men and women who tried to bring Southern textile workers, lumber men, iron workers, and rubber workers, to name but a few, into the CIO in those years. Her contribution was crucial in achieving the modicum of success that did result, and if she is known at all, it is because of her union work. However, she did not join the CIO until she was an elderly woman. Much of her lifetime had already passed. Moreover, her interests, even during her years with the labor movement, were much broader than simply her work with the union. As her lineage provided the young sheriff with a course in Virginia history, so her life provides us with a kaleidoscope of Southern liberal activity. The purpose of this chapter is to try and show what aspects of southern and, indeed, American history this life helps explain. Where does she fit in the general story of southern liberalism, and of southern feminism, for her sex and its implications is crucial to an understanding of her activities and attitudes?

Lucy Randolph Mason was born on July 26, 1882, in Clarens, Virginia, the second child and first daughter of the Reverend Landon Mason, an Episcopal minister, and his wife, the former Lucy Ambler, daughter of a clergyman. Born into a profoundly Christian family she herself was to remain a devout Episcopalian all her life. In 1891, the Reverend Mason was called to Grace Episcopal Church in Richmond, Virginia, where he served until his retirement in 1917. It is in Richmond, then, that she was formed. Later, Lucy was to describe her parents as "practical Christians," and this indeed seems to have been the case. Her mother, in particular, was active in a number of areas of social concern and was particularly influential in advocating the cause of prison reform. Indeed, Miss Mason recalled that she turned the rectory into a halfway house for prisoners who had served their time; often the guest room which was next to her bedroom was occupied by recently released inmates. At times, she said, she feared them, but nothing ever happened.[2]

Lucy Mason was educated in private schools in Richmond, but unlike many women of her class at that time, she did not go on to college. Instead, she joined the reputable law firm of Braxton and Eggleston, where she worked as a stenographer until 1914. During those years, however, her social concerns were heightened by the experience of teaching Sunday school classes in Richmond's seediest districts, and then running a club for the girls who worked in the city's tobacco factories. Through them, she was first aware of the harshness and hazardous nature of industrial life in the "New South." Her feminist instincts were first aroused, as were those of so many other women, by the suffrage movement. By 1911 she was writing letters and pamphlets in favor of women's suffrage, usually under an assumed name in order not to embarrass her father. In 1912, anonymity finally cast aside, she was elected to the board of the Richmond Equal Suffrage League. She later became its president, to her father's distress. Thus two of the concerns to which she was to dedicate her life, equality of treatment for her sex in public life, and the reform of the conditions under which women worked in the South were already giving direction to her activities.[3]

In 1914, she was given the chance to bring these concerns together, when, after the death of Mr. Braxton and the subsequent winding up of the firm's affairs, she joined the staff of the Richmond YWCA as its industrial secretary. The history of the YWCA in the South remains to be written, yet it can already be said that its contribution to the story of southern reform is seminal. Most of the women who worked for change in the South in the decades before the civil rights revolution had started with the YWCA, indeed, most of them had had a spell as an industrial secretary. These were the people whose responsibility it was to develop programs of relevance to working girls, as opposed to the middle class young women most generally associated with YWCA activities. These industrial secretaries were dedicated women, usually more radical than the other officials of the "Y," increasingly determined, as they observed the bleak lives of the young people with whom they worked, to do what they could to bring change. Lucy Mason was no exception. During her years as industrial secretary she worked ceaselessly on behalf of the women factory workers of Richmond. Indeed, she became well enough known as an advocate for the rights of women industrial workers that in 1917 when America entered World War I, and the Council of National Defense was created to coordinate the home front effort, she was appointed chairman of Virginia's Committee on Women in Industry.[4]

In 1918, however, her mother died suddenly of a heart attack, and, as the only unmarried daughter, she felt a clear obligation to care for her father, who was in failing health. Thus, she gave up her YWCA work. From then until his death in 1923, she said, she scarcely spent a night away from home.

She managed, however, to continue her activities in the suffrage area. When that battle was finally won, she became the first president of the Richmond League of Women Voters and chairman of the State League's Committee on Women in Industry. Her work was sufficiently distinguished for the League's national vice-president to ask her to accept the chairmanship of the National Committee on Women in Industry, an office she was forced to decline because of her father's health. It was during this time that she produced, under the auspices of the League of Women Voters, "The Shorter Day and Women Workers," a pamphlet which stated the case for legislation restricting hours of work for women with such cogency that Edward Costigan, U.S. commissioner for tariffs, wrote congratulating her on the "balance, restraint and comprehensiveness of your treatment."[5]

In 1923 her father died, and she was again free to work for social reform. Back she went to the Richmond YWCA, this time as its general secretary, the person responsible for the day-to-day administration of the institution. She had scarcely begun her new duties, however, when Florence Kelley, the redoubtable general secretary of the National Consumers League (NCL), asked her to join that organization as its southern secretary. Reluctantly, Miss Mason refused. She could scarcely leave the YWCA so soon, she said, besides, she was not yet ready to leave Richmond. Mrs. Kelley, unused to being turned down, was not happy. "I consider it a calamity of national dimensions that, at this moment, you are bending your best energies to the work of a local organization of any kind," she wrote, "instead of sharing the vast opportunity to modernize the Supreme Court and the U. S. Constitution." "However," she continued, "I hasten to point out that I waited nine years for Miss Dewson, and on one occasion four years for Pauline Goldmark, and in the end both came to this office. So I am girding on the armour of patience for a year, trusting that the situation will be such that you will consent to become secretary for the Southern States." It took nine years, actually before she came to the League. By that time, Mrs. Kelley had died, and Miss Mason was to be her successor.[6]

As general secretary at the YWCA, her responsibilities were much wider than those she had had when she first worked there. She had to concern herself with a range of activities, from the lunch program to fund raising.

Nevertheless, she continued her interest in industrial legislation for women and children, and she also broadened the scope of her social concerns. Through her close friend, Katherine Gerwick, a member of the YWCA's national staff, she became active in the peace movement, while her position as general secretary inevitably drew her into Richmond community affairs and into the interracial movement. As a member of the Virginia Inter-Racial Development Committee, she became active in promoting better relations between the races, and was thus inevitably drawn into the long struggle for racial justice in the South. In 1929 she was the only white woman to do public battle with the Richmond City Council, in an unsuccessful attempt to prevent the passage of a highly restrictive residential segregation ordinance, something for which she received the unstinting plaudits of the black community. Indeed a measure of the Richmond blacks' regard for her can be gauged from their reaction when she left the city in 1932. At a special appreciation service held in her honor, speaker after speaker paid tribute to her courage, her sense of fairness and justice, and her energy. "She wears no air of complex superiority," said one such, "she does not talk down to people but with people, whether they be white or black." Gordon B. Hancock, chairman of the Department of Economics and Sociology at Virginia Union University and organizer of the meeting, talked of "the spirit of a New South which is embodied in the life and labors of this Christian-hearted white woman." A testimonial scroll, signed by 124 sponsors, was presented to her at this meeting.[7]

Mason's decision to leave Richmond was the result of a number of factors. First, a profound personal crisis, of which more later, had left her shaken, in a state of prolonged emotional shock, and anxious to leave familiar and now painful surroundings. Second, she was growing increasingly dissatisfied with the routine work at the YWCA—"I am fearfully tired of finances and cafeterias and residences," she wrote a friend in 1931. This sense of discontent was heightened in that year, when she spent two months working for the Southern Council on Women and Children in Industry, her salary paid by the National Consumers League. Her job was to travel the South, talking mainly to textile manufacturers, urging them to support state legislation setting maximum hours of work, and the prohibition of night work for women and children in the mills, pointing out that it made good economic sense to rationalize the industry in this way, quite apart from the general social betterment that would result. She also organized local chapters of the Council amongst Southern women's groups to keep up the pressure for reform. "We women are going to keep on talking and getting the facts until something does happen," she warned one mill owner. Later, she published a pamphlet arguing the case for these reforms. She had not worked harder for years than during these two months, and she revelled in it. Going back to the routine of "Y" work was hard to bear.[8]

Fortunately for her, she did not have to stay there for long. Florence Kelley, the Consumers League's guiding light since its foundation, died in 1932. She herself had long wanted Mason to join the organization and in 1931 had told Molly Dewson that she favored Lucy as her successor. "She is known all over the South, very favorably and carries great weight there," she said. "She is a fine speaker and is consecrated to the work. I think she would take it." Upon Kelley's death, the League's board offered Mason the job, and, after ascertaining that she could reorient the league's work in such a way as to place greater emphasis on southern problems, she accepted, and left Richmond for New York City.[9]

She was joining an organization which had had a long history of activity on behalf of labor and social legislation, and on women's issues. Founded in 1899, it had done noble battle in the progressive period on behalf of such causes as state laws limiting hours for women and children, for the establishment of the Children's Bureau, for regulation of the meat packing industry, and for a host of other reform measures. Like other social feminist groups, in particular its companion body, the Woman's Trade Union League, it lost support in the 1920s due both to the climate of the times and the split within the women's movement itself between those who favored the removal of all legal distinctions between the sexes, and those who wanted protective legislation for women. Nevertheless, it maintained its presence as an active pressure group for reform, concentrating on the Child Labor Amendment. Many of the women who were shortly to move into the ranks of New Deal officialdom had passed through it, people like Molly Dewson, Josephine Roche, and, of course, Frances Perkins, the first woman cabinet member. She, in fact, remarked of her appointment as secretary of labor, that she did not feel that she had personally been so chosen, "but that it was the Consumers League who was appointed, and that I was merely the symbol who happened to be on hand, able and willing to serve at the moment." The Consumers League, therefore, was a vital component of what Susan B. Ware has characterized as the women's network.[10]

In the early days of the New Deal, Mason spent most of her time in Washington, testifying at National Recovery Administration (NRA) code hearings trying to ensure that they included the best possible labor provisions. Indeed, she once complained that she had "read codes until I can't think any more." Later she spent more time in the field, principally in the South setting up regional branches of the League and lobbying for state wages and hours bills, and for protective legislation for women. The Consumers League had a file of "model bills" on such issues, some of them drawn up by Felix Frankfurter, some by the Department of Labor's Division of Labor Standards and these she promoted whenever possible. She maintained close links with various departments and divisions of the expanded federal government, where, of course, many ex-league members were now working, exchanging information, and, at times, performing research tasks as well as publicizing New Deal programs. As she once told Mrs. Roosevelt, whom she first met at this time, "I am sure you agree with us that nongovernmental instruments for creating public opinion are still needed in a democracy and that private organizations can do some things impossible for government bodies. We work in closest cooperation with various divisions of the U. S. Department of Labor, as well as with state labor departments. We also work with state Federations of Labor, bringing to the support of some of their progressive measures an entirely different group of people." The Consumers League under Mason was a staunch supporter of the New Deal, hardly surprising at a time when so many of the League's positions were now becoming legislative reality. Nevertheless, despite the favorable climate, the Consumers League did not flourish in the 1930s partly because much that it had advocated over the years had now come to pass. As Mason said, "the popular impression in these days is that 'government will do it', and support for private agencies is no longer necessary." There also were more particular reasons, but the result was that by 1937 the NCL was in serious financial trouble. Contributions had dropped off to such an extent that a drastic reduction in office staff and general activities was essential. Henceforth Mason would not be able to spend time in the South or travel about lobbying on behalf of labor legislation. She would have to stay at home and mind the store.[11]

This she was not prepared to do. She hated office work, and avoided it whenever she could. What she had enjoyed most about the Consumers League work was the chance it had given her to work for labor reform in the South, and this she was not willing to give up. Moreover, during the previous few years, she had made contact with a number of labor union officers, including some from the Textile Workers Organizing Committee (TWOC), now just beginning a drive to organize southern workers under the aegis of the lusty, young CIO. She had admired these men, and wished to be part of their effort. Fortunately, she had a connection with John L. Lewis, president of the CIO, which she could exploit. Her brother-in-law was Lewis's banker in Alexandria, Virginia, while her sister Ida was president of the local gardening club which Mrs. Lewis desperately wanted to join. A meeting was arranged at her sister's house. The result was that Lewis arranged for her appointment to the TWOC organizing drive as public relations representative. Reportedly, he was impressed by the advantage both her lineage and her appearance gave her to at least get a hearing for labor's point of view. In 1940, her job was redesignated public relations representative for the CIO in the South. Accordingly, in October 1937 she left New York for Atlanta where she was to be based for the rest of her life.[12]

The nature and emphasis of her work changed considerably during her fifteen years with the CIO, but essentially there were always four main components to it. The first was a general public relations aspect, which manifested itself in a score of different ways, from answering antilabor editorials in newspapers to speaking to church groups about the aims of organized labor. At all times her emphasis was on the reasonableness of labor's demands and the social benefits that unions can bring. She prepared regular digests of labor news for distribution to editors, answered questions about labor policy, gave radio broadcasts, and attempted to prevent antilabor hysteria whenever she could. "I have put in some intensive work with both Atlanta papers on the witch-hunting campaign started by the Georgia governor," ran one of her regular reports to CIO headquarters. "I have also quietly brought to church and other groups' attention the need for preserving civil liberties and sanity and helped in producing some very favorable action in the way of statements, sermons and group action." Mason was particularly effective with church groups, where her own obviously sincere Christianity and her prim respectability had a disarming effect, and on college campuses. She related well to young people and was a popular and regular campus speaker and panelist. During her years with the CIO she logged hundreds of thousands of miles, usually in her battered old Chevrolet, visiting colleges and churches, organizing "fellowship dinners" between clergymen and labor representatives, taking part in workshops and retreats, and speaking to various clubs and societies. It was always an essential part of her work.[13]

The second component was to act as a one-person advance guard before an organizer moved into a town or mill village. Often she would be asked to go into the town first to make contact with community representatives. If it were a mill village, she would talk to the mill owner—whom sometimes she knew personally—and explain what was about to happen. She would see the local law enforcement officers, attempt to secure guarantees that the rights of the organizers would not be interfered with, and if that was not forthcoming warn them of the consequences of violating their civil rights. She would visit the local editor and attempt to get him on her side; she would talk to the clergymen. If the union was to try and organize blacks as well as whites, as was sometimes the case, especially during World War II in such industries as ship building, she would attempt to set up structures to accommodate both races before organizing began, while at the same time reassuring the local leadership that the CIO had no wish to break down the southern caste system. She was not always successful in persuading people to permit union activity, but the demands from organizers for her services in this area were always many more than she could handle, and give a clear indication of the value they placed on this aspect of her work. Organizing the South was a hard task, and anything that could make it easier was to be keenly sought.[14]

A third component of her work involved dispute-settling, which again she would attempt to deal with only upon request by the state CIO chief. Sometimes these disputes were jurisdictional, more often they involved problems within unions that had recently become integrated. Memphis, Tennessee, provided an example of her efficacy in this area. The CIO unions, generally, but principally the rubber, ship building, and lumber unions had at first had many more black than white members. But with the coming of war industries to the city, white membership increased dramatically, and there was considerable tension. Mason spent a lot of time in the city in 1942 and 1943, and largely as a result of her work, and, in particular, her obvious concern for the black workers, "the CIO unions," as she put it in 1943, "now combine both races in the same locals and both races attend the same meetings... thousands of white and colored workers meet together at regular intervals to plan through their unions for the economic interests of both races."[15]

But by far the most important part of her dispute-settling work involved her activity in situations where police interfered with the civil rights of organizers, a common occurrence in the South. She would descend upon the particular town or village, as she did in Vicksburg, Mississippi in 1944, where the southern director of organization of the International Woodworkers of America had been arrested for "organizing the Negroes," demand to see the chief of police, in this case "a general stuffed-shirt called Hogaboom," and insist that the civil rights of organizers be henceforth respected. She would also report all violations to the civil rights division of the Department of Justice. Sometimes the threat of an investigation was enough, more often than not though, she had to keep pressing Washington for action and this she did relentlessly. She had an ally in Mrs. Roosevelt, who often, on Mason's request, applied her own particular brand of pressure to Justice Department officials. Of course, Mason was not able to stop the harrassment of union officials in small southern towns, it would have taken an army to do that in the 1940s, but she did get the Department of Justice to carry out several investigations, and launch a number of prosecutions, some of which were successful. Moreover the very pressure of an irate Mason in a town, refusing to leave until a particular wrong had been righted; badgering the police chief, the mill owner, the mayor or the editor; lecturing them on civil rights; reminding them who she was, so obviously respectable in her pince-nez, her grey hair tied in a bun, and her sensible shoes, often had the desired effect. She was, after all, a determined lady. If a strike were involved, she would usually take a spell on the picket line. Never once was she arrested. As Myles Horton, himself a former organizer, said many years later of her ability to badger people into "stopping all their indecencies," "Boy, she was a power. We would all yell for Lucy anytime we needed help and she would come into the toughest situation and was great. She played a tremendous role, a tremendous role."[16]

The fourth component of her work was to maintain liaison with the federal government. This she did in various ways, through service on government boards and bodies, such as the President's Commission on the South which produced the famous 1938 report on southern economic problems, through her connections with Mrs. Roosevelt, through her links, often forged during her Consumer League days with government officials like Frances Perkins, and through her involvement in Democratic party affairs. Moreover, she was active in a wide variety of organizations quite apart from the CIO. Indeed, just about every liberal institution and agency in the South had a Mason connection. She was on the executive committee of the Southern Conference for Human Welfare, a director of the Southern School for Women Workers, and on the board of the Highlander Folk School both of which provided short courses for local labor leaders, and both of which stressed the need to bring southern women fully into the labor movement. She also had close connections with the Southern Regional Council. She was absolutely tireless in her pursuit of social change.[17]

By 1950, after four hectic years working for "Operation Dixie" the CIO's postwar drive to organize the South, her body had begun to wear out. She was no longer able to travel as she had done, and she spent most of the next two years working on her memoirs, still on the CIO payroll. The book was published in 1952, entitled *To Win These Rights*, with a foreword by Mrs. Roosevelt. She retired the next year, and died in an Atlanta nursing home in 1959.

What are the general historical points that her public life illuminates? What aspects of southern history does it help understand? Some of the answers are clear enough. Miss Mason's story obviously helps flesh out the neglected story of southern labor. Through her, and her activities, valuable insights into the personalities, the procedures, and the problems involved in the labor movement in those years can be gained. Similarly, the years with the Consumers League tell something about the fate of private reform agencies when they succeed too well, or rather when government expands and takes over their function. They are left without a role and they begin to wither. More subtly, through Mason's life, something about southern liberalism in general, its roots and its impulsions, can be learned, and, in particular, about the connections between women and reform. Through her, we can explore the YWCA's influence as a training ground for liberal activity. The position of industrial secretary is particularly important, for the more one learns about a particular group of southern women of whom Miss Mason was a representative, all of whom in one way or another could be described as dissidents, all of whom opposed the prevailing mores of the region, in one way or another, one commonality immediately obtrudes. The bulk of them had had some connection with the YWCA, indeed many of them had served as local or regional industrial secretaries. Then, Miss Mason's life introduces us to certain liberal agencies specifically oriented toward women's issues. Most interesting is the Southern Summer School for Women Workers, itself a direct outgrowth of the YWCA's work, through its industrial secretaries, with the largely unorganized female work force in the southern textile mills and tobacco factories. Founded by two dedicated women, Lois MacDonald and Louise McLaren, both of whom had been industrial secretaries, it lasted from 1927 until 1951, providing in the words of Mary Frederickson, "young workers from the textile, garment and tobacco factories with the analytic tools for understanding the social context of their lives, the opportunities to develop solidarity with one another, and the confidence for full participation in the emerging southern labor movement." Each year it provided selected women with courses in economics, political theory, and other labor-related areas, as well as encouraging them to think about their lives as women, and their relationship to their families, their communities, and their workplaces. Miss Mason was on the board of the Summer School from its inception to its disbandment. She was always intensely supportive of its work, she frequently taught courses on labor economics there, she knew intimately the women who ran it over the years, these southern members of the women's network.[18]

Then there was the Southern Conference for Human Welfare (SCHW), the most important of all liberal institutions in the South during the New Deal period. Founded in 1938 in the wake of President Roosevelt's declaring the South to be the nation's number one economic problem, it lasted for ten turbulent years, constantly under attack for its policies on race, "red-baited" continually, always short of funds, its future ever in doubt. Yet it achieved some results, focusing national attention on many of the injustices of southern life, occasionally scoring victories in its efforts to reform some of these, most notably in the campaign to outlaw the poll-tax. Almost all the region's leading liberals belonged to it at one time or another. Mason was a charter member, and served on the board of directors for all but two years of its existence. The Conference depended considerably on her administrative skills just to keep things going. She was constantly urging the imposition of a more rigorous bureaucratic structure on what was a notoriously poorly administered body. More important, the Southern Conference, though never dominated by members of the Communist Party, as was often alleged, certainly had communist members, who at times tried to take over certain key committees and posts. Mason always fought them hard, more than most other board members. She was concerned about the "taint" communist association always placed on liberal organizations, and it was partly over this issue that she resigned from SCHW in 1947.[19]

What was it that turned Lucy Mason toward social reform, that made her such "a fearless fighter for social justice," in the words of Mrs. Roosevelt? Was she, as Virginia Durr, herself one of the most splendid of southern liberal women, once said "fighting for her own emancipation?" How representative was she of a certain class or caste of southern women? These questions are much harder to answer. One can say, however, that there were linking themes in her public life, in its three phases, in Richmond, New York, and Atlanta. Throughout her life, whether as industrial secretary, president of the League of Women Voters, or with the Consumers League or CIO, she struggled constantly on behalf of her sex, generally through the advocacy of special, protective legislation for them. She was the epitome of the social feminist. A second linking theme was clearly her region. She was always a southerner. Even when working for a national body like the Consumers League, she devoted most of her attention to the South. In that sense, she never acquired a national view, she never stepped outside her region emotionally, even during those five years, the only time in her life that she did so, when she lived outside it geographically. Related to this is a third linking theme, that of race. It did not dominate her thinking as it did some of her liberal colleagues, nevertheless a concern for racial justice permeates all her work, from Richmond to Atlanta, and in so doing sets her apart from the prevailing view of her region.[20]

So far only Miss Mason's public life has been discussed. She did, however, have a private life, jealously guarded while she was alive, with fragments only available yet to the researcher. Still, these intensely personal fragments illustrate further general points about southern women of the time, and this essay will conclude with a brief discussion of two of these, conscious always of that feeling of violating privacy, yet confident that Miss Mason wanted these areas uncovered. Lucy Mason was very cautious, especially about personal matters. Often, for example, she would ask the recipients of letters in which she had made comments of a personal nature to destroy them once they had been read. Fortunately, this advice was rarely followed.

The curator of manuscripts of the Perkins Library, Duke University, where her papers are located, said that Mason personally went through the whole collection before donating them to the library, removing all material she considered to be sensitive. Yet, she left a number of intensely personal letters, passionate letters, often moving letters, addressed to the great love of her life. The implication clearly is that she wanted people to know that she, too, had loved, and had been loved, that this most important of human experiences had not been denied her. An extract from one of these gives some indication of their character.

You remember how we would look into each others eyes those years ago, seeing beyond the shining surface, seeing into the soul that lay beyond the eyes, nothing veiled in me from you, nor in you from me. We saw each other in all that potential best which is spirit animating matter. . . . In you nothing is hid from me, when those clear moments came, and in me you see the scroll unrolled, you read me as I truly am—weak, blind, dull yet aspiring, seeing, perceiving the ideal that lies enwrapped within me—within all human souls. No place is strange, for you are there; no task is impossible, for you share it, no defeat is defeat, for you help me find the lesson defeat would teach me. . . . Without you, what would life be? I cannot know, for in fact life as far as I can remember has never been without you.[21]

This letter, as were all the others, was directed to Katherine Gerwick, a fellow YWCA worker, with whom Miss Mason began what was clearly an intense relationship in 1923. These letters start in 1929, and the last one is dated 1944. There is nothing unusual about the fact that they were written to a woman. As Susan B. Ware and others have pointed out, many of the public women of this generation reserved their most intense emotional relationships for those of their own sex. Molly Dewson, for example, lived with Polly Porter for nearly fifty years, in a long, devoted and fulfilling relationship; in the South, there was Lillian Smith and Paula Snelling. It was easier then for two women to live together, without arousing prurient suspicion. Marriage for various reasons, not necessarily only sexual preference, was often not possible for these women, and heterosexual involvement outside marriage was not countenanced. Thus they sought and found fulfillment with members of their own sex. There was even a term to describe these relationships, "Boston marriages." Mason's relationship with Katherine Gerwick clearly fits this pattern.[22]

What is unusual, however, is that at the time the letter quoted above was written, as was the case for all the letters referred to, Gerwick was dead. She had died in 1927, following complications after routine surgery. Mason was distraught, she suffered a nervous breakdown, and one of the reasons that she was desperate to leave Richmond was her inability to adjust to life there after Katherine's death. She wrote to her, and, according to her own testimony, talked with her regularly until 1944, when she entered into another permanent relationship, again with a woman, which lasted until her own death in 1959. Moreover, Gerwick was not the only dead person she communicated with, she often talked to her mother and her sister Ida, after their deaths. For Lucy Mason, despite her profound Christian belief, or perhaps because of it, was a spiritualist, a mystic. "Death was," she said, "but one little door to greater being," a divide of the utmost unimportance. Not only was it possible to communicate freely across the divide, either through the use of a medium or directly, but she believed that people who had died could still influence events in the world directly. "Another thing I believe," she wrote a friend in 1930,

is that if people on the other side of life have someone, or several people here who love them a lot it helps them to direct energy into our world. Especially if there is some one person very, very close, who understands and loves them tremendously and who believes that love and life can pass the barriers of death, I think they can use that person as a sort of fulcrum to influence other people here. Such a person gives them a sort of power house or base of energy. It has seemed very real to me since Katharine [Gerwick] died—we go on as co-partners in enterprises that are worthwhile, and she can get at lots of other people better because she has my brain and heart as a human center.[23]

This conviction that people who had died were no more than "on the other side of life," and could still reach and be reached, sustained her throughout her life and, incidentally, helped her sustain family and friends when they themselves were bereaved. It was not a belief she kept private, and though some scholars and interviewers have found it bizarre, her contemporaries were not similarly bothered. Brownie Lee Jones, who had been industrial secretary of the Richmond YWCA when Mason was general secretary, and who was later to direct the Southern Summer School, was one of her closest friends. When interviewed for the Southern Oral History Project in 1977, she scoffed at the interviewer's suggestion that there was something odd about Miss Mason. Agreeing that "she used to always tell me about talking to her friends you know, those what were long gone," she nevertheless insisted that she was "a liberated Southern woman," a "real social force" in the South, and a woman with her feet very firmly on the ground. Perhaps her mysticism seems stranger now than to her contemporaries because there were others like her, or at the very least, such beliefs among southern middle-class women, while not general, were at least not unique. Perhaps they could quite readily be fitted into a profoundly religious frame of reference. After all, the hard-nosed labor men with whom she associated from 1937 on found nothing odd about her.[24]

Let us say nothing more than this. The life of Lucy Randolph Mason, in its public and its private aspects, does have much of a general nature to tell us about southern liberalism in the twentieth century, about the growth of the southern labor movement, and about southern women. It is also the story of a fascinating human being, in itself well worth telling.

NOTES

1. Lucy Randolph Mason, *To Win These Rights* (New York, 1951), introduction. See also Lucy Randolph Mason Papers, Perkins Library, Duke University (henceforth Mason Papers), drafts of autobiography.

2. Ibid.

3. Ibid. See also Lucy Cary, *The Religious and Social Aspects of the Suffrage Movement* (Equal Suffrage League of Virginia, May 1912) in Mason Papers, Printed Materials, Folder 1.

4. *Richmond Times Dispatch*, March 23, 1914; Mary Evans Frederickson, "A Place to Speak Our Minds: The Southern School for Women Workers" (Ph.D. diss., University of North Carolina, 1981), pp. 16–38; Mason to Miss Anne Pridmore, March 26, 1940, Mason Papers, Box 1, Folder 4; Mason, *To Win These Rights*, pp. 5–6.

5. Mason Papers, drafts, League of Women Voters Papers, Library of Congress (henceforth LWU Papers), Series 1, Box 2, Newsletter of Committee on Women in Industry, No. 3, December 28, 1922, No. 4, January 20, 1923; Belle Sherwin to Mason, July 17, 1922, Edward Costigan to Mason, December 26, 1922, both in Mason Papers, Box 1, Folder 1.

6. Florence Kelley to Mason, September 5, 1923, Mason Papers, Box 1, Folder 1; Mason, *To Win These Rights*, pp. 6–7.

7. Mason, *To Win These Rights*, pp. 6–10; *Richmond Times Dispatch*, January 15, February 1, 5, 12, 1929; "An Appreciation by Her Friends," Mason Papers.

8. Mason, *To Win These Rights*, pp. 8–10; Mason to Rufus, April 6, 1931, to W. M. McLaurin, February 14, 17, 1931, to Donald Comer, January 23, February 14, 1931, Mason Papers, Box 1, Folder 1.

9. Mary Dewson to Emily Marconnier, October 16, 1931, Mason Papers, Box 1, Folder 1; Dewson to Mason, March 27, 1931, Mason Papers, Box 7, Folder 3; Louise Catterall to Mason, May 28, 1932, Mason to Board of Directors, Richmond YWCA, June 14, 1932, Mason Papers, Box 1, Folder 2; Mason, *To Win These Rights*, pp. 11–12.

10. William L. O'Neill, *Everyone Was Brave: A History of Feminism in America* (Chicago, 1969), pp. 95–98, 152–53, 232–40; Susan B. Ware, *Beyond Suffrage: Women in the New Deal* (Cambridge, Mass., 1981), p. 35.

11. Mason, *To Win These Rights*, pp. 13–17; Mason to Clara Beyer, Division of Labor Standards, November 1, 17, 1935, Beyer to Mason, November 12, 1935,

Records of the National Consumers League, Library of Congress (henceforth NCL Records), Group B, Carton 24 (henceforth B/24); Mason to Eleanor Roosevelt, February 10, 1937, NCL Records, B/21.

12. Mason to Frank P. Graham, May 15, June 10, 1937, Frank P. Graham Papers, Southern Historical Collection, Wilson Library, University of North Carolina at Chapel Hill (henceforth Graham Papers); Mason to Nicholas Kelley, May 28, 1937, NCL Records, A/1. Interview with Virginia Durr, Wetumpka, Alabama, December 9, 1981 (henceforth Durr Interview).

13. Mason, *To Win These Rights*, passim; Mason to Allan Haywood, July 12, 1940, Mason Papers, Box 2, Folder 1.

14. Mason, *To Win These Rights*, passim; Mason to Eleanor Roosevelt, May 2, 1941, Papers of Eleanor Roosevelt, Franklin Delano Roosevelt Library, Hyde Park, New York (henceforth Eleanor Roosevelt Papers), Box 813.

15. Mason to Haywood, March 6, 1943, to Dr. Charles S. Johnson, Fisk University, April 14, 1943, both in Mason Papers, Box 3, Folder 1.

16. Mason to Victor Rotnem, Chief, Civil Rights Section, Department of Justice, March 10, 31, 1944, Mason Papers, Box 3, Folder 2; Toxey Hall to Mason, May 17, 1944, George Brown to Mason, May 17, 1944, Mason to Toxey Hall, to Eleanor Bontecou, May 24, 1944, all in Mason Papers, Box 3, Folder 3; Interview with Myles Horton, Southern Oral History Collection, Wilson Library, University of North Carolina at Chapel Hill (henceforth SOHC).

17. See Mason to Eleanor Roosevelt, September 23, 1942, January 3, 1943, Mason Papers, Box 3, Folder 1; Mason to Mrs. Roosevelt, August 18, 24, 1943, to Sidney Hillman, August 17, 1943, Mason Papers, Box 3, Folder 2.

18. Frederickson, "A Place to Speak," Introduction, passim.

19. On the Southern Conference, see Thomas E. Krueger, *And Promises to Keep: The Southern Conference for Human Welfare* (Nashville, 1967), passim. On Mason's role, see especially the Papers of Carl and Anne Braden, State Historical Society of Wisconsin (henceforth Braden Papers), Boxes 17–20.

20. Durr Interview, December 9, 1981.

21. Interviews with Dr. Mattie Russell, Curator of Manuscripts, Perkins Library, Duke University, July–November, 1981; Mason to Katherine Gerwick, January 25, 1931, Mason Papers, Box 1, Folder 1.

22. Ware, *Beyond Suffrage*, pp. 26, 167.

23. Mason to Cecil Scott, October 1930, Mason Papers, Box 1, Folder 1; to Rev. Walker, March 24, 1940, Mason Papers, Box 1, Folder 4.

24. Interview with Brownie Lee Jones, SOHC.

PART III
The Way of the Lord

7

After Scopes: Evolution in the South

WILLARD B. GATEWOOD, JR.

Whether the so-called monkey trial at Dayton, Tennessee, in July 1925 was a decisive moment in the history of Christianity as William Jennings Bryan suggested or "an obscenity of the very first calibre" as Henry L. Mencken believed, it was the biggest and best newspaper story in the decade after World War I. On hand to witness the trial of John Thomas Scopes, the local football coach and high school teacher accused of violating Tennessee's new law against the teaching of Darwin's theory of evolution, was a larger contingent of newsmen than covered the naval limitation conference in Washington four years earlier. The principal attraction in the sleepy town in the Tennessee hills—"forty miles from the nearest city and a million miles away from anything urban, sophisticated and exciting"—was not young Scopes, but rather two nationally known verbal pugilists, William Jennings Bryan, whom the World's Christian Fundamentals Association dispatched to assist the prosecution, and Clarence Darrow, who headed the legal team sent by the American Civil Liberties Union to defend Scopes.[1]

The Scopes trial quickly took its place alongside the Ku Klux Klan as a standard ingredient in the version of a Benighted South that emerged in the 1920s. That the South was the scene of a succession of well publicized battles over Darwin's theory and the only region of the country that kept monkey laws on the statute books for over forty years lent credence to the view that militant opposition to biological evolution was as southern as racism and states' rights. In one form or another the idea that campaigns against Darwin were rustic capers by ignorant religious zealots of the southern hinterlands has persisted since the 1920s. Such a view, while not without elements of truth, tends to distort the role of the South in the controversies over evolution that have periodically erupted in the twentieth century and to obscure the scope and meaning of these struggles.

To interpret the disturbances over Darwin as rural in origin, much less as mere regional phenomena, is to fly in the face of considerable evidence to the contrary. The antievolution campaigns, whether in the form of laws banning the theory from public schools in the 1920s or of acquiring "equal time" for creation science more than a half century later, were not isolated local efforts by a handful of untutored clerical zealots hostile to science per se. Rather they represented the most publicized aspect of a larger, more complex movement known as fundamentalism, a version of evangelical Protestantism that emerged in the late nineteenth century. Northern and urban in origin, fundamentalism was a supernatural, biblically-based faith, often with a premillenialist orientation and always militantly opposed to liberal theology and the cultural changes it accommodated. Constituting a formidable coalition by the end of World War I, fundamentalists embarked upon a nationwide offensive in the 1920s that for a time filled the air with the sounds of ferocious combat and that polarized American Protestantism into warring camps.[2]

Until the 1920s, as George Marsden has noted, fundamentalism in the North developed independently, but along parallel lines, with conservative Protestantism in the South.[3] After World War I, when northern-based fundamentalists mounted their offensive to unseat liberals and modernists and to capture control of the major denominations, their efforts elicited broad sympathy and support among southerners who ultimately comprised a significant element in the fundamentalist coalition. The fundamentalist theology that came to maturity in the era of World War I was in many respects similar to what Victor I. Masters, a prominent southern Baptist, described in 1915 as "the Anglo-Saxon evangelical faith" of the South.[4] Essential in both was a belief in a divinely inspired, errorless Bible as the source of all that was "decent and right in our civilization." For fundamentalists, their battle for the Bible was a battle for civilization. In the South, where the "Anglo-Saxon evangelical faith" was linked with cultural conservatism, the battle for the Bible easily became a battle for the southern way of life.

By 1920 southerners had long been accustomed to describing their region as a Garden of Eden. Whatever the characteristics this biblical metaphor was used to project, it almost invariably included the notion of God-fearing, Bible-reading people allied in "common defense of the truth and common warfare upon iniquity." In no other respect was the region so deserving of the label Solid South as in its commitment to a Bible-centered, individualistic, low church Protestantism which provided a religion of certitude unencumbered by the "theological vagaries" of liberalism and modernism that flourished elsewhere in the country.[5] An abundance of "theological vagaries" existed in the region in the form of independent and radical sects, but they tended to cluster at the opposite pole of the religious spectrum. As a result, the same southern Baptists considered conservative by their brethren in the Northern Convention were viewed as liberal apostates by many sects within the South.

The strong antimodernist impulse, evident throughout southern Protestantism, early identified Darwin's theory as a threat to the integrity of the errorless Scriptures. Among the victims of the bias against evolution in the late nineteenth century was James Woodrow, an uncle of Woodrow Wilson, who in 1886 was dismissed from the Southern Presbyterian Seminary in South Carolina for insisting that evolution was compatible with the book of Genesis.[6] Concern about the dangers of the "new theology" that accompanied the emergence of fundamentalism not only caused southerners to be on guard against its appearance in their midst but also prompted greater attention to what was viewed as a critical component of that theology, namely evolution.

Although northern fundamentalists concentrated on doctrinal matters and manifested relatively little interest, at least at first, in Darwinism per se, they recognized it as an integral part of the modernist theological structure and therefore as "false doctrine." Neither the route by which evolution became the focus of the fundamentalist struggle nor the role that southerners played in that process is easily explained. What is obvious, however, is that fundamentalist leaders came to recognize evolution as an issue that would enable them to reach a mass audience and rally to their cause those who possessed little interest in, or understanding of, the doctrinal concerns emphasized in various sets of statements known as "the fundamentals." Two other points worth noting are: first, when southerners became a part of the national fundamentalist coalition they brought with them a tradition of hostility to Darwin's theory; second, those national fundamentalist spokesmen most vocal in opposition to the theory and most influential in elevating it to a position of primacy were individuals who were either native southerners or had been educated in the South. Among these were William B. Riley, Amzi C. Dixon, J. Frank Norris, Jasper C. Massee and John Roach Straton.[7]

Whatever the significance of the southern connections of these men, they succeeded in transforming the character of fundamentalism and in making the defense of the "true faith" dependent on opposition to the theory of evolution and the mind it represented. As a result, individual fundamentalists as well as interdenominational organizations, such as the World's Christian Fundamentals Association, embarked upon a nationwide campaign to outlaw the teaching of evolution in public schools. The decision of William Jennings Bryan to assist in this effort transformed it into a popular crusade of national dimensions. In no other section of the country was his role more influential than in the South, where he had long enjoyed the status of a folk hero.[8]

Bryan's entry into the antievolution campaign marked the beginning of a season in which the region was obsessively preoccupied with Darwin's theory and its implications. A host of traveling evangelists, such as Baxter F. "Cyclone Mack" McLendon of South Carolina and Mordecai F. Ham of Kentucky, joined lay and clerical spokesmen in the major southern denominations in alerting the region to the dangers of "the slime theory." Of the latter none generated more controversy and dissension, especially among southern Baptists, than J. Frank Norris of Texas, whom the liberal *Christian Century* described in 1924 as "probably the most belligerent fundamentalist now abroad in the land." Norris and other opponents of Darwin's theory in the South quickly transformed evolution into a code word whose meaning embraced the whole range of modern infidelities.[9] In their view it was the foundation stone of modernism and other deviant theologies parading under the label of Christianity that were responsible for the contemporary "journey into apostasy." "The beast jungle theory . . . ," Amzi C. Dixon told an audience in his native North Carolina in 1922, "robs man of his dignity, marriage of its sanctity, government of its authority and the church of her power and Christ of His glory."[10] On occasion the antievolution crusade assumed the character of a patriotic effort to save elements of the southern way of life that lay beyond the strictly religious realm. This was especially true of those who linked Darwin's theory to the ever-present race question on the grounds that it threatened white supremacy by making "a Negro as good as a white man," and those who held "Yankee professors" and "imported faculties" in southern universities primarily responsible for the spread of the Darwinian heresy in the region.[11]

In a region so proud of its reputation as "the stronghold of orthodox Christianity in this country" and traditionally hostile to Darwin, the antievolutionist rhetoric proved extraordinarily effective in galvanizing public opinion in favor of statutes to outlaw evolution. The crusade against evolution in the South, as Wilbur J. Cash observed, was not the work of a "small, highly organized pressure group," but rather "an authentic folk movement."[12] Even southerners who questioned the propriety of antievolution legislation were likely to be hostile to Darwin's theory. Although numerous devices, from rulings by state boards of education to actions by local school officials, were employed throughout the United States in the 1920s to eliminate evolution from classrooms, only in the South did fundamentalists achieve their aims by statutory means. Ultimately five states—Oklahoma, Florida, Tennessee, Mississippi and Arkansas—enacted antievolution measures. More remarkable, perhaps, in view of the regional obsession with Darwin, was the failure of similar legislation elsewhere in the South.[13]

If evolution was the issue that allowed organized fundamentalism to attract a mass audience and broad support for a time, it was also the issue on which the movement foundered. The ridicule and derision heaped upon fundamentalists in the wake of the Scopes trial, coupled with the loss of their most popular and prestigious spokesman with the death of Bryan shortly afterward, disrupted their coalition and diminished their influence. Diffused among rival organizations and individuals with a penchant for the sensational and bizarre, fundamentalism began to conform to its new image as the representative of "the forces of organized ignorance."[14]

Emerging from the struggles of the 1920s without capturing control of a single major denomination and stereotyped as combative eccentrics existing on the fringes of modern culture, fundamentalists were no longer newsworthy by the early 1930s. Contrary to pronouncements by some liberal religious journals, neither fundamentalism nor hostility to evolution disappeared. The latter for a time went into "remission," but fundamentalism put down roots outside the mainline denominations and ultimately developed into what has been termed "a second wing of Protestantism" whose growing numerical strength and influence went largely unnoticed in the secular press until after World War II.[15] Nor did fundamentalism remain static. In the decades after the 1920s it came to include a succession of separatist groups that continued to wear with pride the "fundamentalist" label and nurtured other, more moderate elements known as evangelicals.

The combativeness of rival contenders for the faith often obscured the broad areas of agreement among diverse fundamentalist groups. The worldly pessimism, otherworldly hope, and sense of suffering that characterized much of southern religion was nowhere more evident than among fundamentalists. These traits coupled with their status as out-groups, frequently derided by nonsoutherners and either ignored or treated with condescension by middle-class southerners who controlled the mainline denominations, tended to encourage a common identity among the disparate fundamentalist elements in the region. Whatever changes southern fundamentalism experienced in the era after the Dayton Affair, its antimodernist impulse remained intact and strong. Just how strong became evident in the response to the Revised Standard Version of the Bible that appeared in 1952. Martin Luther Hux, a Baptist minister in Rocky Mount, North Carolina, went so far as to burn a copy of the new Bible, which he described as "a deliberate attack on the historic faith" and as "a scheme by the modernists to make the Lord Jesus Christ the son of a bad woman."[16]

Although the traditional citadels of fundamentalism in the North and the Midwest continued to exert a powerful influence in the era after the Scopes trial, the emergence of new centers of strength below the Potomac tended to give the movement "more of a Southern accent." As early as 1930 a prominent southern Baptist noted that the South had "all but preempted the Bethels of fundamentalism."[17] Viewing themselves as a faithful remnant surrounded by infidels and false prophets and no more reconciled to Darwin's theory than their forebears, fundamentalists in the South as elsewhere concentrated their energies on establishing an institutional base outside the major denominations. Rather than mounting crusades against evolution, they dedicated themselves to organizing churches, seminaries, colleges and Bible schools, mission programs, and publishing and broadcasting concerns. The results, by any standard of measurement, were spectacular.[18]

In terms of long-range influence one of the most significant aspects of fundamentalist development in the South in the wake of the Scopes trial was the emergence of numerous educational institutions. In addition to dozens of Bible institutes, the region by 1960 had more than fifty institutions classified as Bible colleges. Though often ridiculed as "chicken coop colleges," they turned out increasing numbers of graduates trained in defending "the Bible as the Word of God against all attacks of modern infidelity." Preeminent among fundamentalist institutions of higher education in the South were Bob Jones University and Dallas Theological Seminary. both founded in the 1920s, which exerted influence far beyond the boundaries of the Old Confederacy. Shortly after the death of Bryan in 1925, friends launched plans to establish a university as a memorial to him. The result was William Jennings Bryan University in Dayton, Tennessee which opened in 1930 but which scarcely fulfilled the ambitions of its founders. Careful to remain untainted by "modern heterodoxies," such institutions adhered rigidly to a belief in a divinely inspired, inerrant Bible and stood ready to combat all false teachings, including evolution, that "masqueraded under the guise of science." Whether at Columbia Bible College in South Carolina or at a fledgling independent Baptist seminary in Little Rock, "standing firm for Genesis" in a matter of creation and human origins was the posture of fundamentalist educational institutions. They rejected evolution not only because it was unscriptural but also because it was, in their view, unsupported by scientific evidence.[19]

In 1942 the well-known journalist and observer of southern affairs, Virginius Dabney, made a survey of colleges that espoused an antievolutionist position with the obvious intention of demonstrating that Darwin's theory was no more unpopular in the South than in the Midwest. As a result he dismissed the growth of fundamentalist educational institutions below the Potomac as of little consequence. "Their influence upon southern thought is almost nil," he noted, "and they are eclipsed in the public mind by the many progressively oriented and competently manned colleges and universities in the region." Like other middle-class southern liberals embarrassed by the presence of fundamentalists and antievolutionists in the region, Dabney viewed them as representatives of ignorance and illiteracy. When he spoke of "southern thought" and the "public mind," he obviously did so in a highly restricted way.[20] Evidence that fundamentalism and antievolutionism were essential ingredients of the popular mind in the South was omnipresent on the radio, in the cinder block churches that dotted the regional landscape, and in the ballads of the plain people that mourned the death of Bryan—who died at Dayton "defending our dear Lord" and fighting "the evolutionists, the infidels and fools ... trying to ruin the minds of children in our schools."[21]

During the fifty years following the Dayton Affair the South witnessed the emergence of numerous independent churches, sects, and religious organizations of a fundamentalist variety. The separatist tendencies that prompted the exodus of fundamentalists from the major denominations persisted in the continual division and subdivision within their own ranks later. For example, an infinite variety of independent Baptist churches came into existence after 1920. Among these were the American Baptist Association, centered in Arkansas, Texas, and Tennessee, whose founders included Ben Bogard, a leader in the antievolution fight in Arkansas in the 1920s; the World Baptist Fellowship, one of several fundamentalist organizations inspired by J. Frank Norris; and the Southwide Baptist Fellowship, organized in 1956 at the huge (thirty-three hundred members) Highland Park Baptist Church in Chattanooga, Tennessee.[22] Scarcely less dramatic than the proliferation of independent Baptists in the twentieth-century South was the rapid growth of other groups, notably the Churches of Christ and Pentecostals, which also exhibited a strong antimodernist impulse.[23] To a greater or lesser degree all of these groups, sects, and emerging denominations, not to mention the Seventh Day Adventists and Jehovah's Witnesses, in the South included Darwinism evolution in their lists of false doctrines.

Magazines, tracts, and various other publications that poured forth from fundamentalist presses in the region, sometimes in multiple printings of more than one hundred thousand copies, regularly reminded the faithful of the dangers inherent in Darwin's theory. For a generation beginning in 1934, for example, John R. Rice, a Baptist revivalist and radio preacher with headquarters in Murfreesboro, Tennessee, waged war on the theory, especially in his publication *The Sword of the Lord* and in the tracts and books published by his Sword of the Lord Press. The author of 124 books and pamphlets with a combined circulation of thirty-six million, Rice consistently argued that evolution was an "infidel guess" and a "part of the doctrine and ideology of Communism."[24]

Individuals active in the antievolution crusade of the 1920s who continued to oppose Darwin's theory throughout the quarter of a century afterward kept the issue alive and prepared the soil in which creation science would flourish in the 1970s. For example, Mordecai F. Ham, the evangelist who crisscrossed the South in the 1920s condemning evolution and linking it to "the Red Flag of Bolshevism," remained a foe of Darwinism until his death in 1961. Among his estimated one million converts was a sixteen-year-old North Carolinian named Billy Graham who drank deeply from the springs of southern fundamentalism at Bob Jones and Florida Bible Institute before making his way to Wheaton College in Illinois.[25] Ben Bogard, an independent Baptist preacher, lecturer, and perennial debater, who spearheaded the drive against evolution in Arkansas, remained hostile to the theory throughout his long career. After his death in 1952, the seminary that he founded in Little Rock perpetuated his antievolutionist legacy.[26] Far more significant was the flamboyant, controversial J. Frank Norris of Texas, editor of *The Fundamentalist* and "the epitome of the independent fundamental Baptist" who exerted a powerful influence in fundamentalist circles for almost three decades after the Scopes trial. A whole generation of preachers and evangelists were "inspired by his example" and "hundreds of churches" organized through his influence. By his own admission one of his most notable achievements was his war on evolution that resulted in the purging of the Baylor University faculty of "seven evolution professors." The ever broadening base of southern fundamentalism and the virile legacies bequeathed by Ham, Bogard, Norris and others insured the survival of antievolution sentiment in the South.[27]

Class differences tended to obscure the substantial areas of agreement that existed between conservatives in the mainline southern churches and the more militant, separatist fundamentalists.[28] Although those independent Baptists outside the Southern Baptist Convention viewed those inside as "false prophets" or compromisers, the southern Baptist fold itself as well as other mainline denominations included many whose beliefs and attitudes intersected at various points with those of their more separatist-oriented fundamentalist brethren. Their similarities became evident in 1968 in a book entitled *Why I Preach the Bible Is Literally True*, written by W. A. Criswell, the pastor of the First Baptist Church in Dallas and president of the Southern Baptist Convention.[29] The point was that many southern churchmen, though repelled by the bizarre antics of some fundamentalists and resentful of the ridicule heaped upon the South as a result of the Scopes trial, were nonetheless in sympathy with the intent of antievolution legislation, which in the words of the Tennessee governor in 1925 was "to protest the tendency to exalt science and deny the Bible." For many, laws banning evolution essentially represented efforts to save their children—the future generation—from the corrosive influence of a false doctrine that "crushed the soul." Since conservatives as well as fundamentalists generally considered soul saving the primary function of the church, the elimination of evolution appeared altogether consistent with the church's mission.[30]

Those embarrassed by the "spectacle at Dayton" and unwilling to risk its reenactment elsewhere in the South attempted to address many of the same issues involved in the passage of monkey laws by supporting legislation requiring Bible reading in public schools. As early as 1928, the Tennessee delegation to the General Federation of Women's Clubs successfully campaigned to win the organization's endorsement of a movement to introduce Bible study in the public school curriculum. By its own admission the delegation was motivated by a desire "to modify the drastic evolution law . . . which brought about the famous Scopes Trial" and so much unfavorable publicity for Tennessee.[31] By 1931 five southern states required Bible reading and six others permitted it. Except for Louisiana, where a large Catholic population precluded a Protestant consensus, Bible reading became virtually a universal practice in public schools throughout the South.[32] While the pattern in regard to the teaching of biological evolution was probably less uniform, there is substantial evidence to indicate that Darwin's theory was a topic that teachers in the region either chose to ignore altogether or to approach with great caution.

After the enactment of the Arkansas antievolution measure in 1929, which marked the end of legislative activity for almost fifty years, a common observation, especially by apologists for the South, was that the existence of monkey laws in three states posed no threat and were in fact meaningless. Such an argument echoed the sentiment of Governor Austin Peay, who upon signing the Tennessee antievolution law, declared: "Nobody believes that it is going to be an active statute."[33] The governor was correct if he meant that teachers would not be hauled into court whenever they mentioned Darwin's theory. What most teachers understood, however, was that the statute reflected majority opinion and could at any time be invoked. Watson Davis, who covered the Scopes trial in 1925, observed upon his return to Dayton in 1960: "No teacher who wants to hold his job teaches evolution." Rather than being prosecuted, an evolutionist in the Tennessee classroom was likely either to find that his contract was not renewed at the end of the term or the climate so uncongenial that he would resign.[34] Noting the care with which the state textbook commission "screened" school books to "make sure that the theory doesn't slip through," a biologist at the University of Tennessee emphatically denied in 1961 that the state's antievolution statute was a dead letter law as many insisted. "School supervisors," he argued, "must report to their superintendent in the observance of 'school laws,' among them the anti-evolution law specifically."[35]

The mere existence of antievolution laws not only acted as a deterrent to free discussions of evolution, but they also made available to disgruntled citizens legal instruments for disciplining teachers and administrators they found objectionable on other grounds. In 1929, for example, a high school principal in Fentress County, Tennessee, who incurred the enmity of two citizens because he suspended their children from school for a fireworks prank, was brought to trial and accused, among other things, of teaching evolution. Although the evolution charge was obviously added in an attempt to arouse community opinion against the principal, he was ultimately cleared of all charges. "It must now appear plain," the Memphis *Commercial Appeal* editorialized regarding the Fentress County case, "that the [anti-evolution] law is not going to be permitted to enjoy a dead letter status."[36] Somewhat similar to the Fentress County case was a suit filed in 1967 by a group of taxpayers in Izard County, Arkansas, charging the superintendent with misusing funds and with "allowing textbooks that teach evolution in the schools in violation of the law." Again evolution "was thrown in to add comfort to the other charge" against the superintendent.[37]

Nor were the state-supported institutions of higher education in Tennessee, Arkansas, and Mississippi altogether immune from the implications of the antievolution statutes. Several science professors at the University of Arkansas openly violated that state law in a futile attempt to be arrested and thereby provide the basis for a test case, but faculty members in other state institutions in the South were more cautious.[38] In 1946 Vera Jacobs described how as a student at Mississippi State College for Women she first became aware of the state's antievolution law. When she purchased her Western Civilization textbook at the campus bookstore, "the clerk tore out four or five pages (those discussing Darwin) before handing it" to her.[39] Most college and university authorities concerned about the antievolution laws developed more subtle strategems for circumventing them.

Not merely in the classrooms of the three states that possessed monkey laws but throughout the South evolution was a sensitive issue for teachers and administrators. A study sponsored by the Union of American Biological Societies (UABS) and published in 1942, which revealed how widespread the lack of attention to Darwin's theory was nationally, identified the forces that discouraged treatment of it. The overwhelming majority of southern respondents to the study's questionnaire indicated that community opinion, personal beliefs of teachers themselves, state laws, school administrators, and board of education regulations, in that order, functioned as the principal restraints on the teaching of evolution. Significantly the teachers' objections to Darwin's theory constituted a major factor in the lack of attention to evolution.[40] The fact was that teachers in the South often shared the antievolutionist opinion of the larger community and agreed with the sentiment of the Tennessee legislator in 1939 who in opposing the repeal of the state's monkey law, remarked: "I don't want my children being taught something I don't believe."[41]

The widespread acceptance of such a view in the South was sufficient to intimidate teachers and administrators who were sympathetic to evolution. The UABS survey revealed that biology teachers from North Carolina, a state that defeated evolution laws in the 1920s and prided itself in being in the vanguard of southern progressivism, were acutely aware of the risks involved in frank discussions of evolution in the classroom. Darwin's theory was, according to one teacher in the state, "a taboo subject to most people in the state"; others agreed and indicated that they avoided any treatment of it in order not "to stir up trouble."[42] In 1971, thirty years after the UABS survey, popular hostility to Darwin's theory may have subsided but had scarcely disappeared in North Carolina. In that year Gaston County school officials summarily dismissed George Ivey Moore, a student teacher in a junior high school, "for having responded to students' questions with answers approving the Darwinism theory, indicating personal agnosticism and questioning the literal interpretation of the Bible." Moore filed suit in federal court and won. The judge ruled that Gaston County school authorities had violated the establishment clause of the First Amendment by officially approving, in effect, "local orthodoxy" in regards to Darwin's theory of evolution. As the judge noted, the very word "evolution" still "struck a nerve" in Gaston County.[43]

In view of the lucrative market in school textbooks it is hardly surprising that publishers were careful to avoid striking the same nerve. As a result, during the decades following the Scopes trial high school biology textbooks underwent significant revision in deference to antievolution opinion in the United States. The new and revised books deemphasized evolution, treated it under different terminology or dropped references to it altogether. The role of the South in these revisions was all the more significant in view of "the fact that a higher percentage of southern high school students study biology than in other regions of the country presumably because of the South's agricultural orientation."[44] The altered contents of biology textbooks, coupled with the antievolution opinion in many southern communities and the presence of teachers who personally objected to Darwin's theory, acted as a powerful deterrent to the spread of "false doctrines" among the future generations of the region.

Throughout the fifty years after the Scopes trial various individuals and organizations, including scientific and academic groups, attempted in vain to secure the repeal of the monkey laws in Tennessee and Arkansas. In addition to references to freedom of inquiry and to the scientific validity of evolution, the most frequent argument invoked against such laws was that they tarnished the image and damaged the reputations of these two states in particular and the South in general.[45] In Arkansas the ban on the teaching of evolution had scarcely been enacted when Robert E. Lee Maxey, an attorney and native of the state living in New York, filed suit in 1929 to enjoin its enforcement. After protracted delays the case was finally dismissed in 1932 at Maxey's request. Seven years later, a bill introduced in the Arkansas legislature to repeal the antievolution law died quietly without fanfare at the hands of the House Committee on Education, whose members, like many public school teachers throughout the South, realized that a reopening of the debate on evolution was likely "to stir up trouble."[46] Twenty-two years later, in 1959, when Mrs. Gordon Oates, a legislator from Pulaski County (Little Rock), made a second attempt to repeal the monkey law, the reaction to her measure was, in her words, "as if someone had dropped a bomb" in the legislative hall. Inundated with telephone calls and letters protesting her repeal measure and advised by her legislative colleagues that the people "would never go along with something they did not believe in," she reluctantly withdrew the bill on the grounds that a majority of her constituents opposed it.[47]

A bill to repeal the Tennessee antievolution law in 1929 met with no more success than those in Arkansas. Later efforts to repeal the Tennessee measure in 1931, 1935, 1939, 1951, and 1961 also failed but not before sparking legislative debates remarkably similar in content and tone to those during the 1920s. Legislators favoring repeal spoke as advocates of liberty and enlightenment who deeply resented the injury to "the good name of the state" prompted by the antics of what they called "a few narrow, prejudiced religious fanatics." Those who opposed repeal included some who preferred to leave the monkey law "quietly and peacefully sleeping" rather than remind the world of its existence. But the majority of the opponents still believed that Darwin's theory was incompatible with their religious faith and a serious threat to morality, ethics, and decency.[48] "If this act is repealed," a Tennessee legislator declared in 1931, "we may as well close our Bibles, turn our backs on Christian people and let this state go to hell."[49] Thirty years later Tennessee legislators, among many others throughout the South, voiced identical sentiments.

In the half century after the Scopes trial the South underwent dramatic social and economic changes; industrialization, urbanization, a steady climb out of education deprivation, a Second Reconstruction that destroyed the legal foundations of racial segregation and prompted references to a "postracial south," and increased per capita wealth substantially reduced some of the statistical disparities that traditionally distinguished the region from the rest of the nation. Much of the progress in education that commentators in the 1920s considered essential to overcome public hostility to evolution in the South had been achieved by a half century later, but somehow more and better public schools failed to eradicate opposition to Darwin's theory. Notwithstanding the preference of chambers of commerce and other regional boosters for the label "sunbelt," the South remained the Bible Belt. A sociologist writing in 1972 concluded that there was no substantial decrease in "Southern religious peculiarity in the recent past and no prospects for the decrease in the near future."[50] In 1925 Henry L. Mencken observed while returning to Baltimore from Dayton that one could throw a brick out of the train window anywhere in route and hit a fundamentalist on the head. Allowing for Mencken's imprecise use of "fundamentalist" as a pejorative term for a broad spectrum of southern churchmen, his observation possessed considerable validity—and still did a half century later. The typical nonsouthern image of southern Baptists as late as 1967, according to a denominational paper, was that of "fundamentalists and hillbillies," devoted to "ideas and practices of day-before-yesterday," but who somehow appeared "too well dressed."[51] Southern fundamentalists in the 1960s and 1970s were, in fact, different from those of Mencken's era: their ranks exhibited greater affluence and respectability, higher levels of education and sophistication, a broader institutional base, and an increasing political consciousness. The fundamentalism bequeathed by the generation at the turn of the century that was primarily northern and urban in origin lost something and gained something in its sojourn in the South. Hence, the fundamentalism that the South fed back to the nation after World War II, while deeply indebted to those who had formulated the doctrinal statements known as "the fundamentals," was not quite the same. From the ranks of this southern-type fundamentalism emerged the likes of Billy Graham, Jerry Falwell, Oral Roberts, and others who presided over expensive, nationwide religious empires and whose collective influence resulted, to an extraordinary degree, in what David Edwin Harrell, Jr., has termed "the southernization of American evangelicalism."[52] Their message and style revealed the unmistakable influence of those who battled modernism and evolution in the generation of the Scopes trial. The idea of the South as "the nursery, the training ground, the granary, the source of supplies" for evangelizing America and the world was thoroughly familiar for them.[53] Although Graham and most others associated with the post–World War II religious revival in the United States largely ignored Darwin's theory, they contributed significantly to a cultural milieu that nourished antievolutionism.

In the 1960s southerners had reason to believe, perhaps even more than other Americans, that their world, like Willa Cather's forty years earlier, had "broken in two." A war in Vietnam raised questions about the notion of national invincibility, while a succession of social and cultural traumas, including a sexual revolution, a counterculture, a "now generation" scornful of the past, and a radical theology that spoke in terms of "the death of God" profoundly disturbed those wedded to the traditional, evangelical faith and the system of values that rested upon it. The presence of a well-known advocate of the "death of God" theology on the faculty of Methodist-related Emory University merely confirmed the convictions of southern fundamentalists that the mainline denominations had capitulated to infidelity.[54] That a civil rights revolution aimed at dismantling the apparatus of racial segregation and thereby eliminating what most churches and sects of all varieties had sanctioned as a pillar of the southern way of life coincided with these threats to the region's "pure and undefiled" religion only heightened the anxiety level of southerners. For many the whole complex of changes in the 1960s, from the "death of God" theology to the sexual revolution and the civil rights crusades, represented a coordinated effort to destroy southern "civilization." In the midst of such stress the call went forth: back to the Bible. The Bible not only held the answers to modern civilization's problems but it also provided guidance in combating the latest crop of infidelities. "We in the deep South," John R. Rice wrote in 1966, "are so old fashioned we still believe in the Bible.... We generally are against socialism and communism and modernism, and so leftwing newsmen and modern preachers love to deride the South."[55] For Rice and numerous other fundamentalist spokesmen in the region, the South clearly remained the one place in America with a religious faith sufficiently pure and robust to spearhead a campaign to lead the nation back to its moorings.

In the calculation of many southerners, outside as well as inside fundamentalist ranks, the Supreme Court of the United States belonged among the "godless forces of the anti-Christ" that threatened the region. More than unpopular rulings regarding racial desegregation prompted the proliferation throughout the South of billboards that read: "Impeach Earl Warren." In no other section of the country did the Warren Court's decision banning prayer and Bible reading in public schools in 1962 and 1963 prompt such widespread condemnation as in the South. In Congress southerners were among the most vocal critics of the decisions, which Senator Herman Talmadge of Georgia described as having the effect of "putting God and the devil on an equal plane." Senators James O. Eastland of Mississippi and John McClellan of Arkansas joined Talmadge in sponsoring a constitutional amendment that sanctioned both prayer and Bible reading as "part of the program of any school." The evidence suggests that their action met with broad popular approval in the South. In Tennessee, for example, a survey indicated that 78 percent of the state's public school teachers objected to the court decisions.[56]

In the midst of what Max Lerner later called the "unraveling of national cohesion" in the 1960s—a phrase used to signify, among other things, growing concern over a victory-less war in Vietnam, a host of environmental problems, decaying cities, the loss of a sense of community and the discovery that poverty and racism were national rather than merely southern problems—there emerged the concept of a Redemptive South that for a time enjoyed considerable popularity. It rested primarily on the belief that the South's experience with poverty, defeat, and racism, coupled with its natural resources, sense of community, and quality of life-style, uniquely prepared the region to contribute to a national renewal or at least to serve as a model for those outside the South to "gain a better relationship with things, places, people, ideas and organizational structures." Among the most fervent proponents of the Redemptive South theme were the members of the L. Q. C. Lamar Society, organized in 1969 and made up of middle-class and upper-middle class southerners.[57]

Parallel with, but wholly distinct from, the Lamar Society and similar groups were others in the region, substantially more numerous and far less likely to belong to the country club set, who, without articulating it as such, pursued their own version of a Redemptive South. Poverty, urban blight, despoiled landscapes and similar problems received little if any of their attention; rather redemption to them meant something more basic—it meant leading the nation away from false doctrines and back to God. As representatives of a rejuvenated, southern-based fundamentalism, they stood ready to save the nation's soul. Not the least among those that hoisted aloft the fundamentalist banner was Jerry Falwell of Lynchburg, Virginia, an independent Baptist and a self-proclaimed "separatist, premillennialist, pretribulationist sort of fellow."[58] As Falwell's career demonstrated, the resources and popular appeal of the fundamentalism broadcast over several hundred radio and television stations from the Thomas Road Baptist Church were considerable.

For those who like Falwell still believed that Darwin's theory represented a cardinal infidelity, the appearance of textbooks prepared by the Biological Sciences Curriculum Study (BSCS) was the signal for mobilization and action. These books, as a part of the frenzied effort to reform the science curriculum of American schools in the wake of the Soviet Union's launching of Sputnik in 1957, possessed a forthright evolutionary orientation. The response of a variety of evangelical and fundamentalist groups to the BSCS textbooks that appeared early in the 1960s was one of militant hostility. In the South the fight against the books was especially intense in Texas where representatives of Baptist groups and Churches of Christ mounted a well-organized campaign. The Texas embroglio prompted numerous references to the "renewal of the monkey war" as did similar outbursts in Kentucky, Florida, and Alabama. Except for Mississippi and Alabama, all southern states ultimately included the BSCS textbooks on their approved lists, an action that did not, of course, require local schools to use them.[59]

Despite the furor in the South over the BSCS textbooks and the court decisions on prayer and Bible reading, the region was not the birthplace of the revived crusade against evolution. That distinction apparently belonged to California where the so-called creation science or creationist movement first flourished early in the 1960s. Although some observers, in referring to the "flatness of the accents" of those involved in the California fracas, implied that transplanted southerners, presumably second generation Okies and Arkies, were primarily responsible, the evidence is too sketchy to speak with precision on that score.[60] What is clear is that southerners were prominent in creationist organizations from the beginning. The two most important such organizations, both formed in 1963, were: the Creation Research Society, the scholarly arm of the creation science movement, organized at Asbury College in Kentucky and headquartered in Michigan; and the Bible Science Association, founded in Idaho by Walter Lang, a Lutheran minister, which was more inclined to political activism. Most notable among the southerners involved in these efforts was Henry M. Morris, a native of Texas and a Baptist, who was professor of engineering at Virginia Polytechnic Institute. A founder of the Creation Research Society and an architect of the creation science movement, Morris was the author of *The Genesis Flood* published in 1961 which has remained one of the most authoritative sources of scientific creationism. In 1972 he became head of the Institute for Creation Research (ICR) in California, the most important single agency in challenging evolution on scientific rather than religious grounds.[61]

Notwithstanding the scientific emphasis of creationist arguments, clearly more was at stake than the scientific validity of Darwin's theory. The creationists' campaign, no less than that of antievolutionists of an earlier generation, was scarcely a single-issue protest; rather it represented a reaction to changes that occurred in the previous several decades. The works of Henry M. Morris, for example, insisted that "most of the world's modern problems" could be traced to the widespread acceptance of evolution.[62] Even more explicit in linking Darwin to the breakdown in morality was Braswell Dean, Jr., presiding judge of the Georgia Court of Appeals and a Methodist active in various creationist organizations, who described evolution as "the cause of permissiveness, promiscuity, pills, prophylactics, perversions, pregnancies, abortion, pornotherapy, pollution, poisoning and proliferation of crimes of all sorts."[63]

The new assault on Darwin's theory, coupled with the controversy created by the publication in 1961 of *The Message of Genesis*, a conservative but nonliteral interpretation of creation by Ralph Elliott of the Southern Baptist seminary in Kansas City, rekindled interest in the evolution issue, especially in those states that still had monkey laws.[64] In Tennessee and Arkansas this revived interest prompted those opposed to monkey laws to renew efforts to repeal them and emboldened those in favor of such legislation to enforce them. In 1967, in the midst of a movement to repeal the Tennessee law, led by representatives from Nashville and Memphis, the Campbell County board of education fired a young teacher, Gary Scott, for teaching evolution. The threat of "another Scopes trial" and more unfavorable publicity figured significantly in the repeal of the forty-year-old monkey law in 1967. The Memphis *Commercial Appeal* and other urban dailies expressed relief that "the monkey law was now history."[65] That such a view was not shared universally by all Tennesseans became abundantly evident six years later.

In Arkansas the revival of interest in evolution in the 1960s resulted in a direct confrontation between those anxious to repeal the state's monkey law and those who perceived it as a defense against infidelity. Elliott's *Message of Genesis* provided the occasion for the *Baptist Challenge*, a "voice of independent Baptists" published in Little Rock and edited by M. L. Moser, Jr., the militantly fundamentalist minister of the city's Central Baptist Church, to speak out forcefully against evolution. Convinced that atheistic Darwinism was "winning the battle," the *Challenge* in 1965 warned its readers of "the peril to all freedom and liberty inherent in this satanic theory." Moser also used his influence with the Metropolitan Little Rock Association of Ministers, an organization formed during the racial integration crisis by clergymen who opposed as too liberal the stand taken by the city's regular ministerial association on matters relating to race, to secure a resolution favoring retention of the state's antievolution law. To repeal it, Moser argued, would play into the hands of the "socialistic and atheistic conspiracy" to undermine American education.[66]

When a bill to repeal the monkey law again died in the Arkansas legislature in 1965 without coming to a vote, Forrest Rozzell, executive secretary of the Arkansas Education Association (AEA), determined to resolve the question of the antievolution law's constitutionality by instituting a suit in state court. Backed by the AEA and several major newspapers, including the influential *Arkansas Gazette* of Little Rock, Rozzell initiated a public discussion of the issue at the same time that he quietly prepared for a test case. Fundamentalist clergymen were quick to denounce his suggestion that the Arkansas evolution law should be repealed.[67]

On September 10, 1965, Orval Faubus, in his sixth term as governor, entered the fray with a ringing statement against any tampering with the monkey law. He wanted it "as a safeguard to keep 'way out' teachers in line."[68] "I accept," the governor declared, "the theory of the Bible on the creation of man as related in the Book of Genesis." In his view evolution was incompatible with the Bible and was, in fact, atheistic.[69] Privately he described Rozzell as "an atheist," who, like the editors of the *Arkansas Gazette*, believed that intellectual progress was impossible without a belief "in the theory of evolution, intermarriage of the races and other extreme viewpoints . . . contrary to the ideas . . . of decent people."[70] The avalanche of letters and petitions from throughout the state that poured into the Governor's office indicated overwhelming approval of his position. A substantial portion of this correspondence came from ministers and laymen in independent Baptist groups and the Churches of Christ. Some enclosed copies of Henry Morris's latest work on creation science with the suggestion that it mightily strengthened "the case against evolution."[71]

Approval of the governor's stand was not, of course, limited to Arkansas. Among the large number of congratulatory messages from outside the state was a lengthy letter from Walter Lang of the Bible Science Association who took the occasion to acquaint Faubus with his own organization. Lang insisted that "socialism or communism or the new [im]morality" could not be defeated without first eliminating the concept that "we ascended from lower forms of life."[72]

Amid the fierce debate over evolution Rozzell, having persuaded Susan Epperson, a young biology teacher in Little Rock "with an impeccable Arkansas background" to become the plaintiff in a test case, filed suit to secure a declaratory judgment that the state's monkey law was unconstitutional. In May 1966 Chancery Court Judge Murry O. Reed ruled in Epperson's favor, but following an appeal to the Arkansas Supreme Court by the State's Attorney General Bruce Bennett, who attacked evolution as "a crackpot theory," the state's highest court upheld the constitutionality of the antievolution law as a "valid exercise of the state's power to specify curriculum in its public schools."[73] By the time of the court's decision the agitation over evolution in Arkansas had become intense: the State Association of Missionary Baptist Churches endorsed "biblical creation"; Moser and his church sponsored a mammoth "creation seminar" in Little Rock conducted by members of the Creation Research Society; and a series of "Evolution Debates" in the city attracted capacity crowds.[74] Despite evidence of popular opposition to Darwin's theory, Rozzell and others interested in the Epperson case pressed toward a resolution of the issue by appeal to the United States Supreme Court. In 1968 the court struck down as unconstitutional the forty-year-old Arkansas antievolution statute and by implication the Mississippi law.[75]

Although many heralded the decision as a victory for academic freedom, the principle of church-state separation, and enlightenment, opponents of Darwin's theory greeted it as another defeat for "true Christianity" at the hands of the same body that had attempted to eliminate prayer and Bible reading from public schools. M. S. Moser, Jr., described the Epperson decision as another evidence of the court's intention to remove all doctrines "recognizing our nation as a Christian nation . . . and substituting . . . the doctrines of atheism" in their place.[76] If the Epperson decision had little effect in altering the opinions of antievolutionists, it did force a change in tactics. Rather than advocating legislation to ban the teaching of evolution, they concentrated instead on securing "equal time" or "balanced treatment" for creationism, an approach that had broad appeal as an expression of fair play and democratic values.

Spearheading the new campaign were the Creation Research Society, the Bible Science Association, and the Institute for Creation Research which were joined by dozens of more local or specialized groups. The renewed struggle against Darwin also received important support from powerful organizations such as Jerry Falwell's Moral Majority and Family Life, America Under God (FLAG) whose primary concerns lay elsewhere. Of considerable significance in the new drive against evolution was the role of "evangelical scientists" on the faculties of fundamentalist colleges and seminaries, as well as some state institutions, in the South. A few were members of the Creation Research Society, and most had ready access to its steady stream of creationist literature. For example, Russell Artist, a biologist and a member of the CRS who taught at David Lipscomb College, a Church of Christ institution in Nashville, fought against the use of BSCS textbooks and for the enactment of a creationist law in Tennessee.[77]

Despite strenuous efforts in states in the West and Midwest, creationists secured "equal time" legislation only within the South where their lectures, seminars, debates, and literature struck responsive chords. While creationist organizations probably converted few evolutionists to their cause, their activities were important in mobilizing those unreconciled to evolution. Not only did they provide "scientific arguments" with which to combat the theory, they also linked it to "secular humanism," a term of reproach signifying a wide range of modern evils. The result was a proliferation of grass roots organizations throughout the South, such as the Fair Education Foundation in North Carolina and Citizens for Another Voice in Education (CAVE) in Georgia, that took up the crusade for legislation to insure that creationism would at least have "equal time" with evolutionism in public school science classes.[78]

The first legislative success of the "equal time" advocates occurred in Tennessee in 1973, which six years earlier had repealed its antievolution law. In the same year a similar measure passed the Georgia state senate only to die in the lower house. Despite a federal court decision in 1975 that declared Tennessee's "equal time" statute unconstitutional "on its face,"[79] creationists continued their lobbying efforts with school boards and labored to formulate a "equal time" or "balanced treatment" statute that would pass the scrutiny of the courts. No one was more active in seeking such "foolproof" legislation than Paul Ellwanger of Anderson, South Carolina, the head of a small lobbying group known as Citizens for Fairness in Education, who viewed "the whole battle as one between God and anti-God." After collecting various proposed legislative acts, including one drafted by Wendell Bird, an attorney for the Institute for Creation Research, Ellwanger prepared his own model statute which called for the "balanced treatment" of scientific creation and evolution. He sent copies to acquaintances in Arkansas and Louisiana, who had his model legislation introduced in their respective state legislatures. Supported by the state chapters of FLAG and the Moral Majority, as well as various religious groups including the Greater Little Rock Evangelical Fellowship, Ellwanger's "balanced treatment" measure sailed through the Arkansas legislature and was signed into law in 1981. The Louisiana legislature enacted a somewhat different version in the same year.[80]

In December, 1981 in Little Rock—a bustling New South city with high rises and shopping centers, whose boosters preferred to call it the buckle on the Sunbelt rather than the Bible Belt—the curtain opened on a courtroom drama that the press insisted upon labeling Scopes II. At issue was the constitutionality of Arkansas's "balanced treatment" law. When, on January 5, 1982, federal judge William R. Overton rendered his decision striking down the statute, one observer, a creationist, remarked that he had seen "the Creator go to court and 'lose.' "[81] Despite an attempt at the Little Rock trial to make the struggle appear a confrontation between two sciences, "creation science" and "evolution science," rather than between religion and science, John T. Scopes would have had little difficulty in recognizing the basic issues. What might have appeared strange to him were the roles assumed in the proceedings by representatives of the mainline denominations and by those who during his own trial in 1925 were dismissed as eccentric groups existing on the fringes of southern culture.

That officials of the major Protestant denominations—Southern Presbyterian, Methodist, Southern Baptist, and Episcopal—as well as other groups spearheaded the legal contest that declared Arkansas's "balanced treatment" law unconstitutional suggested the extent to which the battle lines over evolution in the South had shifted since the 1920s when Darwin's theory prompted tumultuous struggles and sharp divisions in such denominations. But to say that the issues associated with the struggle over evolution were no longer disruptive in mainline denominations did not mean that religious forces played little part in the controversies of the 1970s and 1980s. Just the opposite, of course, was the case. But the strongest and most articulate support for creationism came from sources outside what continued, perhaps inaccurately, to be called mainline Protestantism: it came from fundamentalist groups whose numbers and influence dramatically increased in the decades following the Scopes trial. Those whom journalists in the era of Dayton indiscriminately included under perjorative labels such as Fundamentalists and Holy Rollers, had sixty years later emerged as powerful forces both nationally and regionally. They had moved nearer the mainstream in terms of wealth, education, and power without abandoning the antimodernist impulse of their faith that expressed itself, among other ways, in opposition to Darwin's theory. Clearly, too, the quest for status, evident in the hostility toward the perceived elitism of orthodox scientists by scientific creationists, figured significantly in the struggles of the 1970s and 1980s. It may be, as Michael Novak has suggested, that "the lawsuits over creationism are more a conflict over cultural status than a conflict between science and religion."[82]

Although the South was the scene of noisy struggles over Darwin's theory and the only section of the country to invoke the coercive power of the state to ban it from the classroom, the region was never monolithic in its hostility to evolution. Those in the South intent upon enacting monkey laws encountered strong opposition from some conservative churchmen, including Southern Baptists, as well as from academic, scientific, and diverse other groups. Among Southern Baptists there were always leaders who boldly and eloquently opposed antievolution statutes as inconsistent with the denomination's historic commitment to religious liberty and to the principle of church-state separation.[83] But the popularity of the antievolution position in the South meant that those who spoke against such laws, especially elected officials, did so at considerably greater risk than those elsewhere. In the South one was almost certain to be condemned and ostracized as a cultural scalawag who had sold out to alien forces bent on obliterating the southern way of life. Most opponents of antievolution legislation in the region recognized, as did Wilbur J. Cash, that such measures were usually "the focal point of attack for a program, explicit or implicit, that went far beyond evolution laws."[84]

Despite a tendency to identify opposition to Darwin as "an anachronistic movement limited to a few backward Southern states," popular hostility to his theory has never been confined to the South. In 1927 Maynard Shipley, an indefatigable foe of fundamentalists, antievolutionists, and others whom he classified as the "forces of obscurantism," estimated that more than half of the total church membership in the United States, or twenty-five million Americans, found Darwin's theory unacceptable.[85] The results of nationwide public opinion polls conducted during the next half century, which indicated substantial increases in fundamentalist influence and the persistence of antievolutionist sentiments among a broad spectrum of the American population, suggests that Shipley's estimate may have been conservative.[86] In 1968 Howard Zinn insisted that southern fundamentalism and the antimodernist impulse that it so dramatically exhibited on occasion represented "only an intense form" of what existed in the entire nation.[87]

Yet the fact remained that the South's response to evolution has been more intense, noisier, and more productive of coercive legislation than that of the rest of the country. Explanations of the region's exceptionalism on this particular issue have usually included references to two of the three R's of southern distinctiveness in general, ruralism and religion, and on rare occasions to the third R, race. Undoubtedly the South's rural character, low church, Bible centered, individualistic Protestantism, relatively low level of literacy and traditional educational deficiencies, as well as the existence in the region of a populist bias against established authority and elitism, have influenced its reaction to the theory of evolution. Perhaps more important, however, has been the peculiar relationship between regional faith and culture, a relationship in which consensual attitudes have been equated with a divinely ordained order of things.[88] Whatever else antievolution and scientific creationist laws may have symbolized, as Clarence Cason observed in 1935, southerners perceived them as devices "to conserve their customs" and protect "the church about which their social patterns, their essential culture, foregathered to an important extent."[89]

NOTES

1. H. L. Mencken to Raymond Pearl, July 14?, [1925], in *The New Mencken Letters*, ed. by Carl Bode (New York, 1977), 188; Sheldon N. Grebstein, *Monkey Trial: The State of Tennessee vs. John Thomas Scopes* (Boston, 1969), 200; on the Scopes Trial see L. Sprague de Camp, *The Great Monkey Trial* (Garden City, 1965), Ray Ginger, *Six Days or Forever? Tennessee v. John Thomas Scopes* (Boston, 1958).

2. The best analysis of fundamentalism is George M. Marsden, *Fundamentalism and American Culture: The Shaping of Twentieth Century Evangelicalism* (New York, 1980), which I have relied upon heavily.

3. Ibid., p. 103.

4. Victor I. Masters, "As to Immigration," *Baptist Advance* 9 (January 21, 1915): 2.

5. John M. Moore, *The South To-day* (Nashville, 1916), pp. 171–72.

6. Clement Eaton, "Professor James Woodrow and the Freedom of Teaching in the South," *The Journal of Southern History* 28 (February 1962): 3–17. See also Larry Hayward, "F. E. Maddox, Chaplain of Progress, 1908," *Arkansas Historical Quarterly* 38 (Summer 1979): 146–66.

7. Marsden, *Fundamentalism and American Culture*, pp. 103, 169–179, 258.

8. Willard B. Gatewood, Jr., *Controversy in the Twenties: Fundamentalism, Modernism and Evolution* (Nashville, 1969), pp. 18–21; Lawrence W. Levine, *Defender of the Faith: William Jennings Bryan, The Last Decade, 1915–1925* (New York, 1965), pp. 271–72.

9. Willard B. Gatewood, Jr., *Preachers, Pedagogues and Politicians: The Evolution Controversy in North Carolina, 1920–1927* (Chapel Hill, 1966), pp. 40–45;

James J. Thompson, Jr., *Tried As By Fire: Southern Baptists and the Religious Controversies of the 1920's* (Macon, 1982), pp. 103–4, 143.

10. Quoted in Gatewood, *Controversy in the Twenties*, p. 124.

11. Wilbur J. Cash, *The Mind of the South* (New York, 1941), p. 339; Gatewood, *Preachers, Pedagogues and Politicians*, p. 154.

12. Cash, *Mind of the South*, p. 338.

13. Kenneth K. Bailey, *Southern White Protestantism in the Twentieth Century* (New York, 1964), pp. 72–91.

14. Marsden, *Fundamentalism and Modern Culture*, pp. 188–91; Gatewood, *Controversy in the Twenties*, pp. 39–46.

15. Willard B. Gatewood, Jr., *Science and Religion: The Controversy over Evolution* (St. Charles, Mo., 1970), pp. 13–14; Paul Carter, *The Twenties in America* (New York, 1968), pp. 79–80.

16. Liston Pope, *Millhands and Preachers: A Study of Gastonia* (New Haven, 1942), chapters 6 and 7. On Hux see Ralph Lord Roy, *Apostles of Discord* (Boston, 1953), pp. 203–4; Editorial, *Christian Century* 69 (December 17, 1952): 1460.

17. Marsden, *Evangelicalism and American Culture*, p. 194; Joseph Martin Dawson, "Religion Down South," *Christian Century* 47 (June 25, 1930): 811.

18. Joel A. Carpenter, "Fundamentalist Institutions and the Rise of Evangelical Protestantism, 1929–1942," *Church History* 44 (March 1980): 61–75. See also Louis Gasper, *The Fundamentalist Movement* (The Hague, 1963), chapters 5 and 6. An indication of these developments in the various southern states appears in Samuel B. Hill, ed., *Religion in the Southern States: An Historical Study* (Macon, 1983).

19. S. A. Winter, *The Bible College Story* (Manhasset, N.Y., 1962), pp. 48–56; George W. Dollar, *A History of Fundamentalism in America* (Greenville, S.C., 1973), pp. 89, 270–72; Virginius Dabney, "Standing Firm for Genesis," *The Nation* 154 (March 14, 1942): 310–12.

20. Dabney, "Standing Firm for Genesis," pp. 310–12; see also Virginius Dabney, *Liberalism in the South* (Chapel Hill, 1932), chapter 16.

21. Howard W. Odum, *An American Epoch: Southern Portraiture in the National Picture* (New York, 1930), p. 210.

22. Dollar, *History of Fundamentalism*, pp. 216–17, 226, 242–44.

23. Charles Roland, *The Improbable Era: The South Since World War II* (Lexington, 1975), pp. 122–24; William Woodson, *Standing for their Faith: A History of Churches of Christ in Tennessee, 1900–1950* (Henderson, Tenn., 1979), pp. 131–34.

24. David Edwin Harrell, Jr., *White Sects and Black Men in the Recent South* (Nashville, 1971), pp. 28–29; Dollar, *History of Fundamentalism*, p. 355; John R. Rice, *Evolution or the Bible—Which?* (Murfreesboro, Tenn., n.d.); John R. Rice, *Bible Doctrines to Live By* (Murfreesboro, 1968), pp. 184–87.

25. Dollar, *History of Fundamentalism*, p. 326; Bob Arnold, "Billy Graham: Superstar," in *On Jordan's Stormy Banks: Religion in the South*, ed. Samuel S. Hill, Jr. (Macon, 1983), pp. 15–22.

26. On Bogard's long career see L. D. Foreman and Alta Payne, *The Life and Works of Benjamin Marcus Bogard*, 3 vols., (Little Rock, 1965–1966).

27. Gasper, *The Fundamentalist Movement*, pp. 17–18; Jerry Falwell, et al., eds., *The Fundamentalist Phenomenom: The Resurgence of Conservative Christianity* (Garden City, 1981), pp. 92–95; Bobby D. Compton, "J. Frank Norris and Southern Baptists," *Review and Expositor* 79 (Winter 1982): 63–84.

28. One of the most provocative statements of class and religion in the South appears in Harrell's, *White Sects and Black Men*, especially chapter 5; on fundamentalism and Southern Baptist Convention see Leon McBeth, "Fundamentalism in the SBC in Recent Years," *Review and Expositor* 69 (Winter 1982): 85–104.

29. W. A. Criswell, *Why I Preach the Bible Is Literally True* (Grand Rapids, 1968). See also "Battle of the Book," *Newsweek* 73 (May 5, 1969): 96–97; W. A. Criswell, *The Issues We Must Face* (Grand Rapids, 1953), especially chapter 4, "Curse of Modernism," pp. 41–51.

30. Gatewood, *Controversy in the Twenties*, pp. 26–27, 331.

31. *New York Times*, June 8, 1928.

32. Ward Keesecker, *Legal Status of Bible Reading and Religious Instruction in Public Schools*, U. S. Department of the Interior, Office of Education, Bulletin, 1930, No. 14 (Washington, 1930); Alvin W. Johnson, "Bible Reading in the Public Schools," *Texas Outlook* 24 (March 1940): 23–24; "Should Churches Seek Public School Credit?" *Christian Century* 69 (September 17, 1952): 1053.

33. Quoted in *The Nashville Banner*, March 24, 1925.

34. Watson Davis, "Antievolution Not Dead," *Science Newsletter* 78 (August 13, 1960): 103.

35. Wilma Dykeman and James Stokely, "Scopes and Evolution—The Jury is Still Out," *New York Times Magazine*, March 12, 1961, pp. 72–76.

36. Memphis *Commercial Appeal*, January 10, 12, 1929.

37. *Arkansas Gazette* (Little Rock), July 21, 31, 1967.

38. Leo Sweeney, "The Anti-Evolution Movement in Arkansas" (Master's thesis, University of Arkansas, 1966), p. 118.

39. Vera Jacobs, "Expurgation of Evolution from Textbooks in Mississippi," *School and Society* 63 (February 2, 1946): 82–83.

40. Oscar Riddle, et al., *The Teaching of Biology in Secondary Schools of the United States* (n.p., Union of American Biological Societies, 1942), pp. 69–75.

41. Quoted in Memphis *Commercial Appeal*, February 17, 1939.

42. Riddle, *Teaching of Biology in Secondary Schools*, p. 73.

43. For the decision rendered on March 7, 1973, see *Federal Supplement*, 1973 (St. Paul, 1973) Volume 357, pp. 1037–44; see also *Charlotte Observer* March 8, 1973.

44. Judith V. Grabiner and Peter D. Miller, "Effects of the Scopes Trial: Was It a Victory for Evolutionists?" *Science* 185 (September 6, 1974): 832–37.

45. Dabney, *Liberalism in the South*, p. 308; Memphis *Commercial Appeal*, June 11, 1931, February 17, 1939; *New York Times*, January 26, February 20, 1935.

46. Sweeney, "Anti-Evolution Movement in Arkansas," pp. 116–18.

47. Ibid., pp. 123–24.

48. Memphis *Commercial Appeal*, June 11, 1931, February 20, 1935, February 17, 1939; "Tennessee Sticks to Genesis," *Literary Digest* 60 (July 11, 1931): 21–22; *New York Times*, January 26, February 20, February 21, 1935, March 11, 1951; "A Story for Ham," *The Reporter* 24 (March 30, 1961): 12–14.

49. Memphis *Commercial Appeal*, June 11, 1931.

50. John Shelton Reed, *The Enduring South: Subcultural Persistence in Mass Society* (Lexington, 1972), p. 79.

51. R. D. Goodwin, "That's Not Our Image," *Arkansas Baptist* 66 (August 3, 1967): 5.

52. See David Edwin Harrell, Jr., "The Roots of the Moral Majority: Fundamentalism Revisited," *Occasional Papers*, Institute for Ecumenical and Cultural Research, No. 15, May, 1981, pp. 1–11; David Edwin Harrell, Jr., "Southern Revivalism From Graham to Falwell," unpublished paper delivered at the Center for Arkansas and Regional Studies, University of Arkansas, March 10, 1983; Editorial, "Fundamentalist Revival," *Christian Century* 74 (June 19, 1957): 749–51.

53. From the Southern Baptist Convention Home Mission Board in 1924 quoted in Thompson, *Trial As By Fire*, p. 72.

54. See *Baptist Challenge* 5 (December 1965), p. 4.

55. Quoted in Harrell, *White Sects and Black Men*, p. 54.

56. Paul Blanchard, *Religion and the Public Schools: The Great Controversy* (Boston, 1963), pp. 53–55, 171; Charles E. Bryant and C. Kenneth Tanner, "Public School Religion in Tennessee," *Church and State* 24 (May 1971): 8–10.

57. On the Lamar Society and Redemptive South idea see one of its publications, H. Brandt Ayers, et al., *You Can't Eat Magnolias* (New York, 1972); Robert H. McKenzie, ed., *The Rising South* (Tuscaloosa, 1976), pp. 11, 2–6.

58. Frances Fitzgerald, "A Disciplined, Charging Army," *The New Yorker* 57 (May 18, 1981): 60.

59. Arnold B. Grobman, *Changing Classroom: The Role of the Biological Sciences Curriculum Study* (Garden City, 1969), pp. 203–19; *Richmond Times Dispatch*, October 12, 1964; Eliot P. Tucker, "The Anti-Evolutionists of 1964," *Science Education* 51 (October, 1967): 371–78; *New York Times*, August 2, November 11, 1964.

60. On the California struggle see Dorothy Nelkin, *Science Textbook Controversies and the Politics of Equal Time* (Cambridge, 1977), pp. 81–101; John A. Moore, "Creationism in California," *Deadalus* 103 (Summer, 1974): 173–87; Calvin Trillin, "U.S. Journal: Sacramento, California, A Hearing on the Origin of Species," *New Yorker* 48 (January 6, 1967): 55–58.

61. Ronald L. Numbers, "Creationism in 20th Century America" *Science* 318 (November 5, 1981): 541–43; William J. Tinkle, "Creationism in the Twentieth Century," *Creation Research Society Quarterly* 10 (June, 1973): 44–47.

62. Henry M. Morris, *The Troubled Waters of Evolution* (San Diego, 1974), pp. 36–37, 156–57, 161–68.

63. Quoted in Kenneth S. Saladin, "Sixty Years of Creationism in Georgia," *Society* 10 (January-February 1983): 20.

64. Bailey, *Southern White Protestantism*, pp. 155–48.

65. Memphis *Commercial Appeal*, April 13, 21, May 1, 14, 15, 16, 17, 18, 1967.

66. E. C. James, "Baptist Theologians and Their Books," *The Baptist Challenge* 2 (February 1962): 1–3; Editorial, "Just Where Do They Stand," ibid. 2 (December, 1962): 2; Ray Mason, "Was Your Grandmother An Ape?" ibid. 4 (November, 1964): 7; Editorial, "Darwin Is Winning the Battle," ibid. 5 (January, 1965): 2.

67. Cal Ledbetter, Jr., "The Anti-evolution Law: Church and State in Arkansas," *Arkansas Historical Quarterly* 38 (Winter 1979): 315–16.

68. Quoted in *Arkansas Gazette*, September 11, 1965.

69. Orval Faubus to Harold K. Brown, September 21, 1965, to Sam Griffith, October 1, 1965, Orval Faubus Papers, University of Arkansas Library, Fayetteville (henceforth Faubus Papers).

70. Orval Faubus to Marion E. Rice, November 8, 1965, Faubus Papers.

71. See the large number of letters and petitions in the folder marked "Evolution File" in Faubus Papers.

72. Walter Lang to Orval Faubus, September 17, 1965, Faubus Papers.

73. Ledbetter, "The Anti-evolution Law," pp. 316–22.

74. *Arkansas Gazette*, October 18, 20, November 5, 1965, June 29, 30, 1966, March 6, 1967; M. L. Moser, Jr., "Creation or Evolution," *Baptist Challenge* 6 (May 1966): 1–6; "Creation Seminar," ibid. 7 (February 1967): 1, 4.

75. Ledbetter, "The Anti-evolution Law," pp. 322–27.

76. *Arkansas Gazette*, November 13, 1968.

77. "Textbooks in Tennessee," *Creation Research Society Quarterly* 7 (December 1970): 160.

78. Saladin, "Sixty Years of Creationism in Georgia," p. 21.

79. Nicholas Wade, "Evolution: Tennessee Picks a New Fight with Darwin," *Science* 182 (November 16, 1973): 696; Christine Russell, "Victory for Evolution," *BioScience* 25 (July 1975): 420; *New York Times*, March 17, 1973.

80. *Bible Science Newsletter* 17 (June 1979): 7; Dorothy Nelkin, "Legislating Creation in Arkansas," *Society* 20 (February 1983): 13–16; "Creationism in the Schools: The Arkansas Decision," *The Northwest Arkansas Times*, January 2, 3, 4, 5, 6, 1982.

81. Norman L. Geisler, *The Creator in the Courtroom: The Controversial Arkansas Creation-Science Trial* (Milford, Michigan, 1982), p. x. See also the entire issue of *Impact*, No. 105, March, 1982, the regular publication of the Institute for Creation Research, and Edward J. Larson, *Trial and Error: The American Controversy Over Creation and Evolution* (New York, 1985), pp. 156–71.

82. Michael Novak, "False Foes," *Society* 20 (January-February 1983): 34.

83. See Thompson, *Tried As By Fire*, chapter 7.

84. Cash, *Mind of the South* p. 339.

85. Maynard Shipley, *The War on Modern Science* (New York, 1927), p. 370.

86. *Christianity Today* 9 (January 1, 1965): 347. Nelkin, "Legislating Creation in Arkansas," p. 16.

87. Howard Zinn, *The Southern Mystique* (New York, 1968), p. 243.

88. Samuel A. Hill, Jr., in his *Southern Churches in Crisis* (New York, 1966) emphasizes this point.

89. Clarence Cason, *90° in the Shade* (Chapel Hill, 1935), p. 62.

Dry Messiah Revisited: Bishop James Cannon, Jr.

ROBERT A. HOHNER

"Damn him all you please," wrote H. L. Mencken in 1930, "the fact remains brilliantly plain that Monsignor James Cannon, Jr., LL.D., is the chief figure in American public life today." Making allowance for Mencken's characteristic hyperbole, it is nevertheless true that Cannon, largely forgotten today, was the most powerful and best known American clergyman of his time. A southern Methodist from Virginia, he was a social activist and ecumenical leader in a church and region noted for its conservatism, parochialism, and narrow preoccupation with the saving of individual souls. Plunged into the maelstrom of secular politics by his dedication to the cause of Prohibition, Cannon proved himself a shrewd and resourceful tactician, a political preacher who often bested the politicians at their own game.[1]

Cannon succeeded in large part because he was tough-minded and indefatigable. Endowed with an exceptional capacity for work, he routinely held several jobs at once and pursued an often bewildering variety of causes simultaneously. When he was elected a bishop in 1918, for example, he was principal of Blackstone College, a secondary school for girls in Southside, Virginia; superintendent of the Southern Methodist Assembly at Lake Junaluska, near Asheville, North Carolina; owner and editor of his conference newspaper, the *Baltimore and Richmond Christian Advocate*; superintendent of the Virginia Anti-Saloon League; principal owner of the Richmond *Virginian*, a daily newspaper; owner of a summer hotel at Junaluska; and chairman of the national legislative committee of the Anti-Saloon League of America, which required frequent trips to Washington.[2]

Of medium height and unimpressive physical appearance, Cannon was a brusque, cold, and disciplined man with a keen mind, a combative temperament, and unusual powers of self-control. His extraordinary composure and calmness under fire or provocation invariably disarmed opponents. One exasperated opponent exclaimed, "I think you come as near sitting on a block of ice as any man I ever saw." Confrontation was central to Cannon's style, and his dominant personality, aggressive tactics, and flair for controversy evoked strong emotions. However much his brethren respected his energy and capacity for effective work, many of them feared and disliked him, and for years opponents worked to deny him the episcopacy. He was finally elected a bishop at the General Conference in Atlanta in 1918 only by virtue of unusual circumstances. Although Cannon had stood fourth on the initial ballot, when the six bishops to be elected were chosen, he was not among them. One of those selected then stunned the conference by refusing the position, an almost unprecedented event which reopened the balloting and led to the election of Cannon as a replacement.[3]

Cannon's public persona was stern and forbidding. There was another side to the Virginia leader, however. An older Methodist colleague observed of him that "the cultivated Christian women that a few years ago were poor girls, and must have remained uneducated but for his kindly and timely aid," saw a gentler and more attractive figure. Their parents and others had entered the educator's "hospitable home and seen the strongest evidences of consecrated Christian character manifested there." To them, "far-reaching in sympathy and in soul, another and nobler Cannon lives." Of all the activities in which he engaged, Cannon was happiest as a schoolmaster, and after his temperance and episcopal duties removed him to a national and world stage, he often looked back upon his years at Blackstone with nostalgia. Most of the "Blackstone girls" admired him, and they remained intensely loyal throughout his long and stormy career.[4]

The Virginia journalist J. A. Leslie, Jr., once a reporter for Cannon's daily newspaper, confirmed that the Methodist leader "could be an attractive and often delightful companion. He had fine intelligence, was informed on almost everything, and when he doffed his professional mantle he was an extremely pleasant person to be with. He was thoughtful of others, and seemed interested in people and what they were doing." In conversation, Leslie observed, Cannon "could dominate any group if he chose to do so because his spongelike mind absorbed information, and with his poised and completely polished manner he could make himself extremely agreeable." Leslie conceded, however, that Cannon could also be "pretty hard-boiled." The bishop, he observed, "knew what he wanted and didn't let anything stop him," and his adversaries discovered that when Cannon "entered the arena, he was a bad man to tangle with."[5]

Cannon has not fared well in historical writing. Virginius Dabney's biography, *Dry Messiah*, reinforced the stereotype of the Virginia cleric as a narrow and unscrupulous fanatic and hypocrite, a view already implanted in the popular mind by a hostile press. Dabney was a columnist, and later, editor for Cannon's archrival, the wet Richmond *Times-Dispatch*. He had nearly finished his biography in 1929, but the appearance of various charges of wrongdoing against Cannon added a new dimension to his subject. Fearful of the prospect of a libel suit, Dabney put the project aside, completing it only after the bishop's death. "Now that the Doctor has been gathered to his fathers," he observed in 1946, "it is much safer to be caustic and incisive." Privately Dabney made no secret of his intense dislike of Cannon and of his determination to expose the bishop as a scoundrel. Cannon, he told Alfred A. Knopf, was "an old crook and hypocrite."[6]

With a strong bias, a journalistic proclivity for the sensational, and a lack of available manuscript evidence, Dabney not surprisingly caricatured his subject. Despite its partisanship, however, *Dry Messiah* has set the tone for subsequent historical writing on Cannon. Other popular writers, unable to consider the temperance movement seriously or to resist exploiting the colorful events of Cannon's later years, have produced similarly unflattering portraits. Nor have scholars, usually relying heavily on Dabney, been immune to crude characterizations. The English historian Sean Dennis Cashman depicts Cannon as a "malevolent genius," the "most dishonest" of the dry leaders, and a man guilty of "nefarious activities" on Wall Street and elsewhere. In similar fashion, a recent history of drinking in America denounces him as a man guilty of "scurrilous bigotry." In his history of Prohibition Andrew Sinclair is more temperate, although he ultimately characterizes Cannon as an extremist and a fanatic. Even Norman H. Clark, author of the best general work on Prohibition, characterizes him as a bigot and "self-indulgent hypocrite."[7]

There are some exceptions to the prevailing trend, however. Thirty years ago Richard L. Watson, Jr., the editor of Cannon's autobiography, wrote a balanced essay on the Methodist leader which appeared as an introduction to the bishop's memoirs. In recent years Prohibition has of course become the subject of serious scrutiny by scholars. In this period of significant revisionism in temperance studies, one can return anew and with special appreciation to Watson's piece, which remains the best account of Cannon's life and career. More recently, Jack Temple Kirby has provided a fair-minded and stimulating assessment of Cannon in his study of southern progressivism.[8]

Cannon was above all a Methodist clergyman. Promoting the work of the church and protecting its interests remained his paramount concern. Yet within the southern Methodist church he was always something of a maverick. In a denomination which tended to regard higher education as a hindrance to a successful ministry, Cannon was a graduate not only of Randolph-Macon but of Princeton Theological Seminary, and he was marked from the outset as different. (As late as 1927 only a small minority of southern Methodist preachers were college graduates, and only a handful had completed seminary.)[9] Although he married well, Cannon, a native of Maryland, remained an outsider to many Virginians. Early in his ministry, he established a reputation as a challenger to the establishment within the church, and in later years his social activism and penchant for controversy and headlines made most of his fellow bishops uncomfortable. His senior colleagues in the episcopacy, Warren A. Chandler of Atlanta and Collins Denny of Richmond, the principal guardians of the traditionalism and conservativism of southern Methodism, strongly opposed clerical involvement in politics, and they were especially hostile to Cannon throughout most of his career.

By virtue of background, education, and travel Cannon was the least parochial of the southern Methodist leaders. Cooperation between Christian groups, national and international, was of vital importance to him, and he brought an ecumenical dimension to a church noted for its isolation from other denominations and broader concerns. Cannon's ecumenical interests stemmed in part from his youth in the border South. Salisbury, his home town, was on the Eastern Shore and in the commercial orbit of the Northeast, and young Cannon came into frequent contact with northern people. He had twice visited Philadelphia with his family, and the daily newspaper in the Cannon home was the Baltimore *Sun*, which was broader in scope than most southern newspapers. When he entered seminary, it was not the fledgling theological school of his own church, Vanderbilt, but a northern institution instead, and a Presbyterian one at that. Cannon emerged from Princeton still very much a southern Methodist, but his years there broadened his outlook, introduced him to other denominations, and tempered his regional and denominational loyalties. He later participated in the formation of the Federal Council of Churches, and he was one of the few southern churchmen active in that organization and its successor, the National Council of Churches.[10]

Early in his ministry, Cannon's attendance in 1891 at the Second Ecumenical Methodist Conference in Washington, D.C., had made him aware of a larger stage of Christian activity and the need for greater cooperation between Methodist groups. In his own hometown he had witnessed the wasteful duplication and senseless rivalry between separate Methodist churches, northern and southern. It is not surprising that he became an early advocate of Methodist unification, serving on the Joint Commission on Unification from 1918, and with Bishop Edwin D. Mouzon, spearheading the movement for unification which so bitterly divided the southern church in the mid–1920s. His dedication to the cause of Methodist unification represented a typically progressive impulse toward efficiency, centralized control, and uniformity.[11]

One of Cannon's chief interests was missions, and after becoming a bishop, he spent much of his time abroad, supervising southern Methodist missionary work in Mexico, the Belgian Congo, Cuba, and Brazil. During World War II he visited England and France to investigate the moral conditions confronting American soldiers and sailors, and at the Paris Peace Conference in 1919 he lobbied for temperance provisions in the peace treaty. Throughout the 1920s he attended the opening session of the League of Nations in Geneva, and he frequently participated in international church conferences, such as those in Stockholm in 1925 and Laussanne in 1927. His work for such organizations as the World League Against Alcoholism and Near East Relief also required frequent visits to Great Britain, Europe, and the Near East. Given his extensive travel abroad, Cannon's conspicuous presence in public and church affairs at home seems remarkable. On a trip to the Congo in 1927 he contracted malarial fever, and for the remainder of his life nervous disorders and severe arthritis afflicted him.[12]

Although Cannon sometimes took his wife and members of his family abroad, his constant absences from home placed an added strain on his family life. His children had many problems, and it was common knowledge among church insiders that Mrs. Cannon had raised them with little help from their absentee father. In 1919 a military court convicted one of Cannon's sons, a member of the U. S. Naval Aviation Corps, of forging checks and sexual misconduct. The bishop was then abroad, and in pleading with the Secretary of the Navy for clemency his anguished wife confessed that "the church, the state, and the nation have made such demands upon Mr. Cannon's time, that the training of the children has fallen more heavily upon me than most mothers." From Paris Cannon wrote the secretary, Josephus Daniels, who was also a prominent southern Methodist, to express his distress over the conduct of his "very wayward" son. The fact that his own boy was a victim, Cannon said, would only strengthen his determination to destroy the traffic in liquor and vice.[13]

Cannon's temperament and interests embroiled him almost constantly in controversy. As a young upstart in the Virginia Conference, he had quickly challenged the domination of that body by a small clique of senior presiding elders, and his attacks were deeply resented by the old guard. One of his chief antagonists within the Virginia Conference was Paul Whitehead, a prominent figure in southern Methodism. The two men clashed repeatedly, and in 1898 Whitehead brought a formal complaint against the editor for articles which he considered "unjust, uncharitable, and offensive." An investigating committee concluded that although Cannon had intended no offense, his language was sometimes "so strong and uncompromising" as to produce that effect. The committee advised him to "guard his utterances" in the future "to avoid even the appearance of unkindness." Whitehead, however, was unsatisfied. Cannon, he complained privately, "has very little feeling and no disposition to act justly towards an adversary."[14]

Whitehead and others in the conference viewed Cannon as a disturber of the peace who would stop at nothing to achieve his goals. "Our unalterable policy," confided the associate editor of the conference newspaper, "is utterly to ignore Mr. Cannon. To treat him as one would a dead dog. It is the only way to kill him off." Others took a more charitable view. In 1900 A. Coke Smith, a highly respected member of the Virginia Conference and later a bishop, provided a perceptive early appraisal of Cannon. The deep division within the conference disturbed Smith. Although both sides were to be blamed, he wrote privately, "Cannon precipitated it and his course has embittered it. He is one of those men who are conscience bound—whose consciences unfortunately get into everything. He seems to think the world is wrong and he is called to set it right. He is not a bad man; on the other hand, he is a good man. He has in him the Spirit of a martyr—but will go to the stake for a prejudice when he thinks he is going for a principle." Cannon, Smith added, had "mistaken force for the power of love. I wish he did not have the means at his command which he has—or that he had more of the milk of kindness in his nature."[15]

His stern devotion to the cause, regardless of personal consequences, deprived Cannon in time of many of his close friends. As a young clergyman his patron in the church had been Bernard F. Lipscomb, his boyhood pastor in Salisbury. A leading member of the Virginia Conference, Lipscomb took the young preacher under his wing, giving him encouragement and help. Lipscomb's style and temperament were more conciliatory than Cannon's, however, and their relationship became strained as the younger man rose to prominence. The editor's conduct in a bitter and prolonged dispute over control of the Randolph-Macon system of schools and colleges had especially alienated Lipscomb. Years later, when Cannon was charged with various moral offenses, Lipscomb's estrangement became complete. In 1931 he privately expressed approval of the efforts of Cannon's accusers to bring the bishop to trial.[16]

Cannon's chief protagonist in the struggle over Randolph-Macon was William Waugh Smith, the builder of the system, president of Randolph-Macon Woman's College, and a pioneer in southern education. Like Lipscomb, Smith had taken a deep interest in his able younger colleague. They had worked closely together for many years, and Smith had considered Cannon his natural successor as head of the distinguished Lynchburg school. The editor's vehement opposition to the participation of the Woman's College in the pension plan of the Carnegie Foundation, however, ruptured their long friendship. Smith dreamed of creating in Lynchburg an institution of national reputation, with a constituency broader than southern Methodism alone. Cannon's insistence instead on stronger church control led to an acrimonious dispute which was finally resolved only by the courts, seven years later. Smith especially resented Cannon's charge that he and Randolph-Macon trustees had betrayed a sacred trust for Carnegie money. Cannon's attacks, he declared, were "calculated to show distrust and dissension in the Church . . . and to undo the work to which I have given almost my whole active life." Smith died before the Randolph-Macon dispute was resolved, a martyr to the cause of higher education free from ecclesiastical interference.[17]

Almost from the outset of his career, Cannon had made it a practice to control a newspaper through which he could promote his views and champion causes, unhampered by outside interference. With considerable justification, he regarded such control as his "right arm of power." To their surprise and consternation, Cannon's opponents learned in early 1904 that he had become the owner and editor of the newspaper which served both the Virginia Conference and the neighboring Baltimore Conference. "What do you think of *Jim Cannon* editing the 'Balt. And Rich'd Christian Advocate'?" asked Paul Whitehead of a leader of the other conference. "Will your brethren . . . stand having *an 'organ'* of Balto Conf. edited by J C Jr.?"[18]

Many members of the Baltimore Conference shared Whitehead's dislike of Cannon and feared his influence, and his ownership of the *Advocate* prompted that body to start its own newspaper. Such action seemed justified when Cannon, during the Randolph-Macon dispute, vigorously exploited his control of the conference organ, bombarding his readers with a constant flow of articles and editorials which kept the college issue alive and his opponents on the defensive. "The leader of those fighting for the Church control owns the church paper," complained Robert E. Blackwell, the president of Randolph-Macon College, "and it is impossible to get the Trustees' point of view before the people we wish to reach."[19]

Control of his own newspaper became especially important when Cannon assumed leadership of the temperance movement in Virginia. His outspoken leadership quickly incurred the wrath of the wet press in the state, and in the columns of the *Advocate* he vigorously responded in kind. Soon the hostility between the crusading dry leader and most of the Virginia dailies became intense. Among his antagonists in the press, none could rival Virginia's leading newspaper, the Richmond *Times-Dispatch*. As wet as Cannon was dry, the *Times-Dispatch* waged unremitting war on the Methodist cleric. In 1911 it attacked him as a "base slanderer," a master of the art of billingsgate, a blackguard, a fanatic, and a fool. Cannon of course expected opposition from most of the secular press, but he deeply resented the attacks of the *Times-Dispatch*, which he regarded as especially unfair. To counter the influence of the wet press more effectively, Cannon in 1909 raised $100,000 to found a dry daily, the Richmond *Virginian*. For ten years his newspaper offered Virginians an alternative to the wet dailies, as it strongly championed prohibition and other moral causes.[20]

Cannon once called himself a "Christian Socialist." Although the description was inaccurate it reflected the emphasis he placed on the social role of the church. Cannon vigorously embraced social Christianity, and in this respect, he was unlike most other southern religious leaders of his day. He fought for the establishment in his church of a Commission on Temperance and Social Service, and when the General Conference created that agency in 1918, Cannon was the natural choice as its chairman. In 1927 he lashed out publicly at the textile operators in a manifesto entitled "An Appeal to Industrial Leaders in the South." This statement, prepared covertly with the Federal Council of Churches and signed by forty-one other southern churchmen and civic leaders, called attention to low wages, long hours, employment of children and women, the absence of labor representation, and company control of the mill towns. Predictably, it brought down on Cannon the wrath of the southern textile industry. Public criticism of the business leaders of the region by southern churchmen was rare, and Bishop Chandler, horrified by his colleague's indiscretion, attempted to pacify the outraged textile owners and to blunt the force of Cannon's attack. The strident response of the mill owners and their supporters emphasized the difficulty facing those attempting to improve working conditions in the South.[21]

Cannon's manifesto focused attention on a significant social problem. The chief expression of his social concern, however, was the temperance movement. For him, Prohibition *was* the social gospel, and he quickly became the dominant force in the Virginia Anti-Saloon League. "You know how relentless Cannon is," complained one Virginian Congressman, "and the rest are his creatures." Cannon gradually mobilized public support, and in the classic fashion of the League, proceeded to dry up the state, step-by-step. A realist, he aligned himself and the League, not with the reform element in Virginia politics, but with the dominant political organization headed by Senator Thomas Staples Martin. Bowing to the inevitable, the organization in 1914 acquiesced in Cannon's demand for a state referendum on prohibition. Driving himself to the point of physical exhaustion, Cannon led the drys to an overwhelming victory in the campaign which followed.[22]

His alliance with Martin led Cannon in 1917 to support for governor, not the dry and able John Garland Pollard, but the mediocre candidate of the organization, who was personally wet but pledged to Prohibition. Such expediency won Cannon both the lasting enmity of Pollard and the grudging respect of many Virginia politicians, especially Martin and his chief lieutenant, Congressman Henry D. Flood of Appomattox. They recognized in the Methodist cleric a man who understood power and the realities of practical politics, and they respected his energy, tactical skill, and resourcefulness.[23]

Cannon's success in Virginia led to his increasing prominence in the national Anti-Saloon League as well. When the Democrats came to power in 1913, Cannon became chairman of the League's national legislative committee. In that capacity he played a major role in securing enactment of the important temperance legislation of the Wilson years, culminating in the Eighteenth Amendment. In Washington Cannon found his Virginia political friendships invaluable. Southerners now dominated Congress, and the Virginians held key positions of power. Martin became chairman of the Senate Appropriations Committee and later, Senate majority leader, and Flood was the chairman of the House Foreign Affairs Committee. In pressing for temperance legislation, Cannon often worked closely with the Virginia leaders. During the debate over the Lever Food and Fuel Control Bill in 1917, for example, an impasse over the beer and wine provisions threatened to disrupt the war effort. With Senator Martin as an intermediary, President Wilson secured from Cannon and the Anti-Saloon League's legislative committee a compromise agreement which broke the deadlock.[24]

Cannon is best known for his role in the presidential election of 1928. After the Democratic convention in Houston nominated Governor Alfred E. Smith of New York, Smith declared in his telegram of acceptance his intention to press for basic modifications to national Prohibition. Cannon, who at the convention had successfully fought for a simple law enforcement plank, then accused the nominee of repudiating the party's platform. Feeling betrayed, the Virginia leader acted quickly to mobilize dissident Democrats in the South against the wet candidate. "I went to Houston," Cannon explained,

and in the intense heat and turmoil fought for our principles, and secured an action which I thought would prevent the injection of the prohibition question into the campaign. The nominee of the Democratic party realized that his only hope of election was to inject the prohibition issue into the campaign, and he ruthlessly did that very thing.

Although he was in poor health and his wife was terminally ill, Cannon led the Anti-Smith Democrats in a vigorous crusade throughout the South against the New York governor. On election day the Solid South was shattered, with the Republican victor, Herbert Hoover, carrying five former Confederate states.[25]

The conundrum of 1928 continues to bedevil scholars and political analysts. The historical literature on this famous election is extensive, and although most scholars agree that no Democrat could have defeated Hoover that year, the relative importance of the issues of Catholicism and Prohibition remains an open question. Cannon indeed distrusted the Roman Catholic Church. He was also offended by the corruption of Tammany Hall, contemptuous of immigrants from eastern and southern Europe, and shocked by the appointment by Smith of John J. Raskob, a wealthy businessman of Republican background, as chairman of the Democratic national committee. For him, however, the fundamental issue was Prohibition. A Smith victory would have threatened the great reform which Cannon and others had secured only by years of struggle and considerable personal cost, and he refused to stand idly by and watch its destruction. "I have been fighting the liquor traffic all my life," he explained. "I do not propose to withdraw from the field in this the greatest battle which we have ever waged in this age-long conflict."[26]

In his commitment to Prohibition, Cannon spoke for much of Protestant America, and Protestant voters had good reason to oppose Al Smith in 1928 on that question alone. Although Cannon had long found the Roman Catholic Church repugnant, he did not oppose Smith on religious grounds. As the campaign became more intense, however, Cannon was accused, notably by Raskob, of using Prohibition as a cloak for bigotry. He deeply resented that charge, and he believed that Protestants were being unfairly blamed for injecting the religious issue into the campaign. "I am not in favor of attacks on Mr. Smith simply because he is a Roman Catholic," he wrote privately, "but I am utterly unwilling that our southern people shall be branded as bigoted and intolerant fanatics in order to whip them into line to vote for Smith." Three weeks before election day, Cannon published a circular entitled *Is Southern Protestantism More Intolerant Than Romanism?* Citing papal encyclicals and other Catholic authorities on such subjects as salvation, marriage, and public schools, he declared that it was the Roman Catholic Church, not Protestantism, which was intolerant.[27]

Cannon has since been depicted in much of the historical literature as a Protestant bigot whose scurrilous attacks contributed substantially to Smith's defeat. This portrait, however, fails to distinguish between the mindless assaults of the Ku Klux Klan and other nativist groups and the legitimate concerns of more thoughtful Protestants about the role of the Catholic church in American life. The record of the Catholic church in Europe and Latin America, its reproaches to liberal Catholics, and the autocratic pronouncements of some American priests provided Protestants with grounds for suspicion. To the extent that he raised the religious question, Cannon spoke, not for the bigots, but for those with responsible and understandable fears about the compatibility of the Roman Catholic church and American democracy.[28]

Unfortunately, in the heat of a highly emotional political campaign, Cannon often resorted to intemperate language. He repeatedly called Raskob, for example, "the wet Roman Catholic Knight of Columbus," and his blunt characterization of the Catholic church as intolerant, in part a political tactic to place his opponents on the defensive, gave needless offense. Cannon vehemently denied that he was anti-Catholic, and he expressed his respect for many aspects of Catholicism, but those offended by his harsh rhetoric found such protestations unconvincing. Cannon in fact shared the traditional suspicion with which most American Protestants viewed Catholicism, and his experiences in Mexico, the Congo, and Brazil had reinforced his prejudices. Nevertheless, his attitude toward the church of Rome remained ambivalent, and in reflective moments he sometimes revealed a grudging respect for it. A few years later, he expressed to Mencken his distaste for the Catholic hierarchy, but he declared that he was not "bitter and unappreciative of many good men and good things in the Roman Catholic System."[29]

Cannon's chief antagonist in Virginia during the 1928 campaign had been his fellow Methodist and dry, the vituperative newspaper owner from Lynchburg, Senator Carter Glass. A mercurial personality, Glass was often impulsive and intemperate in speech and manner, and of all Cannon's adversaries, none approached him with more hostility and vindictiveness. The enmity between the two men was deep and long-standing, dating back to the election of 1909. Glass, then an independent Democrat, had considered running for governor, but decided against it when Cannon threw his support to the organization's candidate. From that point on, Glass was increasingly hostile to Cannon. "Dr. Cannon," Glass charged privately in 1916, "has done nothing but make money out of his church and its institutions and now either directly or indirectly he is seeking to make money out of the prohibition issue." The campaign of 1928 had further embittered Glass against his rival and he left the Democratic party in Virginia in disarray and apprehensive about the future. The remedy was clear: Cannon must be discredited and eliminated as a force in Virginia and national politics.[30]

Cannon's moment of triumph in national politics was short-lived, for when he again bolted the Democratic party in the gubernatorial campaign of 1929, Virginia voters defeated his coalition of Anti-Smith Democrats and Republicans and his old antagonist, John Garland Pollard was elected as governor. In the midst of that contest, the Hearst press revealed that Cannon had been a regular customer of Kable and Company, a New York brokerage firm on trial for operating an illegal business known on Wall Street as a "bucket shop." This unexpected good fortune delighted Carter Glass, who had quietly gathered adverse information on Cannon for years. Glass moved quickly to exploit the situation, making charges public that Cannon had also been found guilty of hoarding flour at Blackstone during World War I. With the encouragement and cooperation of Glass, Congressman George H. Tinkham of Massachusetts accused Cannon of illegal use of campaign funds during the election of 1928. The Senate Lobby Committee then summoned the bishop before it, but Cannon, challenging its jurisdiction, successfully defied the committee. Glass then persuaded Senator Gerald P. Nye to resurrect his moribund Committee on Senatorial Campaign Expenditures and to investigate the Methodist leader.[31]

In the meantime Josephus Daniels and other Methodist laymen had brought charges of stock-market gambling against Cannon, and the bishop narrowly averted a church trial at the General Conference of 1930 in Dallas. After an investigating committee had voted to bring him to trial, he appeared before it and submitted a new statement. He now admitted that he had made a mistake and expressed himself as "sorely grieved" that his actions had brought "pain and embarrassment" to his church. In a rare display of public emotion, he then broke down and wept. After this dramatic moment, the committee reversed itself, dismissing the charges. Collins Denny cynically observed that "nothing can be done with a body of Methodist preachers when they are cried upon." Cannon's respite was only temporary, however. As a result of the Nye committee investigation, he was indicted for violation of the federal Corrupt Practices Act, and after three years of legal battles, he was brought to trial.[32]

Other than Cannon, the chief victim of the bishop's involvement with the stock market was his young stockbroker, Harry Goldhurst, who was convicted of mail fraud and sentenced to five years in prison. The federal parole board granted him an early release, but Carter Glass intervened, convinced that Goldhurst at his trial had shielded Cannon, and the board rescinded its parole. After serving his sentence, Goldhurst changed his name and embarked upon a new career as a writer and editor. As Harry Golden he became a best-selling author, editor of the *Carolina Israelite*, and a popular figure on the American literary scene. Years later, Golden in his autobiography reminisced about the indiscretions of his youth and his tribulations as the stockbroker of the controversial Methodist bishop. "I found Bishop Cannon ... a brave gentleman," he recalled. "He was always loyal. Nothing ever flustered him. The Bishop never whined." Cannon, he added, had "immense presence—he was important and he knew it—but I never found him overbearing."[33]

Shortly after the election of 1928, Lura Bennett, Cannon's wife of forty years, died. Eighteen months later, in London, England, he married his secretary, Helen Hawley McCallum, and the Hearst press immediately published stories which charged in lurid detail that the bishop had committed adultery with Mrs. McCallum before their marriage. This allegation about Cannon's sexual conduct was the last straw for many of the bishop's embarrassed Methodist colleagues. To save their church from further shame and humiliation, four southern Methodist ministers brought formal charges of immorality against him. In poor health, the embattled bishop returned from Brazil to face his accusers. A committee of twelve clergymen, with Bishop William N. Ainsworth presiding, met in secrecy at Mount Vernon Square Methodist Church in Washington, D.C., in February 1931 to hear the charges and Cannon's response. After five days of hearings, the committee found no grounds for a church trial, thus exonerating the bishop.[34]

Cannon's accusers, confident of victory, heard the verdict with disbelief. Their leader, Costen J. Harrell, later a bishop himself, remained convinced to the end of his life that the investigating committee had engaged in a coverup. The official record of the investigation has never been released, and given the intensely partisan source of the allegations, it is difficult to assess Cannon's guilt or innocence with any degree of certainty. Even Virginius Dabney, however, conceded privately that the evidence on the adultery charge was of doubtful reliability.[35]

While Cannon was fending off assaults from all sides, he caught the fancy of H. L. Mencken. The partisanship and vindictiveness of the bishop's accusers offended Mencken's sense of fairness, and he admired Cannon's courage and forthrightness. Mencken reported on Cannon's skirmishes with his tormentors in a series of pieces in the *Baltimore Sun*, cheering on the beleaguered cleric in articles with such colorful titles as "The Woes of a Holy Man," "A Martyr Faces the Pyre," and "Pontifex Maximus." In 1931

Mencken interviewed Cannon in his apartment in the Bliss Building on Capitol Hill in Washington. The journalist was pleasantly surprised. "The bishop looks a great deal more amiable than his photographs," he noted. The two men quickly established a rapport, and Cannon took a keen interest in Mencken's articles about him.[36]

In June 1934 the Cannons accepted an invitation to join the Menckens for lunch in Baltimore. The occasion was a great success, and it marked the beginning of a continuing friendship. "You and I are men of a certain bellicosity," Mencken remarked afterward, "but we seem to have been fortunate enough to get very amiable wives." They made an unlikely pair, the Methodist bishop and the wet iconoclast, and they enjoyed the irony of their new relationship. "If I did not think I knew you," Cannon joked, "I would fear that you might permit our pleasant social relations to keep you from your usual caustic—sometimes drastic—always characteristic criticism of me and all my works." In the years which followed, the two men became frequent correspondents, in friendly disagreement on Prohibition and American foreign policy, but relishing their mutual dislike of Franklin D. Roosevelt and the New Deal.[37]

To Mencken's delight, Cannon was ultimately acquitted of all the charges against him, both in the federal courts and ecclesiastical bodies. Nevertheless, the scandals diverted Cannon's energies, undermined his influence, and further discredited the Prohibition movement. Josephus Daniels correctly observed in June 1930 that Cannon "is ended so far as any good influence is concerned."[38]

Although a churchman, Cannon remained strongly secular in outlook and interests. His boyhood ambition had been to become a lawyer and to sit on the Supreme Court of the United States. In later life, the law continued to fascinate him, and he relished the combat of legislative and deliberative bodies, both secular and ecclesiastical. With these interests, it is not surprising that he entered the arena of politics with such enthusiasm and success. The son of a prosperous merchant, Cannon also moved comfortably in banking and business circles. He had himself enaged in stocks and bonds, buying and selling real estate, operating a private school, and owning and operating newspapers. His personal life was plain and frugal, and he was careful not to allow business activities to interfere with his official duties. He was quick to point out that any profits from his business were used, not for personal gain, but in support of the causes to which he was devoted. "I ... deny very positively," Cannon declared in 1929 in a celebrated apologia, that any business transactions "have in any way affected my character or spirituality. I have never loved money for its own sake. I have never hoarded money, but my open record will show that I have tried to make money in order that it might be an instrument for service."[39]

Such explanations were unconvincing to Cannon's critics, however, who argued that the Virginia Methodist was a "lost leader," a churchman who had been corrupted by the material world. Cannon may have been innocent of any legal or moral wrongdoing, but his deep involvement in secular affairs nevertheless violated traditional notions of propriety about the proper sphere of men of the cloth. The spectacle of a Methodist bishop investing in stocks, under investigation for sexual misconduct, and brought to trial for misuse of funds in a political campaign seemed symbolic of the triumph of the materialistic and hedonistic values of the 1920s.[40]

Cannon's enemies attempted unsuccessfully to force his retirement at the General Conference of 1934 in Jackson, Mississippi. In the Great Depression, Prohibition lost its moral force and seemed irrelevant, and with repeal and the end of his public ordeals, Cannon faded into near obscurity. In retirement he remained nearly as active as ever, despite his infirmity, attending church and temperance meetings and writing innumerable letters to the editor. He also began writing his memoirs. When in Baltimore he and his wife had lunch from time to time with Mencken, who read a draft of the unfinished manuscript with apparent interest and encouraged him to complete it. "It would be a book worth reading," remarked the historian Julian Boyd, "for he has been up to a lot of skulduggery in his time."[41]

In 1944 Cannon died at the age of eighty, a forgotten figure from a bygone era. He was buried in Hollywood Cemetery in Richmond, the final resting place of James Monroe, John Tyler, Jefferson Davis, and Henry A. Wise, not to mention such lesser mortals as Cannon's old friend, Bernard Lipscomb. Controversy followed him even in death. Because of hostility between his widow and some of his sons, the bishop's tombstone remained blank for some twenty-five years. A simple inscription was finally added around 1970. It reads, "Minister, Publisher, Educator, Bishop, M. E. Church, South."[42]

No tombstone of course can do justice to the richness of Cannon's long and tempestuous career. The most prominent American churchman of his time, he was a tough and resourceful combatant who won the allegiance and respect of countless followers because he took on the hard tasks of the day and never flinched from duty or responsibility. He was a paradoxical figure, a clergyman who also became a secular leader of national importance. The target of continual public and personal attacks which would have broken weaker men, he bore the heat of battle and survived, undaunted to the end. The tumult of his public life has obscured his real importance. As a social activist and ecumenical leader, Cannon attempted to quicken the social conscience of his church and region. His life and career, when stripped of its flamboyant trappings, remind us that not all southern churchmen have been parochial or indifferent to social questions.

NOTES

1. "Pontifex Maximus," Baltimore *Evening Sun*, June 9, 1930; Samuel S. Hill, Jr., *Southern Churches in Crisis* (New York, 1966), pp. 76–84.

2. James Cannon, Jr., "*Unspotted from the World,*" printed circular (Washington, D.C., August 3, 1929), Frederick DeLand Leete Episcopal Papers, Bridwell Library, Perkins School of Theology, Southern Methodist University, Dallas, Texas (henceforth, Leete Papers).

3. Richmond *Times-Dispatch*, November 11, 1910; Robert Watson Sledge, *Hands on the Ark: The Struggle for Change in the Methodist Episcopal Church, South, 1914–1939* (Lake Junaluska, N.C., 1975), pp. 55–57.

4. W. J. Twilley, "An Open Letter to Rev. James Cannon, D.D., and to E. G. Moseley, Esq., *Baltimore and Richmond Christian Advocate*, November 2, 1911, p. 6; James Cannon, Jr., Travel Journal, March 28, 1922, pp. 50–52, James Cannon, Jr., Papers, William R. Perkins Library, Duke University, Durham, North Carolina (henceforth, Cannon Papers); Lena R. Womack to Cannon, October 17, 1935, Cannon Papers; Bessie Matthews Mann to Cannon, April 5, 1936, Cannon Papers; Inez F. Hudgins, letter to the editor, n.d., Richmond *Times-Dispatch*, September 13, 1944.

5. J. A. Leslie, Jr. to Virginius Dabney, October 11, 1946, Virginius Dabney Papers, Alderman Library, University of Virginia, Charlottesville, Virginia (henceforth, Dabney Papers).

6. *Dry Messiah: The Life of Bishop Cannon* (New York, 1949); Dabney draft letter to prospective publishers, n.d. (*ca.* November 1929), Dabney memorandum, n.d. (*ca.* 1948), Dabney to Alfred A. Knopf, September 5, 1946 and October 13, 1948, all in Dabney Papers.

7. John Kobler, *Ardent Spirits: The Rise and Fall of Prohibition* (New York, 1973), pp. 185–86, 340–41, 347–50; Thomas M. Coffey, *The Long Thirst: Prohibition in America: 1920–1933* (New York, 1975), pp. 85–87, 155, 159–161, 238–39, 258–65, 268–72, 279–82, 295–301, 322–25, 330–31, 335–36, 342; Sean Dennis Cashman, *Prohibition: The Lie of the Land* (New York, 1981), pp. 196–97, 221–27; Mark Edward Lender and James Kirby Martin, *Drinking in America: A History* (New York, 1982), p. 162; Andrew Sinclair, *Prohibition: The Era of Excess* (Boston, 1962), reprinted under the title *Era of Excess: A Social History of the Prohibition Movement* (New York, 1964), pp. 35, 157, 167, 270–73, 275, 291, 299–301, 313, 341–42, 375, 391, 400–1; Norman H. Clark, *Deliver Us From Evil: An Interpretation of American Prohibition* (New York, 1976), pp. 187–88, 198.

8. Richard L. Watson, Jr., Editor's Introduction, in James Cannon, Jr., *Bishop Cannon's Own Story: Life as I have Seen It* (Durham, N.C., 1955), pp. v–xxxi; Jack Temple Kirby, *Darkness at the Dawning: Race and Reform in the Progressive South* (Philadelphia, 1972), pp. 80–88.

9. Kenneth K. Bailey, *Southern White Protestantism in the Twentieth Century* (New York, 1964), pp. 7–8.

10. James Cannon, Jr., Manuscript Autobiography, chapter 1, pp. 20–21, 44–45, chapter 2, pp. 5–6, Cannon Papers; Cannon, *Own Story*, p. 17.

11. Cannon, *Own Story*, p. 77; Sledge, *Hands on the Ark*, pp. 63–64, 90–91, 102–6.

12. Cannon, *Own Story*, pp. 193–208, 214–18, 220–33, 246–55, 259–70, 282–89, 292–93, 300–302, 313–17, 320–22, 349–52, 369–71, 433.

13. Sadie Harmon Blackwell, interview with author, Wachapreague, Virginia, May 9, 1971; Memorandum, Office of the Secretary of the Navy, February 19, 1919, Lura Bennett Cannon to Josephus Daniels, February 7, 1919, and Cannon to Daniels,

February 21, 1919, all in Josephus Daniels Papers, Manuscript Division, Library of Congress (henceforth, Daniels Papers).

14. Methodist Episcopal Church, South, Virginia Annual Conference, *Minutes*, 1898, pp. 16, 69; Whitehead to J. S. Hutchinson, June 7, 1899, Collins Denny Papers, Alderman Library, University of Virginia, Charlottesville. (henceforth, Denny Papers).

15. Herbert M. Hope to J. S. Hutchinson, May 9, 1899, and A. Coke Smith to Collins Denny, April 27, 1900, Denny Papers.

16. Robert A. Hohner, ed., "From the Methodist Parsonage in Charlottesville: Bernard F. Lipscomb's Letters to James Cannon, Jr., 1889–1892," *Virginia Magazine of History and Biography* 83 (October, 1975): 428–74; Lipscomb to Coston J. Harrell, February 10, 1931, Costen J. Harrell Papers, United Methodist Publishing House, Nashville, Tennessee (henceforth, Harrell Papers).

17. James Cannon, Jr., deposition, November 12, 1912, *E. D. Newman and others v. Trustees of Randolph-Macon College, and Others*, Circuit Court of Hanover County, Virginia, pp. 71–72, Cannon Papers; William Waugh Smith, *Dr. Smith's Reply* (n.p., n.d. [1908] 16, Randolph-Macon Woman's College Archives, Herbert C. Lipscomb Library, Lynchburg, Virginia.

18. Cannon, *Own Story*, p. 77; John C. Granbery to Dan __, January 7, 1904, John C. Granbery Papers, Walter Hines Page Library, Randolph-Macon College, Ashland, Virginia (henceforth, Granbery Papers); Whitehead to Collins Denny, January 15, 1904, Denny Papers.

19. B. W. Bond to Collins Denny, March 9, 1904, Denny Papers; Blackwell to George A. Plimpton, October 25, 1910, correspondence files, Office of the Secretary, Carnegie Foundation for the Advancement of Teaching, New York, New York.

20. Richmond *Times-Dispatch*, February 25, 1911; Cannon, *Own Story*, p. 115; *Baltimore and Richmond Christian Advocate*, December 23, 1909.

21. Cannon to H. L. Mencken, June 27, 1934, H. L. Mencken Papers, New York Public Library, (henceforth, Mencken Papers). John Patrick McDowell contends that the social concern of the southern Protestantism was more widespread than has been generally recognized. *The Social Gospel in the South: The Woman's Home Mission Movement in the Methodist Episcopal Church, South, 1886–1939* (Baton Rouge, 1982), pp. 1–5; Sledge, *Hands on the Ark*, pp. 66–67; James Cannon, Jr., et al., press release, March 15, 1927, and Worth M. Tippy to Cannon, March 15, 1927, both in Cannon Papers; Warren A. Chandler to George S. Harris, April 2, 1928, Warren Akin Chandler Papers, Robert W. Woodruff Library, Emory University, Atlanta, Georgia (henceforth, Chandler Papers).

22. Francis Rives Lassiter to Henry D. Flood, June 28, 1907, Henry D. Flood Papers, Manuscript Division, Library of Congress (henceforth, Flood Papers); Robert A. Hohner, "Bishop Cannon's Apprenticeship in Temperance Politics, 1901–1918," *Journal of Southern History* 34 (February 1968): 33–49; Cannon to G. Walter Mapp, September 26, 1914, G. Walter Mapp Papers, Accomac, Virginia, now at the Earl Gregg Swem Library, College of William and Mary, Williamsburg, Virginia (henceforth, Mapp Papers); Cannon, *"Unspotted from the World"*; Robert A. Hohner, "Prohibition Comes to Virginia: The Referendum of 1914," *Virginia Magazine of History and Biography* 75 (October 1967): 473–88.

23. Jack Temple Kirby, "Alcohol and Irony: The Campaign of Westmoreland Davis

for Governor, 1909–1917," *Virginia Magazine of History and Biography* 73 (July 1965): 259–79.

24. Dewey W. Grantham, Jr., "Virginia Congressional Leaders and the New Freedom, 1913–1917," *Virginia Magazine of History and Biography* 56 (July 1948): 304–13; Richard L. Watson, Jr., "A Testing Time for Southern Congressional Leadership: The War Crisis of 1917–1918," *Journal of Southern History* 44 (February 1978): 3–40; Cannon, *Own Story*, pp. 188–90; Woodrow Wilson to Cannon, June 29, 1917, and Purley A. Baker, et al. to Wilson, June 30, 1917, both in Cannon Papers.

25. *Declaration of Principles and Purposes of the Conference of Anti-Smith Democrats*, July 19, 1928, printed circular (Richmond, Va., n.d.), Leete Papers; Cannon to Warren A. Chandler, September 22, 1928, Chandler Papers.

26. The most important recent studies of the election of 1928 are David Burner, *The Politics of Provincialism: The Democratic Party in Transition, 1918–1932* (New York, 1968) and Allen J. Lichtman, *Prejudice and the Old Politics: The Presidential Election of 1928* (Chapel Hill, 1979). James Cannon, Jr., "Leaves from my Notebook—VI," Nashville *Christian Advocate*, April 14, 1922, p. 457; Cannon, "*Unspotted from the World*"; Cannon to Eli Baer, October 29, 1928, Cannon to George N. Conrad, July 17, 1928, and Cannon to John S. Chandler, July 16, 1928, all in Cannon Papers.

27. Robert Moats Miller, "Footnote to the Role of the Protestant Churches in the Election of 1928," *Church History* 25 (June, 1956): 145–59; Cannon to Mrs. L. L. Yost, September 20, 1928, Cannon Papers; *Is Southern Protestantism More Intolerant than Romanism?*, printed circular (Richmond, Va., October 15, 1928), Leete Papers.

28. Burner, *Politics of Provincialism*, 206–7. Allen J. Lichtman classifies Cannon's statements during the campaign, not with those of the bigots and hatemongers, but with "the more temperate, but still primarily emotional, appeals of the Protestant press and clergy." Cannon's rhetoric, Lichtman finds, was tinged with anti-Catholicism. Lichtman, *Prejudice and the Old Politics*, pp. 60, 89–90.

29. Cannon, *Is Southern Protestantism More Intolerant Than Romanism?*, Leete Papers; Cannon to H. L. Mencken, September 1, 1934, Mencken Papers.

30. James R. Sweeney, "Rum, Romanism, and Virginia Democrats: The Party Leaders and the Campaign of 1928," *Virginia Magazine of History and Biography* 90 (October 1982): 417–18, 427; Carter Glass to John Garland Pollard, June 26, 1925, John Garland Pollard Papers, Earl Gregg Swem Library, College of William and Mary, Williamsburg, Virginia (henceforth, Pollard Papers); Glass to Charles D. Bulla, February 8, 1909, and Cannon to Arthur Davidson, May 29, 1934, both in Cannon Papers; Glass to E. F. Sheffey, January 31, 1916, Carter Glass Papers, Alderman Library, University of Virginia, Charlottesville, Virginia (henceforth, Glass Papers); Sweeney, "Rum, Romanism," pp. 425–30; Michael S. Patterson, "The Fall of a Bishop: James Cannon, Jr., Versus Carter Glass, 1909–1934," *Journal of Southern History* 39 (November 1973): 498, 509, 517–18.

31. Alvin L. Hall, "Virginia Back in the Fold: The Gubernatorial Campaign and Election of 1929," *Virginia Magazine of History and Biography* 73 (July 1965): 280–302; Watson, Editor's Introduction, in Cannon, *Own Story*, pp. xviii, xxxiiii.

32. Josephus Daniels to the editor, *Christian Century* July 1, 1930, Daniels Pa-

pers; Watson, Editor's Introduction, in Cannon, *Own Story*, p. xix; Collins Denny to Carter Glass, July 24, 1930, Glass Papers.

33. William D. Mitchell to Carter Glass, August 4, 1931, Glass to Mitchell, August 29, 1931, and Arthue D. Wood, et al., memorandum, November 30, 1931, all in Glass Papers; Harry Golden, *The Right Time: An Autobiography* (New York, 1969), p. 130.

34. Watson, Editor's Introduction, in Cannon, *Own Story*, p. xxi; William N. Ainsworth letter to the complainants and the accused, October 25, 1930, Cannon Papers; Methodist Episcopal Church, South, General Conference, 1934, *Journal*, pp. 23–24.

35. Costen J. Harrell to William M. Speed, February 10, 1931, Harrell Papers, United Methodist Publishing House; Costen J. Harrell, interview with author, Atlanta, Georgia, June 16, 1971. The official record of the investigation, including Cannon's defense was stored for years in the vault of the publishing house in Nashville. In the summer of 1984 it was transferred to the General Commission on Archives and History of the United Methodist Church in Madison, New Jersey. To date, however, the Commission has not opened the record for research. Dabney to Alfred A. Knopf, September 18, 1947, Dabney Papers.

36. Baltimore *Evening Sun*, June 24, 1929, July 29, 1929, and June 9, 1930; H. L. Mencken, "The Bishop Loquitur," Baltimore *Evening Sun*, October 12, 1931; Cannon to H. L. Mencken, June 1, 1934, Mencken Papers.

37. Cannon to H. L. Mencken, June 27, 1934, Mencken to Cannon, June 29, 1934, Cannon to Mencken, July 5, 1934, all in Mencken Papers. Mencken's attacks on Methodism in the 1920s are explored in Lawrence Oliver Kline, "H. L. Mencken's Controversy with the Methodists with Special Reference to the Issue of Prohibition" (Ph.D. diss., Duke University, 1975). Mencken to Cannon, July 14, 1934, May 20, 1936, October 30, 1939; Cannon to Mencken, July 4, 1936, October 27, 1939, all in Mencken Papers. Cannon, who had never forgiven Roosevelt for supporting repeal, considered the president a demagogue and a dangerous opportunist. For a more detailed account of the relationship between Cannon and Mencken, see Robert A. Hohner, "The Woes of a Holy Man: Bishop James Cannon, Jr., and H. L. Mencken," *South Atlantic Quarterly* 85 (Summer 1986).

38. Daniels to G. T. Fitzhugh, June 26, 1930, Daniels Papers.

39. Cannon, *Own Story*, p. 31; Cannon, *Unspotted from the World*, Leete Papers.

40. "The Lost Leader," *Christian Century* 47 (June 25, 1930): 806–8.

41. H. L. Mencken to Cannon, October 30, 1939, and November 3, 1939; Cannon to Mencken, July 3, 1940; Julian Boyd to Mencken, September 28, 1943, all in Mencken Papers. Boyd had been a classmate of two of Cannon's sons at Trinity College (later Duke University).

42. Author's visits, September 9, 1968 and June 4, 1973; Interview with Edward Lee Cannon, Raleigh, North Carolina, June 14, 1972.

PART IV

The Search for the South

A Southern Modernist: The Mind of W. J. Cash

BRUCE CLAYTON

" 'Strictly, the Southerner had no mind; he had temperament,' " said W. J. Cash in concluding the opening section of *The Mind of the South*. Here, in Henry Adams' sentence, is the essence of Cash's book that was immediately recognized for what it was: a bold, angry (even bitter), brilliant, disturbing, intensely personal history. In brief, it was a masterpiece. In 1941 the author was little more than an obscure, southern journalist when the book appeared to rave notices, North and South. Even so, Cash clearly intended to throw a stick of dynamite into the southerner's stream of consciousness; like Nietzsche, one of the gods of modernism, Cash wanted to keep the waters of the mind from freezing. Quite an ambitious task for "a fellow who had never amounted to much." But Cash had been reading and brooding for years—and not just about the South. Precociously, inescapably aware of the vastness between reality in the South and Dixie's myths and pretentions, Cash early on burrowed in to a host of modernist writers—major and minor—who knocked the props from under Victorian certainties and replaced them with liberating, but sometimes troublesome notions about the nature of man and reality.[1]

By modernism I mean a Freudian awareness of the centrality not of reason but of ego; of irrationality, social and personal; of the universe as unpredictable; of the importance of social class and the inherent certainty of conflict both in man and in the social order; of the need for a critical mind, rather than a tribal mind, a mind capable of living with ambiguity, irony, and paradox. If Victorianism assumed, as Henry May has written, that reality was malleable and amenable to control by rational, moral men, and that evil and social conflict resulted from ignorance and lack of rational leadership, modernism makes no such claim, sometimes to its regret. "Whirl is king," said Carl Becker summing up twentieth-century modernism and contrasting it with eighteenth-century rationalism. The best that a modernist can hope for is to make "contact" with an everchanging, usually unpredictable reality. Victorianism posited a duality between man and matter, between reason and emotion, with rationality providing mastery over emotion and matter. Hence progress. Such a comforting dualism is denied to modernists who have learned that they are an integral part of the flux they would control. To a modernist, rationality, as William James said, is a sentiment—one to be cultivated and disciplined, but a sentiment nonetheless.[2]

Oddly, Cash's modernism has been all but ignored by historians. Daniel Joseph Singal concludes his magisterial study of southern modernism saying only that *The Mind of the South* marked "the triumph of southern Modernism." Richard H. King made a brilliant start by concentrating on Freud and Cash and *The Mind of the South*'s "quasi psychoanalytic terminology," and Fred Hobson subtly explored Cash's mind but stopped short, saying that "Cash psychoanalyzed the South old and new." Regrettably, Joseph L. Morrison, Cash's biographer, restricted himself primarily to description and made no attempt to discuss the interior of Cash's mind or book. And as it happens, Cash's most searching critic, C. Vann Woodward, has reproached Cash for being "wrong" about southern history and for not writing intellectual history by analyzing major figures as, say, Perry Miller did in *The New England Mind* (1939). Rejecting Cash's broader definition of mind—as "a fairly definite mental pattern, . . . a complex of established relationships and habits of thought"—Woodward scolds Cash for writing a book about "mind" while denying that the southerner had one. In this Woodward is only half right: Cash discussed modern southern intellectuals. Woodward fails to see that Cash's notion of mind as the "temperament" of the people was the work of a modernist who suspected that the irrationality of the masses—and of the master class—was far closer to true history, to the region's "mind," than any elite's ratiocinations. More to the point, Woodward fails to note that Cash was the first truly modernist intellectual the South produced.[3]

He was born May 2, 1900, in Gaffney, South Carolina in the heart of the Piedmont textile mill country, and named Joseph Wilbur Cash. He later quietly, but defiantly, according to Morrison, reversed his first two names so that he and his father, John William, would have different initials. As a child the son resisted his family's narrow religious fundamentalism, thus beginning his emancipation from Victorianism early on. A voracious reader, he liked the Bible—and Shakespeare—but not the Baptist church. He pleaded in vain with his father, a pious, plain man, quite narrow in his outlook, not to send him to Wofford College, a Baptist school in nearby Spartanburg. After an unhappy year there, "Sleepy," as his schoolmates called him because of his drooping eyelids, persuaded the elder Cash to allow him to go north to attend Valparaiso University, the "people's university" as it was known then. But the Indiana winters were too much for the young lonely southerner who returned at Christmas and reluctantly agreed to give Baptist Wake Forest College a try. It was just another "preacher school," Sleepy grumbled.[4]

To his surprise, Sleepy discovered a cadre of teachers who bravely acknowledged Darwin's existence; read H. L. Mencken and James Branch Cabell, the Virginia novelist who wrote dreamy, naughty books; and quoted W. C. Brann, the now forgotten quixotic transplanted Yankee in Texas who made a career out of shocking his readers. Sleepy's teachers were Christians, to be sure, as was the devout but embattled president, William Lewis Poteat who championed free enquiry, even if it meant reading heretics like Darwin. Like other young moderns in the North, (and a few in the South), Cash found such openmindedness liberating and exhilarating. He also—as did his northern counterparts—used modernism to justify rejecting the certainties of Christianity. What had begun as youthful rebellion and boyhood distaste for Sunday School and know-it-all preachers, had flowered into reasoned rejection of religion, one of the foundation stones of Victorianism.[5]

And just in case someone should miss the point, Sleepy latched on to Mencken, the outspoken advocate of Darwin, Nietzsche, Wagner, German thought and beer—all *verboten* in Gaffney or Boiling Springs, North Carolina where Cash's family had moved when he was thirteen. Tucked away at Wake Forest in tiny, rural Wake, North Carolina, Cash whooped it up for Mencken, applauding gleefully when the Baltimore Sage dismissed the South as "The Sahara of the Bozart." Where others grew red in the face stammering about Mencken, Cash agreed with Mencken: "It *is* a desert—a barren waste, so far as the development of culture and the nurture of beaux arts are concerned, and North Carolina comes near being the dreariest spot in the whole blank stretch." Hitting his stride as editor of the *Old Gold and Black*, the sprightly, literate student newspaper, Cash lashed the state for having produced few writers of merit; and worse "it hasn't even raised up readers for books that others have written." At fault was the state's "provincialism" and its addiction to "money-grubbing and crass materialism." Such shallowness dominated college students whose literary taste seldom took them beyond cheap novels or popular magazines. Not more than one in a hundred college men could even recognize "the most distinguished of modern writers and books."[6]

Following graduation in 1922, Jack Cash, as he liked his new friends to call him—to old friends he was Sleepy, to his family he was always Wilbur—did a fruitless year at Wake Forest's law school, tried a summer of journalism in 1923, taught school for a couple of years, and fell hopelessly in love. None of this, including the dreamy romance, led to anything. Mainly he read and wrote. He reveled in Mencken and Cabell. He loved Cabell's *Beyond Life* (1919), a quirky, rococo defense of the artist's right to soar into realms of the imagination, the keystone of modernist art. Cash continued reading Voltaire, Montaigne, Gibbon, Hazlitt, his joy, and his old love, Shakespeare.

At no time, apparently, did the eclectic, omnivorous Cash read Matthew Arnold or Thackeray, or Trollope—any of the English Victorians, that is,— or any of America's genteel writers. His own abortive writing attempts at this time also reveal his passion for modernists. He tried his hand at several novels (all burned): one in the manner of Joseph Conrad, another a la Theodore Dreiser, and a third in the Dostoievsky mold. Down in Mississippi William Faulkner, whom Singal identifies as a quasi-modernist, was reading the same authors. And up in New York City young Allen Tate, fresh from his brilliant undergraduate years at Vanderbilt where he joined the Fugitive poets who would flee from the modern world, discovered T. S. Eliot in 1922. Smitten by Eliot's modernist verse and the poet's reverence for tradition, Tate began a lifelong struggle with modernism.[7]

During the 1920s, while Tate became the celebrated author of the elegaic "Ode to the Confederate Dead" (1927) and Faulkner penned such neglected novels as *Mosquitoes* (1927), and *Sanctuary* and *Sartoris* in 1929, Cash suffered recurrent health problems, including debilitating bouts of melancholia and depression. His drift from southern certainties continued.[8] His father, equally reverential toward capitalism and Baptist theology, was making it in the mills, having risen to superintendent at Boiling Springs' new hosiery mills in 1923. Here was the mill village paternalism in full bloom: the owners ruled arbitrarily in the manner of the planter lords, even providing cheap housing and credit at the village store. Earlier Cash had accepted the orthodoxy that the workers were happy, that unions were not only unnecessary but evil, a Yankee heresy, and that the owners, being Christian stewards, would provide for their grateful workers.[9]

But in the summer of 1923, Sleepy awoke. He had a summer job as a reporter with the Charlotte *Observer*. In mid-August a walkout at one of the city's largest textile mills turned into an ugly three-week strike. The *Observer*, the city's conservative and staid newspaper, all but ignored the strike and assigned it to Cash. Compared to the lively and liberal Charlotte *News* that put the strike on the front page, the *Observer*'s coverage, tucked away on inside pages, was mild. But Cash saw the wretched conditions with a fresh eye as he listened sympathetically to the workers' complaints. His estrangement from mill village paternalism had begun in a rush.[10]

That estrangement came to completion in 1928–1929 when Cash, temporarily healthy, was a full-time journalist. In 1928 he was in Shelby, North Carolina, not far from Charlotte, editing a local semiweekly, the *Cleveland Press*. Shelby, the home of Clyde R. Hoey and O. Max Gardner, one of the reigning chieftains in the Democratic party and the party's gubernatorial candidate, provided Cash an opportunity to see at firsthand the rough and tumble world of politics in the vitriolic presidential contest between Herbert Hoover and Al Smith. Smith's Catholicism, his stand on Prohibition, his inept campaigning, and the opposition of some Democratic politicians and churchmen like Bishop Cannon, prompted five southern states to vote Republican. For the first time in fifty years the South was not solid. Cash editorialized and campaigned for Smith, attacked the anti-Smith forces, including the clergy. One editorial quoted a Methodist pastor's prayer: "Oh Lord, we ask Thee to give victory to our candidates. We know they are Protestants, Oh Lord, and deserve Thy Support."[11]

Cash came away embittered at what he considered Gardner's reluctant waffling in support of Smith, his demagoguery, and his unconcern for the economic plight of the people. The following year—now unemployed but writing—Cash followed the bitter, controversial strike in Gastonia where politicians and preachers joined hands with mill owners to smear the strikers with charges of "communism" and other forms of treason. Seeing it all up close, Cash lost any lingering respect he might have had for the world his family and most white southerners cherished.[12]

These events, however searing to his conscience, galvanized Cash into writing a series of angry, probing, Menckenesque articles for Mencken's *American Mercury*. From "Jehovah of the Tar Heels," an irreverent snarl at Furnifold M. Simmons, leader of the state's anti–Smith forces; to "War in the South," a bitter exposé of management's tactics in the Gastonia strike; to "Holy Men Muff a Chance," on the clergy's failure to exploit the Depression, Cash lashed out at southern deities. In between had appeared "The Mind of the South," "A Close View of Calvinist Lhasa,"—a back-of-the-hand slap to Charlotte's Scotch-Irish bourgeoisie—and "Buck Duke's University." "The Mind of the South" foreshadowed Cash's later fully developed contention that the southern "mind" was a lamentable concoction of fantasy, individualism, racism, and violence. To complete the circle, and to signal his complete estrangement from southern capitalism's self-congratulatory rhetoric about its philanthropy, Cash denounced James B. ("Buck") Duke, the celebrated self-made tobacco magnate who had recently given millions to transform Trinity College into Duke University. To Cash, a small-d democrat and foe of religious orthodoxy and economic royalism, the new Methodist university was created in Buck's image to make North Carolina safe for laissez-faire capitalism, the American Tobacco Company and the monopolistic Duke Power Company. Blow upon blow, Cash hammered out his repudiation of the Democratic party—just so many reactionary Jehovahs; the Protestant clergy—just so many ignorant, cocksure holy men eager to put their thumb in the eye of free thinkers; and southern capitalists—just so many greedy barons of business who exploited those whom they pretended to love and cherish.[13]

Cut off from believing what his neighbors believed, isolated from any intellectual community such as that clustered around Howard Odum at the University of North Carolina, and tempted to think of himself as an odd duck—never mind that his first *American Mercury* articles brought an invitation from the Knopfs to do a book on the southern mind—Cash teetered on the brink of complete nervous breakdown in the early 1930s. The depression had reduced his family to near destitution. Cash did some free-lancing—Mencken paid well—and tried to win a Guggenheim Foundation fellowship that would allow him to go to Europe and write a novel. Allen Tate had won a Guggenheim a few years earlier on the strength of his quickie biography of *Stonewall Jackson* (1928). Tate used his year abroad to write another equally inconsequential biography of *Jefferson Davis* (1929).[14] But Cash's applications met rejections. So he read and pondered. When Tate, John Crowe Ransom, and Donald Davidson and other former Fugitive poets and writers issued their conservative Agrarian manifesto, *I'll Take My Stand* (1929), a stunning defense of tradition and a nostalgic yearning for an ordered society, Cash felt an even greater sense of isolation. Tate was almost a modernist, certainly he was when he spoke as a literary critic. But his own yearning for tradition and religion, a yearning that would bring him eventually to the Catholic church, prompted him to divorce, once and for all, literary and social comment.[15]

Cash knew he had something strikingly different to say; he had been saying it in bits and pieces since his collegiate days. But he needed information and ideas, mainly ideas. He made his way through the histories by William E. Dodd, William Garrott Brown, John Spencer Bassett, Edwin Mims, Thomas Dyer; their books were useful, but he found their New South optimism (read Victorianism) naive. He found much more to admire in and borrow from the compendious sociological works of Howard Odum, particularly *An American Epoch* and *Southern Regions of the United States*.[16] Cash was also drawn to Odum's disciples and cohorts—Arthur F. Raper's bold work on lynchings and sharecroppers; Harriet Herring's revealing studies of child labor in southern cotton mills; Rupert Vance's probing of the *Human Factors in Cotton Culture* (1929); and Guy B. Johnson's sympathetic interest in black culture and his work on the Klan. Their New South liberalism was moderated by a modernist commitment to exploring the social order critically, to shifting their attention from the individual to his social setting, and to getting at the facts, however unpleasant. But they paid a price. Their modernism, says Singal, sent them beyond Odum but cut them off from the scope of their predecessors—namely Tate and Odum. "Instead of attempting to comprehend all the South at once, their technique generally caused them to focus on one small facet of it." The result was that "minute details frequently absorbed them, while grand visions typically eluded them. It was a price they were willing to pay in their efforts to achieve empirical honesty."[17]

Cash, who did not have an academic bone in his body, was eager to outline, probe, explain a grand vision. He drew on his predecessors and contemporaries for facts, not ideas. (The closest Cash came to being a slavish disciple of anyone was his partial acceptance of Broadus Mitchell's contention in *The Rise of the Cotton Mills in the South* (1921) that the original entrepreneurs had been motivated by an altruistic desire to provide employment for the uneducated white masses.)[18]

For ideas, Cash turned to Marx and Freud. One cannot say specifically what Cash read by either, but as a young college graduate he dove into Freud. He read to understand himself, to heal himself if possible. He suffered from hyperthyroidism; worse, for his ego, he feared that he was sexually impotent, though as a collegian he had, he once admitted, "roistered in Raleigh's red-light district."[19] Freud was in the intellectual air in those days, even in the South. Earlier, during the war years, Freud had made his way into the North, mainly through popularizers, and Cash may even have encountered his work at Wake Forest.[20] Whatever, as *The Mind of the South*, makes abundantly clear, Cash had a comprehensive understanding of Freud's primary concepts, particularly "ego."

Both *The Mind of the South* and Cash's editorials and book reviews in the Charlotte *News* where he worked steadily from 1936 to 1941 reveal a familiarity with Marx. When and what he read is unknown, but it is safe to assume that the omnivorous reader went beyond the *Communist Manifesto*. Yet Cash was never a Marxist, nor ever tempted to be one. Marx's concept of class, of the division of any society into two classes, and of the absolute importance of class bias and prejudices, informed Cash's mind and enlivened the pages of his newspaper writings and his masterpiece. In the 1930s, Cash could see, as some of his contemporaries, such as John Dewey, could see, and what Reinhold Niebuhr would argue forcefully in the 1940s: that for all his sophistication, for all his awareness that rationality was always limited, if not subordinated to class, Marx was a pre-modernist.[21] Marx had his own certainties—that a classless and therefore rational society would, inevitably, evolve. "The whole trouble with the dream," Cash editorialized in 1937, "is that it is too lovely. It assumes that the human race is capable of a high degree of rationality and disinterested cooperation. . . . " Old Karl, says Cash in a Menckenesque mood, was "one of the two or three most naive idealists who have lived on this planet." To Cash, Marx assumed that mankind could live nobly. An individual here or there might, "But for the body of us most of the time: we are not intelligent. We see only to the end of our noses— to the tiny limit of the immediate personal benefit we have in view. We are ruled by *ego*" (emphasis added).[22]

The Freudian notion of ego is the controlling concept of *The Mind of the South*. One will not find the word in the index; and Cash never says he has a "frame of reference," or that he's writing "psychohistory"—the word was not even around in 1941. Nor is *The Mind of the South* psychohistory written to demonstrate the usefulness of a critical apparatus. Cash's book is too complex, too wide-ranging, too original, too personal to be pigeonholed as psychohistory, or given any label, though he did "psychoanalyze the South old and new."

Cash could not have written the book he did without Freud. More accurately still, *The Mind of the South* could not have been conceived and executed by anyone who *had not* escaped southern Protestantism, rejected the quavering quasi-modernism of Tate, the intellectual hesitations of Odum's disciples, accepted Darwin and social evolution, rejected (with Marx) the complacent self-congratulations of southern capitalists and turned to Freud. Nor, given the personal nature of the book which frequently relies on Cash's own experiences for "evidence," could Cash have written as he did without a Nietzschian self-confidence, the sort that emboldens a modernist to believe that one's private vision, no matter how personal, idiosyncratic, or sweeping, is to be argued, passionately and boldly.

The Mind of the South argues, over and over and over, that southerners were ruled not by class—though poor southerners, says Cash, were dominated by the "ruling class" from beginning to end—but by their egoistic needs to identify completely, no matter what the cost, with a grand, romantic, heroic, gallant idea of the South. No one escaped that yearning. The planter ruling class—and Cash, informed by Marx, consistently draws our attention to the ruling class, whether planters or twentieth-century capitalists—was quite small numerically, probably because they were aggressive, self-made men of a crude frontier who believed their rule to be a natural consequence of their struggle to prevail. But mainly they ruled because they were able to implant in the common southerners' mind (and Cash includes blacks as well as whites) that the planters were gallant gentlemen, real southerners, that is.

Yet to Cash, the planters were never a true aristocracy. They were too close to the primitive frontier. Cash was a Turnerian who rejected every Victorian assumption in Turner. The planters, moreover, were painfully aware of their deficiencies, even in their "subsconscious," hence their loud bragging and boasting. Guilt-ridden, but not exclusively over slavery, haunted by a sense of their pretensions to aristocracy, and made the object of contempt by northern abolitionists, the planter created a host of "defense mechanisms," against the accusations which affronted his "ego."[23]

Yankees may not have been taken in by the charade, which even the planters came to accept, but the white masses were. The common white southerners, who owned no slaves and very little land, and who were economically and politically exploited by a social structure built on slavery, looked up to the planters, admired them, saw in them examples of what they might yet become. It was pure fantasy, but a fantasy that coddled the ego, said Cash. Here spoke a modernist who understood that the projections of the common whites' unconscious fantasies served as their "imagination." It surely was not rational for dirt farmers in North Carolina, or sunburned, gap-toothed, illiterate Delta whites to identify the tiny ruling class of planters with the South. But the common southerners' egos, their desire to think highly of themselves, no matter what the odds, dominated and obliterated class consciousness.

Such an imaginative insight—the sort that makes most workaday historians envious—led Cash to one of the his most stunning and controversial conclusions that the common white's willingness to follow the planters and their descendants slavishly was possible because their directions and orders never, until the 1890s, ran counter to his ego. Before that the common white

> identified his ego with the thing called the South as to become, so to say, a perambulating South in little, and hence found in the prescriptions of his captains great expansion for his ego—associated the authority yielded the master class, not with any diminution of his individuality, but with its fullest development and expression.[24]

Here in one dazzling display of modernism Cash confronted what might be termed *the* irony of Southern history: why did poor whites march off to die for a social system that oppressed them? It is easy to overlook the significance of what Cash did. Most commentators on the Old South in Cash's day had pulled their chins wondering why slaves had not rebelled, or why greater numbers had not tried to escape. Cash would have been the first to spy the racism—to say nothing of a lack of knowledge about slavery—that frequently lurks in that question. Cash did not ask those questions because he was not a racist; but more importantly, he did not project on to oppressed slaves an heroic, rational, courageous self-image. Cash whirled the table and asked, by indirection, what could explain why *whites*, who were not in physical bondage, did not rebel. The answer: psychological bondage.

To Cash, ego needs and ego fulfillments obliterated class consciousness in the antebellum South, afterwards, and well into the twentieth century. Not even in the planter's "subconsciousness" was there a sense of caste or class, nor was there any genuine class feeling in the poorest whites. Characterized by a rough frontier social mobility and reassuring racial consciousness, the white South, forced on the defensive by Yankee criticism, lived comfortably, luxuriating in its identification with the national ego. White southerners, planter and cracker alike, participated in the "romantic pattern," and the southern notion of honor, that something "inviolable and precious in the ego, . . . "[25] Later, when whites scrambled for wealth and position in the new industrial age in ungentlemanly ways that were less than honorable, they soothed their consciences by identifying the South with progress and priding themselves on being crafty and "smart." Yankee go-getting was now honor and virtue. It was another example of self-delusion and the South's willingness to believe anything, as long as it coddled the ego.[26]

One does not have to read far in Cash to discover why he had turned to Freud. As a southern white who had grown up sharing in the most reactionary of racist assumptions about blacks, Cash knew the depths of racial consciousness in whites. Thus Cash contends that the common white southerner could latch on to the planter or to progress as the South because implicit in it all was white, racial solidarity, and thereby the expansion of the common man's ego. However much poor whites might scorn and abuse blacks, the sense of racial security that came from identifying with their betters allowed poor croppers and tenants to sit down with the black man, even break bread with him in his kitchen, and "talk with him of the hazards of the seasons and the elements which they faced in common, laugh at his cunningly humble jokes, *and expand their egos* in the comfortable sense of sitting among inferiors" (emphasis added.)[27] This the planter came to understand and exploit in the postbellum years when the white masses threatened, on occasion, to call a strike.

But was Cash preoccupied with whites? Blacks never get extensive or intensive treatment in his pages. And some of his words, if yanked out of context and not understood as Cash's extravagant style, sound racist. The Negro was a romantic, a hedonist, who rolled lovely words in his mouth, heaping "them in redundant profusion one upon another until meaning vanishes and there is nothing left but the play of primitive rhythm upon the secret springs of emotion." And there was an incident, says Morrison, when Cash—just eighteen and away in the North, away from home for the first time—when a Negro sat down beside him. Cash turned him away rudely, saying he was not about to "sit with a nigger." Nor would he "as long as he lived," says Morrison—a statement many who knew Cash find hard to believe.[28]

Whatever, one should notice "that whatever critical comments Cash made about blacks he attributed the same or worse to whites," says Richard King.[29] Also in Cash's probing, deeply sympathetic analysis of blacks in the modern South he acknowledged and saluted black demands for education, for the vote, for jobs. He argued that in spite of soul-destroying obstacles some blacks were climbing the economic ladder. But Cash had no desire to use any of this to minimize white prejudice. He wrote movingly about exploitation and racial oppression and argued that slums and ghettos were the cause of crime.[30] Yet King mistakenly criticizes Cash for failing "to make the plausible move to the observation that the Negro, because he existed in two worlds, was far from the simple and uncomplex figure he was assumed to be."[31] Such contentions overlook the fact that Cash never for a moment embraced the white South's cherished fantasy that it "understood" the Negro. And Cash went even further. Like W. E. B. DuBois, whom he cites, he was aware that blacks hid their true feelings behind a veil, a mask. But what was behind that mask, that was the question that bedeviled even the commonest whites, said Cash. Whites boasted that they knew the Negro, but they boasted too much. Inwardly they shuddered at what must be going on behind that grin. "What was back there, hidden? What whispering, stealthy, fateful thing might they be framing out there in the palpitant darkness?"[32]

The man who wrote that was no racist. And Fred Hobson is surely right when he observes that Cash, who was in reality the soul of modesty, would have thought it highly presumptuous of him to "explain" the black mind. Modesty and modernism kept Cash from taking on the New South liberals' assumptions that they understood the Negro. Even the most benign, well-meaning liberals of the preceding generation, such as Edgar Gardner Murphy and Woodrow Wilson, sincerely believed that *they* understood the Negro. The masses, with their irrational, prejudiced, easily-inflamed minds obviously did not. Thus, before Cash, racism was a problem "out there" in the ignorant, unwashed white masses or in the bestial Negro rapist. The race problem would be remedied through public—if segregated—schools and a reformed white electorate. Cash would have none of this Victorianism.

In fact, in his unflinching documentation of racism, particularly the violent lynchings that disgraced the South before World War I, Cash consistently blamed the planters and their descendants—"men of the better sort," said New South liberals, men who could never be guilty of gross or brutal prejudice. Cash even went so far as to argue that lynchings had declined since 1920 because the "better sort" had come to see that extreme racism was no longer in their economic self-interest. Lynchings bred unruliness in whites; lynchings were likely to sweep blacks into "mass hysteria" and shake them out of their "submissiveness."[33] And then, as though he had become aware that he had, a la the New South liberals or Marxists, attributed too much rationality or evil purposefulness to the ruling class, Cash backs off to find the "real" source for the decline in lynchings in Progress and its ultimate symbol, the machine, the embodiment of order and rationality, the opposite of an irrational lynch mob.[34]

Regarding rape, Cash was more circumspect. He restricted himself to the past, to the nineteenth century, saying there was some legitimacy in the white South's anxiety and anger, and fear of the black rapist. Still, he argued as New South liberals had and as Arthur F. Raper documented in *The Tragedy of Lynching* (1933) that the fear was all out of proportion to the facts. Rape was rarely the real cause of lynchings and white racism. But being a Freudian modernist, he could not stop there, particularly since he refused to blame the "ignorant" white masses. He labels the whole matter the "rape complex" and hints (but only hints, he was a gentleman of his time, after all) that some of the rape complex was merely a projection of the sexual fantasies of neurotic, even hysterical old maids and young girls. Such things, said Cash the analyst, were simply not understood then for what they were.[35]

By the time he wrote *The Mind of the South* Cash was sustained somewhat by the thought that modernism was taking root in the South. The better colleges and universities, revitalized by young academics who had been trained abroad or in the North, were revamping their curriculums and introducing modern ideas. A student in Dixie now had a chance to hear Marx quoted, said Cash, and to hear his professors speak approvingly of Freud, Adler, Jung, John B. Watson, John Dewey, Veblen, Nietzsche and Spengler—even Mencken. Younger professors now yawned at Thomas Nelson Page and suggested Ellen Glasgow or James Joyce or T. S. Eliot. From such halls of learning returned young men and women who could be heard saying that Darwin was right, and so was Freud, the man god-fearing southerners thought must be "in the pay of the Kremlin, . . ."[36]

Some students abused modernism, said Cash the grown-up. They confused it with license. They reveled in drunkenness and sexual promiscuity. But the majority of students and schools still adhered to the "ancient framework." There was a remnant of modernists everywhere—in the arts, in journalism, in editorial positions. But Cash was far from sanguine. For all his hope that modernism was undermining the "ancient pattern," he was aware that modernism had a precarious hold on the South. Should modernism ever directly challenge the white South's cherished myths, particularly racial myths, it would be roundly rejected. Let "free enquiry," as the proponents of modern thought liked to say, be associated with Yankee racial equality, said Cash, and it will be silenced, branded as the "logical culmination" of "atheistic Communism." Even the commonest white, Cash wrote, saw in modernism (which as Willard Gatewood has shown was frequently subsumed under the scare word "evolution") "a menace to his interests, or at least to his ego, once it had been called to his attention by his masters." Even so, Cash saw some reason to hope. He believed, certainly he wanted to believe, that the modern mind had begun to penetrate the folk mind and had left some doubt, even in the mind of the Klansman and fundamentalist.[37]

More than this Cash was unwilling to say. In fact, as he neared the end of his masterpiece, he retreated some, saying that while there was a palpable modern mind it had not converted the masses, or even the supposed leaders, the politicians and businessmen. The South's angry response to Roosevelt's contention in 1938 that the region was "the nation's number one economic problem," a contention based on facts, many supplied by Odum, infuriated Cash. He ended saying that the mind of the South was "almost wholly unarticulated with the body of the South." After all, in 1939, despite two decades of modernism, Margaret Mitchell's *Gone With the Wind* was embraced as "a sort of new confession of the Southern faith."[38]

But what about W. J. Cash himself? Did he stand outside the stream of southern consciousness? Was he implying that his mind—a modernist mind—could emancipate itself from history and probe psyche, ego, temperament? He would probably say no, and probably point to his own "extravagance," as Woodward has said in showing that Cash was, at least partially, a reflection of the very mind he deplored. And it is easy to point out the obvious: that were Cash truly a modernist he would understand, as

Reinhold Niebuhr has said, that there is no unprejudiced mind transcending history.[39] A modernist like Cash, aware that all southerners were in history together, would agree. His reply would be that his words were not truth but a striving for truth, for insight, for the best questions. Armed with such self-consciousness, the very hallmark of modernity, the Jack Cashes of this world try not to deceive anyone—most of all themselves.

Paradoxically, few native sons were ever more "southern" than Cash. Unlike Tate, Ransom, Warren, Woodward, and the region's most distinguished intellectuals of his era, Cash refused to leave the South. Like Lucy Randolph Mason, Cash preferred to live in Dixie. He chose, though, to die elsewhere. Just months after his book appeared to rave reviews, Cash, newly married and honored—at last—with a Guggenheim grant, took his life in Mexico City. His journey through the mind of the South had been a fearless attempt at therapy, at cure. That it did not save his own mind is but one more tragedy, one more bit of waste.

Both in what he wrote and when and how he died W. J. Cash made us all doubly aware of southern waste.

NOTES

1. W. J. Cash, *The Mind of the South* (New York, 1941). All references are to the Vintage paperback edition, p. 102.

2. Daniel Joseph Singal, *The War Within: From Victorian to Modernist Thought in the South, 1919–1941* (Chapel Hill, 1982), pp. 6–8; Henry May, *The End of American Innocence: A Study of the First Years of Our Time* (New York, 1959), pp. 1–8; Carl Becker, *The Heavenly City of the Eighteenth-Century Philosophers* (New Haven, 1932), p. 15; William James, "The Sentiment of Rationality," in *William James: The Essential Writings*, ed. Bruce Wilshire (New York, 1971), pp. 25–39.

3. Singal, *The War Within*, p. 373; Richard H. King, *A Southern Renaissance: The Cultural Awakening of the American South, 1930–1955* (New York, 1979), pp. 146–172; Fred Hobson, *Tell About the South: The Southern Rage to Explain* (Baton Rouge, 1983), p. 259; C. Vann Woodward, *American Counterpoint: Slavery and Racism in the North-South Dialogue* (Boston, 1971), pp. 261–84.

4. Joseph Morrison, *W. J. Cash* (New York, 1967), pp. 3–24. For detail, Morrison's biography is reliable and readable.

5. Ibid., pp. 25–36; May, *End of American Innocence*, pp. 1–8. For insight into Brann see *Brann the Iconoclast: A Collection of the Writings of W. C. Brann*, ed. with biography by J. D. Shaw, 2 vols. (Waco, Tex., 1898–1903).

6. W. J. Cash, "North Carolina Culture," *Old Gold and Black*, March 14, 1922; for a comprehensive treatment of Mencken and the South see Fred Hobson, *Serpent in Eden: H. L. Mencken and the South* (Chapel Hill, 1974).

7. Morrison, *W. J. Cash*, pp. 25–47; for Cash on his favorite English writers see W. J. Cash, "It's Unwise to Be too Wise," *Charlotte News*, April 4, 1937; Singal, *The War Within*, p. 157; King, *A Southern Renaissance*, pp. 99–111.

8. King, *A Southern Renaissance*, pp. 100–102; Singal, *The War Within*, pp. 238–41.

9. Morrison, *W. J. Cash*, pp. 35–37.

10. Charlotte *Observer*, August 14, 23, 25, 1923; Charlotte *News*, August 12, 14, 17, 18, 21, 22, 1923.

11. Cleveland *Press*, October 2, 1928; Joseph L. Morrison, *Governor O. Max Gardner: A Power in North Carolina and New Deal Washington* (Chapel Hill, 1971), pp. 48–50.

12. W. J. Cash, "War in the South," *American Mercury* 19 (February 1930): 163–69; for a detailed analysis of the Gastonia strike see Liston Pope, *Millhands and Preachers: A Study of Gastonia* (New Haven, 1942).

13. W. J. Cash, "Jehovah of the Tar Heels," *American Mercury* 17 (July 1929): 310–18; "The Mind of the South," ibid., 18 (October 1929): 185–92; "Close View of Calvinist Lhasa," ibid., 28 (April 1933): 443–51; "Buck Duke's University," ibid., 30 (September 1933): 102–10; "Holy Men Muff a Chance," ibid., 31 (January 1934): 112–18.

14. Singal, *The War Within*, pp. 240–45; King, *A Southern Renaissance*, pp. 102–5.

15. Singal, *The War Within*, pp. 254–60.

16. Hobson, *Tell About the South*, pp. 257–58; Singal, *The War Within*, pp. 115–52; Michael O'Brien, *The Idea of the American South, 1920–1941* (Baltimore, 1979), pp. 31–96.

17. Singal, *The War Within*, pp. 302–38.

18. Cash, *Mind of the South*, pp. 180–81, 216, 332–33, 381–82.

19. Morrison, *W. J. Cash*, pp. 40–44, 48–56.

20. For an excellent analysis of Freud's impact on American thought, and on the American literary mind in general, see Frederick Hoffman, *Freudianism and the Literary Mind* (Baton Rouge, 1957), pp. 44–58. See also Nathan G. Hale, *Freud and the Americans: The Beginnings of Psychoanalysis in the United States, 1876–1917* (New York, 1971), pp. 397–433.

21. Reinhold Niebuhr, *The Children of Light and the Children of Darkness* (New York, 1944), pp. 57–63.

22. W. J. Cash, "Old Karl's Idealism," Charlotte *News*, February 14, 1937.

23. Cash, *Mind of the South*, pp. 62–64.

24. Ibid., p. 115.

25. Ibid., p. 75.

26. Ibid., p. 273.

27. Ibid., p. 317.

28. Ibid., pp. 51–53; Morrison, *W. J. Cash*, p. 21. Interviews with Harriet Doar, September 17, 1984; Irma Drum, August 30, 1984; Charles A. McKnight, September 15, 1984.

29. King, *A Southern Renaissance*, p. 163.

30. Cash, *Mind of the South*, pp. 322–26.

31. King, *A Southern Renaissance*, p. 163.

32. Cash, *Mind of the South*, pp. 325, 326.

33. Ibid., p. 313; for a discussion of New South liberals see Bruce Clayton, *The Savage Ideal: Intolerance and Intellectual Leadership in the South, 1890–1914* (Baltimore, 1972).

34. Cash, *Mind of the South*, pp. 315–16.

35. Ibid., pp. 116–18.

36. Ibid., p. 335.
37. Ibid., pp. 349–50.
38. Ibid., p. 430.
39. Woodward, *American Counterpoint*, p. 283; Niebuhr, *The Children of Light and the Children of Darkness*, p. 144.

With Pen and Camera: In Quest of the American South in the 1930s

BURL F. NOGGLE

Americans in the Great Depression, without at first realizing just what they were up to, set out on a great quest. Bewildered by the economy's collapses, beset with psychic and material insecurity, troubled over what to do—what, if anything, they actually could do about their plight—they carried out a massive inventory, taking stock of themselves, their land, their way of life. Writers and artists and scholars, often singly but more often collectively under New Deal auspices, set out to explore and describe and define America. They took trips and wrote about what they saw. They took photographs and exhibited them. They held interviews with countless Americans, largely the obscure and dispossessed, and transcribed them. They assembled thick guidebooks and inventories of the states and disseminated them. They recorded folklore and folk music. They drew up blueprints and made sketches of American houses and barns, furniture and ceramics, in rich and multitudinous variety of form. They mapped and charted and delineated the nation and its regions and zones, its physical and sociological design. They wrote essays and novels, even plays and poetry, about what they found. And finally, in their quest for understanding themselves and their world of the thirties, they went poking and rummaging into the past and wrote—or rewrote—a goodly part of the nation's history.

This impulse to find the presumed essence of America was not unique to the 1930s. It is an impulse as old as the nation itself. From de Crevecoeur in 1782 asking his classic question, "What then is the American, this new man?" to de Tocqueville in the 1830s looking at *Democracy in America* to David M. Potter in the 1950s pondering over *People of Plenty*, pundits and scholars have been preoccupied with the nature and meaning of America. Joseph Epstein has suggested a name for this engrossment: "What's going on, the way we live now, the search for our national character, the truth about America—all these various preoccupations might come under the rubric of the de Tocqueville Impulse." This impulse has come upon the nation stronger at certain times than at others. In the 1930s it was powerful and pervasive.[1]

In 1939, after the Federal Writers' Project of the New Deal had begun to publish, one by one, its series of *Guidebooks* to each of the states, the writer Robert Cantwell made a telling observation: "The America that is beginning to emerge from the books of the Writers' Project is a land to be taken seriously: nothing quite like it has ever appeared in our literature.... Nothing in our academic histories prepares you for it, and very little in our imaginative writing: none of the common generalizations about America and the American temperament seem to fit it." In 1942 Alfred Kazin elaborated rhapsodically on Cantwell's thought in his stunning survey of American prose since 1890, *On Native Grounds*. In a final chapter on the 1930s—"America! America!"—Kazin sought to characterize the vast body of work done in the depression by writers and artists "whose subject was the American scene and whose drive always was the need, born of the depression and the international crisis, to chart America and to possess it."

Whatever one read or looked at—Works Projects Administration (WPA) Guidebooks, proletarian fiction, documentary studies of the dispossessed, photographs of the land and its people—all "testified to an extraordinary national self-scrutiny.... Never before did a nation seem so hungry for news of itself." To satisfy that hunger, writers and reporters and folklorists and photographers and scholars had, by the end of the decade, compiled a "vast granary of facts about life in America." And this compelling drive toward national inventory soon turned into a celebration of the national culture— witness Pare Lorentz, who prepared a documentary film on floods and erosion in the Mississippi Valley and "caught the image of the river, the spinal cord of the nation, in a chanting litany of American river names, caught it in a burst of celebrant American splendor unparalleled since Whitman." If in the beginning the guidebooks and photographs and other accumulations of data were stocktaking exercises that might reveal solutions to the depression crisis, the rising menace of fascism abroad soon turned that national (and regional) scrutiny into a "thundering flood of national self-consciousness and self-celebration," as "American writing became a swelling chorus of national affirmation and praise.[2]

Just how and why Americans in the thirties came to take the photographs and undertake the travels and make the studies and write the books they did then, and just how conscious they were about taking a great inventory and portraying and celebrating a national (or regional) culture—this is a subject neglected until lately by American historians. Kazin's *On Native Grounds* appeared in 1942. Earl H. Rovit in 1960 published a brief essay in which he suggested that "the twenty-year period following World War I can almost be labelled 'The Rediscovery and Reevaluation of America.' " The "American mind" in the period (and Rovit focused mostly if not exclusively on the thirties) was "forced to turn in on itself—to examine, to criticize, to catalogue, to remember." To Rovit, the "resulting activity marked this period as perhaps the most stimulating, the most creative, and the most frenetic in our national life." Geographers, sociologists, folklorists, anthropologists, philologists, historians, and novelists all went to work. What they turned up and turned out, Rovit only hinted at in a suggestive paragraph or two. In 1973, William Stott published his admirable *Documentary Expression and Thirties America*, the first attempt by anyone to examine, at length and in one sustained study, the documentary photographs, the WPA publications, and the work of social scientists and other contributors to that great quest for America in the 1930s.[3]

During the last decade or so, a number of biographies, studies of photographers and artists and of literary and intellectual figures in the thirties, and anthologies of essays written in the decade, together with life histories and interviews with ex-slaves done by the Federal Writers' Project have come tumbling from commercial and university presses. Scholars and artists have begun to find out a good many things about their counterparts of four decades ago. In what follows I discuss some of this bibliography (and the photographs and interviews and other items under scrutiny in these studies) by way of offering a guide of sorts to those wishing to make their own vicarious journey of the eye and the mind, to launch their own quest into the regions of America in the thirties, and in particular the American South.

I focus on the South primarily because looking for America in the thirties was, in part, looking for regions and subcultures, and in that decade the South more than any region found itself photographed, stereotyped, and scrutinized. Kenneth S. Lynn has recently written that during the thirties, when a "national yearning for a usable past . . . eventually embraced the history of every region on the country," it was the South "that most completely captured the American imagination, as the monster success of *Gone With the Wind*, in print and on the screen, dramatically signified." And there were other Souths, as well, other "images" far removed from Tara and Scarlett and Rhett that fired the American imagination in the thirties. Ever since the South took form, "South-watching," to borrow Fred Hobson's term, has been a favorite pastime, even a preoccupation, for uncounted southerners and outsiders. But in the 1930s some gifted outsiders came south to watch the natives through the lens of a camera, and they recorded some stunning images of southern faces and places.[4]

The term "outsider" calls attention to a significant fact: much of the great photographic documentation of the South in the thirties was the work of artists who were neither native to or residents of the South. David Madden, in an illuminating essay on southern photographs, has asked: "Why are there so few southern photographers compared with southern writers, who have been the most vital in American literature generally?" In fact, "no great artists in any field other than literature, whose work is identifiably southern, have come out of the South. Most of the photographs of the South that are best known... were taken by Yankees." One motive for the Yankee photographer (and a motive that the southern photographer traditionally has rejected) has been to expose or reveal some shortcoming or to perpetuate regional stereotypes or hostilities.[5]

A case in point is "Georgia Nigger," a photograph published in 1932 by John L. Spivak, a renowned reporter in the thirties who, outraged and haunted by a news story of convicts in a cage in North Carolina, went to Georgia early in the decade to write a report on southern chain gangs. He took photographs to accompany and document his powerful exposé. One of his pictures, the frontispiece to *Georgia Nigger*, at first glance appears to be nothing more nor less than a stark and clear documentation of the inhumanity of the convict system. In his 1978 study of southern image making, Jack Temple Kirby saw in the photograph "a young black prisoner in striped suit, with wrists chained to ankles, a wooden pole drawn between his arms and knees, and lying hopeless, nearly catatonic, on his side in the broiling sun." William Stott renders a more complex analysis of this image and of the concept and practice of documentary photography in the thirties. "To right wrongs, to promote social action," says Stott, "documentary tries to influence its audience's intellect and feelings." If documentary is to work social change it must "talk to us, and convince us that we, our deepest interests, are engaged." In the thirties, "documentary constantly addresses 'you',... the audience, and exhorts, wheedles, begs us to identify, pity, participate." Roy Stryker, director of the Farm Security Administration's great photography unit in the thirties, said: "A good documentary should tell not only what a place or a thing or a person *looks* like, but it must also tell the audience what it would *feel* like to be an actual witness to the scene." Stott suggests that photographs such as "Georgia Nigger" made Spivak's exposé of the chain gang "credible" but "did not give it its passion; they documented facts rather than feelings." The prisoners, "suspicious of the camera and of Spivak,... hid their emotion in enigmatic stares." Since the prisoners had feigned indifference, Spivak used his narrative to make the "you" looking at the photographs feel the passion and the outrage that Spivak felt.[6]

The effort to provoke reform was hardly singular to Spivak or unique in the thirties. Jacob Riis and Lewis Hine initiated such socially committed photography earlier, near the turn of the century. Most of the thousands of photographs taken in the South, and the nation, in the thirties were, in one way or another, designed to arouse sympathy and induce reform—almost invariably sympathy for the deprived and the powerless victims of the depression. Yet there were subtle distinctions between the documentary photographs taken and disseminated in the decade. Walker Evans, Dorothea

Lange, Russell Lee, and Arthur Rothstein—to name perhaps the four most talented photographers who went through the South in the thirties—differed from each other in motivation and technique and evoked differing images.

Today Evans is the most acclaimed of all the documentary artists of the thirties. His reputation rests in part upon *Let Us Now Praise Famous Men* that he and James Agee produced in 1941. Although the book suffered neglect for some twenty years following its publication, it is now a classic, celebrated and analyzed both for Evans's photographs and Agee's prose and for the way they complement and reinforce each other's message and imagery. In the summer of 1936, Agee and Evans went to Alabama on assignment from *Fortune* magazine to do a "photographic and verbal record of the daily living of an 'average' or 'representative' family of white tenant farmers." Evans at the time was a member of the Farm Security Administration photography unit and was already an established artist. Agee, who asked for Evans as photographer, had published a few poems and had written a few articles for *Fortune* on the Tennessee Valley Authority. The two men lived for about six weeks with three tenant farm families, sharing their food, their houses, their lives. After *Fortune* chose not to publish their report, Harper and Brothers printed Evans' photographs and offered to publish Agee's manuscript, but he refused to make the revisions the publisher requested. Finally, in September 1941 Houghton, Mifflin published *Let Us Now Praise Famous Men*.[7]

Meantime, in 1937, in *You Have Seen Their Faces*, Erskine Caldwell and Margaret Bourke-White had also juxtaposed text and photographs in a book about the South. Although it became a best seller, the book offended a number of critics at the time and infuriated Evans and Agee. In recent years, *You Have Seen Their Faces* has cheapened in almost inverse proportion to the exalted reputation of *Let Us Now Praise Famous Men*. In April 1936 Caldwell, who had already published his notorious novels, *Tobacco Road* and *God's Little Acre*, set out to do a book on southern sharecroppers that would "show that the fiction I was writing was authentically based on contemporary life in the South." The book "should be thoroughly documented with photographs taken on the scene [by] the best obtainable photographer." This turned out to be Bourke-White, who at the time was the most famous and commercially the most successful photographer in America, due in part to her work for *Life* magazine and for photographs of Soviet Russia and of the drought on the Great Plains. In July 1936 she and Caldwell set out on the southern trip that produced *You Have Seen Their Faces*.[8]

Donald Davidson, one of the Twelve Agrarians who published *I'll Take My Stand* in 1930 and who in the thirties, as for the rest of his life, was the most truculent of the famous Vanderbilt Twelve, published an Agrarian's critique of *You Have Seen Their Faces*. He was only mildly critical of Bourke-White's photographs and in fact at times was downright appreciative, if banal and commonplace in his observations. Davidson was pleased to find "no *erotica curiosa* in the book, no candid camera shots of the harelipped girl tumbling lasciviously in the weeds..., no sharecroppers devoured by the boss's hogs, no old grandmother bumped and flattened by ruthless automobilists;... no Negroes... being hanged in chains or tortured in sweatboxes." *You Have Seen Their Faces* contained "sixty-four excellent photographic studies, on the whole far more romantic than realistic." Davidson labeled romantic "those pictures that give us faces smiling, happy, cheerful, vigorous,... or that suggest the fallen grandeurs and lush natural abundance traditionally associated with the 'Deep South'...." In contrast, some "realistic" photographs show "notable excess of rags, dirt, disease, bad housing, or depressing environment." A third "neutral" type of photograph were faces that Bourke-White had recorded "apparently because they make interesting subjects rather than because they contain any very explicit social message." In general, the photographs were "fair" in the sense that Bourke-White could have shown worse scenes, and she could have shown more "flattering" scenes. But they were "punily, sickeningly incomplete" in another respect: croppers and tenants were not the only tenant problem in the South. "Nearly all Southerners are tenants," and the absentee landlord over them "Is the North." Southerners are "all held in a bondage that is the more subtle because the chains and indentures are not actually visible." Bourke-White did not photograph and Caldwell did not write about this kind of peonage, this colonial dependency on the wicked, exploitative Yankee North.[9]

You Have Seen Their Faces angered other critics, but it remained for William Stott in 1973 to write the most telling criticism of the book and to show how inferior its photographs and text were to *Let Us Now Praise Famous Men*. As Stott points out, the southern sharecropper had been publicized, spotlighted, and appraised for several years before Caldwell and Bourke-White undertook their study. The problem their book treated "was known to virtually everyone who read the book." Caldwell "diminished—brutalised—the sharecropper because his audience expected such a picture, not because he fully believed it." As for the photographs, Bourke-White "made her subjects' faces and pictures say what she wanted them to say." She showed "faces of defeat, their eyes wizened with pain...; people at their most abject: a ragged woman... on her rotted mattress, a palsied child, a woman with a goiter the size of a grapefruit...." Agee treated his sharecropper hosts with respect, even with love. Evans saw beauty and dignity in them. In Bourke-White's photographs, "No dignity seems left them: we see their meager fly-infested meals, their spoiled linen; we see them spotlit in the raptures of a revival meeting...; we see a preacher taken in peroration, his mouth and nostrils open like a hyena's." And if the viewer failed to get the message from Bourke-White's photographs, Caldwell's inscriptions (Evans's photographs had none) under the photograph "made them as abject as possible." Agee wrote of the tenant hovels he and Evans visited: "It seems to me necessary to insist that their beauty... inextricably shaped as it is in an economic and human abomination, is at least as important a part of the fact as the abomination itself." Here, notes Stott, "is the crucial difference between Bourke-White and Evans." She, using whatever lighting trick or bizarre angle was necessary for the job, tried to move her audience and to "expose sharecropper life as an unrelieved abomination." Evans showed its abomination but also, like Agee, its beauty. This was not conventional beauty but tragic beauty and "tragic twice over: because it cannot be recognized or appreciated by those who create it."[10]

You Have Seen Their Faces and *Let Us Now Praise Famous Men* were only two, if the most celebrated two, books of photographs-and-texts done during the thirties. And the photographs by Bourke-White, commercial photographer, and Evans, documentary artist, were only a miniscule portion of the southern images recorded in the decade. The Farm Security Administration (FSA) staff alone, during the years 1935–1942, took more than 270,000 photographs, one fifth or more of them southern images. Eleven people produced 99 percent of the photographs taken by the FSA group during its eight years of work: John Collier, Jack Delano, Walker Evans, Theo Jung, Dorothea Lange, Russell Lee, Carl Mydans, Arthur Rothstein, Ben Shahn, John Vachon, and Marion Post Wolcott. All were talented professionals, and where they went on assignment and what they photographed—to Georgia for photographs of soil erosion or to Vermont for pastoral scenes of winter—depended partly upon their own inclinations and partly upon those of Roy Stryker, head of the Historical Section of the FSA that contained the photography unit.[11]

Stryker himself was not a photographer, but from beginning to end of his term as director, he knew what he wanted photographed. Like several of the photographers he worked with, he exemplified Kazin's writers and artists of the thirties "whose subject was the American Scene and whose drive always was the need... to chart America and to possess it." For a 1973 publication of FSA photographs, *In This Proud Land*, Stryker wrote an introductory essay in which he recalls his excitement about the photographs that came in: "Every day was for me an education and a revelation. I could hardly wait to get to the mail in the morning." It was clear that the FSA collection "was going to be something special.... Still, we had no idea that we were doing anything of the importance that later historians have credited us with." But Nancy Wood, in another essay written for *In This Proud Land*, notes that in Stryker's management of the section, in his suggestions and directions to the photographers, in his approval of some photographs and his rejection of others, "his search was always for facts." It was his goal "to record on film as much of America as we could"—meaning, in Wood's expression, "a fascinating profile of America: courthouses, town halls, gas stations, barber shops, privies..., strikes, auctions, side shows, drinking, gambling, parades, loafing..., the American roadside, interiors, primitive paintings, movies, religion, radio, signs and on and on." John Collier, one of the photographers who worked with Stryker, said, "Artistically and academically Stryker wanted to assemble a model, and each incoming picture was another unit in the puzzle that when assembled was the most sweeping record ever made of the American earth and culture." Jack Delano thought "the great thing about the FSA photographs was that they were all... done in search for the heart of the American people." To Marion Post Wolcott, the only woman besides Lange to join the FSA group, Stryker "widened our horizons by constantly plugging and urging us to record, to document America from the historian's, sociologist's and architect's point of view."[12]

But Stryker's FSA photographers documented some parts of America more than others. Their very purpose, at first, was to photograph America's "rural problems." Given this primary focus, it is little wonder that the South received such thorough and splendid photographic documentation. In 1975, Robert White, a southerner living in Canada, published "Faces and Places in the South in the 1930's: A Portfolio," that contains fifteen pages of White's commentary and sixty-four photographs that White selected from the FSA files. White comments that "the FSA photographers' coverage of the South— and they canvassed the South more exhaustively than any other region—is more representationally inclusive, more generally in accordance with social fact, than their coverage of other regions." In recording "the look of poverty" in the South of the thirties, when the region was, in Roosevelt's classic term, "the nation's number one economic problem," in concentrating upon the rural and small-town life that was "at the time prominent in the South but ... that was destined for quick oblivion," the FSA photographers "managed to capture the essential qualities of life in the South during the 1930's." For White, these photographs "show us... just what it was like to be a Southerner during one of the South's most crucial periods."[13]

The sixty-four photographs that White includes brilliantly reflect and substantiate his evaluation. They also indicate something about the FSA photographers who ventured South in the thirties—Evans was not the only accomplished artist in the group. White includes ten by Evans, among them some of the classics from *Let Us Now Praise Famous Men*. But White also includes nine photographs by Lange, who is often judged second only to Evans in artistry, if not equal to him—as the nine selections might well bear out. The eleven images by Arthur Rothstein, like the eight by Russell Lee, are superb and familiar, and it is no surprise to see them included. But to find seventeen photographs by Marion Post Wolcott is startling—startling for the quantity, almost twice as many as anyone else, and for the quality and the range of subjects she caught. Her photographs merit discussion and description, but most of all they merit reproduction and viewing and contemplative study. Fortunately, the FSA photographs have recently begun to appear one after another in portfolios, anthologies, and other forms of reproduction. By undertaking their particular quest for America in the thirties, the FSA photographers made it possible for students of the South today to carry out vicarious quests of their own.[14]

While the photographers trekked South, other travelers explored the region taking notes. Some of these notes became the basis for books and essays about the region, written and published during the thirties. In his introduction to an annotated bibliography of travel literature in the twentieth-century South, Rupert Vance comments on the "running debate about what an authentic traveller's account is or should be"—an adventure story, journalistic reporting, social study, tourist's account, or "a literary form of minor importance." Vance, not especially concerned with subtle definitions of the genre, listed all kinds of books. But among the travelers who reported on the South during the thirties, the one who perhaps came closest to writing what Paul Fussell has called true "travel Literature" was Jonathan Daniels, in *A Southerner Discovers the South* (1938). Daniels, editor of the Raleigh, North Carolina *News and Observer*, started out from Robert E. Lee's mansion in Arlington, Virginia, and touched every state in the South except Kentucky, looking for evidence of the depression and of the New Deal at work to alleviate it. Vance, although acknowledging that "no one book could have epitomized the South in the great depression," praised Daniels for his "liberal but realistic" tone. "Few travellers, Southern or otherwise, possessed of an equal social consciousness, have been able to deal urbanely with as large a number of controversial topics." *A Southerner Discovers the South* "is likely to remain the definitive travel account of the South in depression."[15]

The label "definitive" is arguable. Perhaps Vance was judging only the "travel accounts" listed in his bibliography, and Daniels's book is clearly one of the best in that list. But along side Daniels and other journalists looking for the South in the thirties, other artistic and scribbling travelers entered the region, and in some ways their work is more nearly definitive than anything by any solitary traveler. These were the notetakers hired by the New Deal to undertake the great inventory that the Federal Writers' Project (FWP) attempted in the thirties. The FWP, along with the Federal Music, Federal Art, and Federal Theatre projects, constituted the Works Progress Administration's "Four Arts Program," created in 1935 to provide jobs for unemployed writers, musicians, artists, and actors. All four of the projects in one way or another illustrate in their activities and output some degree of the cultural nationalism and regionalism that marked the era's quest for things indigenously American. But it was the Federal Writers' Project, above all, that sponsored and nourished this quest and that produced a rich body of material now being reproduced in abundance.[16]

The work of the FWP—work carried on in all forty-eight states and work that made use of the great bulk of FWP employees—was compilation of the state *Guidebooks*. As Daniel Aaron has pointed out, from publication of the first one (Idaho) in 1937 to the appearance of the last one (Oklahoma) five years later, the Guides "received exhaustive comment from . . . admirers and critics." But it soon became "evident that the Guides were not only a compendium of towns and cities and collections of road-tours. They were also a new kind of human and historical geography, a Whitmanesque kaleidoscope of a country as mysterious as China." This quality—a quality that Kazin thought characteristic of thirties literature—is more evident in some of the Guides than in others. The quality, Whitmanesque or otherwise, of each state guide reflected quite directly the quality of the state's project director, and in the South, as in the rest of the country, these varied in quality. One appraiser in 1938 declared Mississippi's guidebook to be "tiresomely sententious" (and also found Maine's "stuffy" but Idaho's "brilliant"). Another reviewer in 1938 praised the Louisiana and North Carolina guides and declared the state directors responsible for their excellence. What Monty Penkower labels "bias and misconceptions" about Negroes and "stereotypes regarding slaves and plantation culture" appeared in a number of the southern state guides—though also in some northern guidebooks.[17]

Ironically it was in these same southern states that FWP workers, sometimes with and sometimes without "bias and misconceptions," conducted an extensive series of interviews with ex-slaves during the years, 1936–1938, and compiled more than ten thousand pages of "Ex-Slave Narratives" that have in recent years become a rich if controversial source of information for students of slavery, black studies, and southern history in general. These narratives, assembled in seventeen volumes, lay all but neglected in the Library of Congress for more than a quarter of a century after they were deposited there in 1941. In 1972 and 1973, Greenwood Press published sixteen volumes of the narratives, along with three other volumes of related material. George P. Rawick, general editor of this series, later discovered or had revealed to him by fellow historians and archivists enough additional narratives to publish twenty-two more volumes.[18]

Various scholars have offered various explanations for the FWP's decision in the thirties to carry on the interviews, for the general neglect of them for twenty-five years, and for their massive multivolume publication in the 1970s. Norman Yetman, for example, mentions the "new appreciation of the indigenous and folk elements in American society fostered by the depression and reflected in the emphases of the Writers' Project." To direct its collection of folklore material, the FWP recruited John A. Lomax, whom Yetman describes as "one of the foremost figures in the development of American folklore" and a man "especially intrigued by the spontaneity and uniqueness of Black Lore." Lomax's work on the FWP "mirrored his personal interest in southern and rural materials," but there developed also "an awakened appreciation during the depression of the richness of the cultural diversity of the American people and a quickened interest in and sympathy for American minority groups." However patronizing and untrained the white interviewers may have been, they were expressing this quickened interest in minority groups in the thirties—and in the folklore of southern blacks that John Lomax instructed them to record.[19]

Ex-slaves were not the only southerners whose lives the FWP sought to study and record. In 1939, the University of North Carolina Press published *These Are Our Lives*, a collection of "life histories" written by southerners working for the FWP. To gather material for their "stories" as W. T. Couch called them, the writers interviewed some four hundred southerners, most of them in North Carolina and Tennessee. Couch, who conceived and directed the life history project in the South, selected from these stories the thirty-five that appeared in *These Are Our Lives*. Couch wanted to offset the image of degeneracy, the "merriment over psychopaths" that Erskine Caldwell had foisted upon the region. Reviewers praised *These Are Our Lives* for defying the Caldwell sterotype. In "Realities on Tobacco Road," Virginius Dabney commented: "One thing which appeals to me . . . is the absence of . . . degenerates. After all, degenerates are the exception, rather than the rule, both North and South."[20]

Like the FSA photographs, like the ex-slave narratives, the life histories written in the thirties have lately begun to receive renewed appraisal and reproduction. From the one thousand or more life histories that FWP workers recorded in the South in the thirties, Tom E. Terrill and Jerrold Hirsch selected and published about thirty of them, along with an excellent introductory essay in *Such As Us*. In 1982, James Seay Brown, Jr., produced a comparable collection, with a comparably good introduction, on Alabama life histories. Meantime, in 1980 Ann Banks selected for publication eighty life histories from a "vast store of unpublished material—the hidden legacy of the Federal Writers' Project—that had been gathering dust since it was deposited in the Library of Congress in 1941." Although her collection depicts Americans from all sections and stations, her introductory essay, her headnotes to each of the eighty histories, and the histories make *First-Person America* a mesmerizing study and a splendid illustration of America's quest for itself.[21]

That quest had at least one more dimension that demands attention: the work of social scientists in the decade. Daniel Joseph Singal has observed that in the early 1920s "it was still possible to count the number of books by southern social scientists appearing in any given year on the fingers of one hand; by the mid-1930s a diligent reader trying to keep up with the literature would have found the task nearly impossible." In 1925, only ten southern institutions of higher learning employed a full-time sociologist. In 1936, when the Southern Sociological Society held its first meeting, some 160 members from southern states attended. The dominant sociologist was Howard Odum of the University of North Carolina, who published in prodigious quantity and who, as academic entrepreneur, had immense influence on the work of fellow scholars both at Chapel Hill and elsewhere.[22]

The key sociological concept associated with Odum was Regionalism, and Chapel Hill was, notes Daniel T. Rodgers, "the hub of the kingdom," the "academic empire," that Odum and fellow Regionalists controlled in the thirties. "Regionalism began in Odum's hands as a descriptive term for a massive factual inventory of the South's assets . . . , grew into an agenda for the social reconstruction of the South, then into a scheme for national planning, and next into a theory of social change"—and "then the whole enterprise vanished with scarcely a trace." But for a time, Odum and fellow Regionalists perfectly exemplified Kazin's Americans of the thirties, hungry for facts that might explain the nation's deficiencies and produce a cure for them—and thus resume the progress that the Great Depression had interrupted.[23]

The Chapel Hill Regionalists were not the only social scientists to assemble impressive factual accounts of the South in the thirties. From Yale, Harvard, and Chicago "half a dozen social anthropologists descended on the South to pry . . . rudely . . . into the region's racial mores and class structures." Each of these groups—the Chapel Hill Regionalists and the Yankee anthropologists—looked for different things and found them in different places. The essentials that the Regionalists sought to inventory were sharecropping, soil erosion, credit, out-migration, and cotton. This meant that they focused on certain key places, in particular the Georgia-Alabama black belt, and all but ignored the Mississippi Delta, although it was even more encumbered with cotton and sharecropping and poverty. "The delta belonged not to Chapel Hill but to the anthropologists," who were in quest of their own set of essential facts, those about race and caste. And rather than statistics, they stressed personal observation and in-depth interviews, and they "came back with one of the most powerful books of social observation to come out of the 1930s, John Dollard's *Caste and Class in a Southern Town*.[24]

The Chapel Hill Regionalists, wary of the race issue, skirted it, and at times even ignored it. Yet the Regionalists, selective though they were in their inventory, drew a picture of the South every bit as grim as that drawn by Dollard, whose book offered a "new sense of how deeply race was embedded in the region's culture and psyche." Odum's hundreds of maps in *Southern Regions*, shaded to demonstrate each state's ranking in economic and social well-being, dramatically "marked off the Southeast from the rest of the nation in everything from libraries and milk production per capita, to wealth, lynchings, and radios and depicted as bleak a picture of poverty and backwardness as the South had seen in a long while."[25]

If social scientists depicted poverty, backwardness, and racism in the South of the 1930s, some historians at work in the decade found these characteristics deeply established in the region's history. The South's most distinguished historian, C. Vann Woodward, came to intellectual maturity and published his first work in the thirties, *Tom Watson: Agrarian Rebel*. For most of his life Woodward has pondered over the distinctiveness of the South. In 1958, he pointed out that in contrast to Americans elsewhere, southerners had historically been people of poverty, not plenty, and had experienced defeat, not victory or success, and had manifested a sense of guilt over slavery and racism, not the "innocence" that white northerners traditionally felt about themselves concerning racial prejudices and injustice. The image of the South limned in the great quest of the thirties was in most respects merely the latest reflection of this distinctive South. Beyond the thirties, of course, lay World War II, the cold war, Vietnam, the onset and demise of the Second Reconstruction, development of the Sunshine Belt, and other fundamental rumblings whereby southerners would lose more and more of their distinctiveness, and northerners would take on more and more of those traits that had once made the South "different." The photographers and writers and scholars who launched their quest for a distinctive American South in the thirties were successful: they found it. A great and comparable quest launched in the 1980s would not enjoy such success.[26]

NOTES

1. Hector St. John de Crevecoeur, *Letters from an American Farmer* (New York, 1957); Alexis de Tocqueville, *Democracy in America*, trans. George Lawrence, ed. J. P. Mayer and Max Lerner (New York, 1966); David M. Potter, *People of Plenty: Economic Abundance and the American Character* (Chicago, 1954); Aristides (Joseph Epstein), "Looking for America," *American Scholar* 45 (Summer 1976): 327–33. It may be more than coincidence that a great revival of interest in de Tocqueville, who had been all but forgotten for years, got underway in the 1930s, the search for America of that decade turning into a search as well for America of a century earlier, as experienced and appraised by de Tocqueville. Cf. James T. Schleifer, *The Making of Tocqueville's Democracy in America* (Chapel Hill, 1980), foreword by George Pierson, p. xvi.

2. Robert Cantwell, "America and the Writers' Project," *New Republic* 98 (April 26, 1939): 323–25; Alfred Kazin, *On Native Grounds: An Interpretation of Modern American Prose Literature* (New York, 1943), pp. 378–406.

3. Earl H. Rovit, "The Regions Versus the Nation: Critical Battle of the Thirties," *Mississippi Quarterly* 13 (Spring 1960): 90–98; William Stott, *Documentary Expression and Thirties America* (New York, 1973).

4. Kenneth S. Lynn, "The Regressive Historians," *American Scholar* 47 (Autumn 1978); *South-Watching: Selected Essays by Gerald W. Johnson*, ed. with an introduction by Fred Hobson, (Chapel Hill and London, 1983).

5. David Madden, " 'The Cruel Radiance of What is': Thoughts on Photographs and the South," *Southern Eye, Southern Mind: A Photographic Inquiry*, ed. Jack and Nancy Hurley (Memphis, 1981), pp. 82–97.

6. John L. Spivak, *Georgia Nigger* (New York, 1932); Spivak, *A Man in His Time* (New York, 1967), pp. 167–81; Jack Temple Kirby, *Media-Made Dixie: The South in the American Imagination* (Baton Rouge and London, 1978), p. 57; Stott, *Documentary Expression*, pp. 26–29, 33–35.

7. James Agee, Walker Evans, *Let Us Now Praise Famous Men* (Boston, 1941).

Stott, whose discussion of LUNPFM is superb, observes that, although Agee's and Evans' "deepest meaning were the same," the photographs and the text are, as Agee himself said, "mutually independent." Pictures and text, "each going separate ways, at moments clarify what the other records." *Documentary Expression*, pp. 266ff. For further observation on the relationship of prose and photographs, see James C. Curtis and Sheila Grannen, "Let Us Now Appraise Famous Photographs: Walker Evans and Documentary Photography," *Winter Portfolio* 15 (Spring 1980): 1–23; and Hilton Kramer, "Walker Evans: A Devious Giant," *New York Times*, April 20, 1975, II: pp. 1, 33. On Agee's contribution to LUNPFM, see a series of essays in *Remembering James Agee*, ed. with an introduction by David Madden (Baton Rouge, 1974), notably Robert Fitzgerald, "A Memoir," pp. 35–94; see also Alan Holder, "Encounter in Alabama: Agee and the Tenant Farmer," *Virginia Quarterly Review* 42 (Spring 1966): 189–206; and Carol Schloss, "The Privilege of Perception," Ibid., 57 (Autumn 1980): 596–611.

8. Erskine Caldwell and Margaret Bourke-White, *You Have Seen Their Faces* (New York, 1937); Caldwell, *Call It Experience* (New York, 1951), p. 163.

9. Donald Davidson, "Erskine Caldwell's Picture Book," *The Southern Review* 4 (Summer 1938): 15–25. Cf. Davidson's Agrarian review with one by a Chapel Hill Liberal, W. T. Couch, "Landlord and Tenant," *Virginia Quarterly Review* 14 (Spring 1938): 309–12.

10. Stott, *Documentary Expression*, pp. 220–71. Many of the people Evans photographed did not see any of this "beauty" or sense any of this "dignity" that Stott finds in LUNPFM. Some forty years after Agee and Evans published their book, a *New York Times* reporter (the Atlanta bureau chief) looked up and talked to members of the three Alabama families who were still living in Alabama. Many of them "abide there yet, still worked to the bone, still, by the standards of their nation, poor and undereducated, and still, many of them, mad as hell at Walker Evans." Said one of them, "Those pictures are a scandal on the family." Others resented the notoriety they had received in contrast to the wealth they (mistakenly) thought that Agee and Evans had received from the book. Howell Raines, "Let Us Now Revisit Famous Folk," *New York Times Magazine*, May 25, 1980, pp. 31ff.

11. The figure of 270,000 is a conventional count, used again and again. Only about 87,000 of these 270,000 negatives have been printed. In 1981, a commercial publisher issued these 87,000 prints on microfiche, arranged by region and by subject in each region. The collection contains 16,917 photographs of the South (compared to 24,125 for the Northeast, the largest, and 8,631 for the Far West, the smallest collection among the six "regions" of the country represented in the collection). See "America, 1935–1946: The Photographs of the Farm Security Administration and the Office of War Information Arranged by Region and by Subject and Published on Microfiche," the brochure drawn up by Chadwyck-Healey, Ltd., publisher of the microfiche edition. See also a printed item accompanying the microfiche edition, *America, 1935–1946. Guide and Subject Index to the Photographs.* . . . From 1935 to 1937, the photography group operated out of the Resettlement Administration, which was transformed into the Farm Security Administration (FSA) in 1937. In 1942, the FSA was abolished, but some of the photographers still with the agency went to work for the Office of War Information for another year or so. F. Jack Hurley's *Portrait of a Decade: Roy Stryker and the Development of Documentary Photography in the Thirties* (Baton Rouge, 1972) is a good history of the FSA's

photography unit. For a comprehensive guide to the unit and its photographers see Penelope Dixon, *Photographers of the Farm Security Administration: An Annotated Bibliography, 1930–1980* (New York, 1983).

12. Kazin, *On Native Grounds*, p. 379; Roy Stryker and Nancy Wood, *In This Proud Land: America 1935–1943 As Seen in the FSA Photographs* (New York, 1973), pp. 7, 14; John Collier, Jack Delano and Marion Post Wolcott, quoted in Hank O'Neal, *A Vision Shared: A Classic Portrait of America and Its People, 1935–1943* (New York, 1976), pp. 298, 240, 176. O'Neal's book contains about 275 photographs, all superbly reproduced, and many of them unfamiliar, since O'Neal tried to use photographs that had not already been printed again and again. O'Neal offers a valuable biographical and critical essay on each photographer, discussing their camera technique, their very notions about what they and the FSA were doing, and how they differed from each other in technique, outlook, and artistry.

13. Robert White, "Faces and Places in the South in the 1930s: A Portfolio," *Prospects: An Annual Journal of American Cultural Studies*, ed. Jack Salzman (Philadelphia, 1975), I: 415–29.

14. Karin Becker Ohrn, *Dorothea Lange and the Documentary Tradition* (Baton Rouge, 1980), pp. xiii–xiv, writes that Lange "was recognized as a great photographer during her lifetime—a reputation based primarily on the photographs she made while working for the FSA in the 1930's. She continues to be recognized as one of the best to work on that outstanding team." Ohrn offers intelligent and insightful commentary on all of Lange's career and presents about one hundred of Lange's photographs, though only a few of them are southern images. A recent collection that includes some of Lange's best photographs of the South in the thirties is *Dorothea Lange: Photographs of a Lifetime*, text by Robert Coles (Millerton, N.Y., 1982). On Russell Lee, who did much of his work in the South, see F. Jack Hurley, *Russell Lee, Photographer*, introduction by Robert Coles (Dobbs Ferry N.Y, 1978), a long overdue tribute to Lee. As Coles points out: "This book, rather obviously, fills (at last!) an aching gap in the social history of documentary photography. We now have on the record books devoted to the works of Dorothea Lange, Ben Shahn, Walker Evans and Russell Lee—giants who stalked the deeply troubled America of the 1930's, taking unforgettable note of a hurt, ailing but so often proud people." *Documentary Portrait of Mississippi: The Thirties*, ed. Patti Carr Black (Jackson, 1982), contains 124 photographs of Mississippi taken by Arthur Rothstein, Ben Shahn, Walker Evans, Dorothea Lange, Russell Lee, and Marion Post Wolcott.

15. Thomas D. Clark, ed., *Travels in the New South: A Bibliography*, 2 vols. (Norman, Okla., 1962), vol. II, *The Twentieth Century South, 1900–1955: An Era of Change, Depression and Emergence*, "Introduction," pp. 3–13, by Rupert B. Vance. Paul Fussell, *Abroad: British Literary Travelling Between the Wars* (New York, 1980), p. 39, distinguishes "travel" from "exploration" and from "tourism." The explorer "seeks the undiscovered, the traveller that which has been discovered by the mind working in history, the tourist that which has been discovered by entrepreneurship and prepared for him by the arts of mass publicity." See Jonathan Daniels, *A Southerner Discovers the South* (New York, 1938).

16. The Historical Records Survey (which was originally part of the Federal Writers' Project but eventually separated from the FWP and became, in effect, a fifth arts project) was quite literally a program designed to take inventory of the nation's public records in courthouses and archives and wherever else they might be found.

On the work of the HRS in the South, see Burl Noggle, *Working with History: The Historical Records Survey in Louisiana and the Nation, 1936–1942* (Baton Rouge, 1982). The Four Arts Program was often labeled "Federal One," since it was the first of six federal projects created within the WPA's Division of Professional and Service Projects. The second of these six, "Federal Two," established the Historic American Building Survey (HABS). This project undertook an inventory of architectural Americana and, unlike the Four Arts projects which ended their work before World War II, has continued to exist in one form or another since its inception. Unlike the FSA photographs, the HABS material has received little attention from scholars. Secondary studies on the HABS scarcely exist, for the South or elsewhere in the nation, though Georgia, Tennessee, and Virginia have received some attention (as have Pennsylvania and one or two other states outside the South). See John Linley, *The Georgia Catalog, Historic American Buildings Survey: A Guide to the Architecture of the State* (Athens, 1982); Thomas B. Brumbaugh, et al., eds. *Architecture of Middle Tennessee: The Historic American Buildings Survey*, photographs by Jack E. Boucher (Nashville, 1974); *Virginia Catalog: A List of Measured Drawings, Photographs, and Written Documentation in the Survey*, Compiled by the Virginia Historic Landmarks Commission and the Historic American Buildings Survey (Charlottesville, 1976).

17. Daniel Aaron, "An Approach to the Thirties," in *The Study of American Culture: Contemporary Conflicts*, ed. Luther S. Leudtke (Deland, Fla., 1977), p. 13; Jared Putnam, "Guides to America," *The Nation* (December 24, 1938): 694–96; E. Current-Garcia, "Writers in the Sticks," *Prairie Schooner* 12 (Winter 1938): 295–309; and Monty Penkower, *The Federal Writers' Project: A Study in Government Patronage of the Arts* (Urbana, 1977), pp. 140–43. William F. McDonald, *Federal Relief Administration and the Arts* (Columbus, 1969) is a huge administrative history of all the Arts Projects. For appraisals of the FWP, see Penkower, *Federal Writers' Project*, and Jerre Mangione, *The Dream and the Deal: The Federal Writers' Project, 1935–1943* (Boston, 1972).

A splendid study of another art program of the 1930s, the Treasury Department's art program, is Karal Ann Marling, *Wall-to-Wall: A Cultural History of Post-Office Murals in the Great Depression* (Minneapolis, 1982). On southern murals, see especially Marling's discussion of the hassle between the muralist and the local establishment of Paris, Arkansas, over just what was appropriate subject matter for the Paris post-office wall (pp. 104–29).

18. George P. Rawick, ed., *The American Slave: A Composite Autobiography*, 19 vols. (Westport, Conn., 1972); Rawick, ed., *The American Slave: A Composite Autobiography, Supplement, Series 1*, 12 vols. (Westport, Conn., 1978); and Rawick, ed., *The American Slave; A Composite Autobiography, Supplement, Series 2*, 10 vols. (Westport, Conn., 1979). See Rawick's introduction to volume one of the *Supplement, Series 1* for an extensive account of his and other scholars' discovery of the additional material. A good history of the compilation and subsequent fate of the narratives is Norman R. Yetman, "The Background of the Slave Narrative Collection," *American Quarterly* 19 (Fall 1967): 534–53. Yetman was one of the few scholars to make use of the narratives before 1970. In the past decade or so, more and more scholars have written some impressive work based on the ex-slave narratives. See Norman R. Yetman, "Ex-Slave Interviews and the Historiography of Slavery," *American Quarterly* 36 (Summer 1984): 181–210.

19. Norman R. Yetman, *Life Under the 'Peculiar Institution': Selections from the Slave Narrative Collection* (Huntington, N.Y., 1976), pp. 347–48. For varying uses and appraisals of the narratives, see C. Vann Woodward, "History from Slave Sources," *American Historical Review* 79 (April 1974): 470–81; John W. Blassingame, "Using the Testimony of Ex-Slaves: Approaches and Problems," *Journal of Southern History* 41 (November 1975): 473–492; Paul D. Escott, *Slavery Remembered: A Record of Twentieth-Century Slave Narrative* (Chapel Hill, 1979); Jerrold Hirsch, "Reading and Counting," *Reviews in American History* 8 (September 1980): 312–317; and *Weevils in the Wheat: Interviews with Virginia Ex-Slaves*, comp. and ed. Charles L. Perdue, Jr., et al. (Charlottesville, 1976).

20. *These Are Our Lives: As Told By the People and Written by Members of the Federal Writers' Project of the Works Progress Administration in North Carolina, Tennessee, and Georgia* (Chapel Hill, 1939); Couch quoted in Daniel Joseph Singal, *The War Within: From Victorian to Modernist Thought in the South, 1919–1945* (Chapel Hill, 1982), pp. 265–301; Dabney quoted in *Such As Us: Southern Voices of the Thirties*, ed. Tom E. Terrill and Jerrold Hirsch (Chapel Hill, 1978), p. xxi.

21. James Seay Brown, ed., *Up Before Daylight: Life Histories from the Alabama Writers' Project, 1938–1939* (Tuscaloosa, 1982); *First-Person America*, ed. and with an introduction by Ann Banks (New York, 1980), p. xiv.

22. Singal, *The War Within*, pp. 302–3. Singal points out that "well-trained sociologists" could also be found at several other southern universities besides UNC by the mid-thirties, but except for Edgar T. Thompson at Duke "these men engaged in little except teaching unless they were connected to Odum's network." Dewey W. Grantham, Jr., "The Regional Imagination: Social Scientists and the American South," *Journal of Southern History* 34 (February 1968): 3–33, is a good, cogent summary statement on the growth of the social sciences in the 1930s.

23. Daniel T. Rodgers, "Regionalism and the Burdens of Progress," in *Region, Race, and Reconstruction: Essays in Honor of C. Vann Woodward*, ed. J. Morgan Kousser and James M. McPherson (New York and Oxford, 1982), pp. 3–26. Alongside Rodgers and Singal's studies of Odum and the Regionalists, a third noteworthy study has appeared recently, Michael O'Brien, *The Idea of the American South, 1920–1941*, (Baltimore, 1979), pp. 31–93. But see also Dewey Grantham's judicious remarks in his 1968 essay, "The Regional Imagination." The most notable of the Regionalist inventories, besides Odum's own *Southern Regions of the United States* (Chapel Hill, 1936), were several studies by Rupert Vance, including *Human Geography of the South* (Chapel Hill, 1932) and Arthur Raper's *Preface to Peasantry* (Chapel Hill, 1936). Rodgers describes Vance as "Odum's best and most loyal graduate student and his principal collaborator in shaping regional sociology." Rodgers, "Regionalism and Burdens of Progress," p. 5. Daniel Singal and John Shelton Reed, eds., *Regionalism and the South* (Chapel Hill, 1982), p. xix., judge Vance to have been "as much the father of regional sociology as was Odum." See also Singal's discussion of Vance in *The War Within*, pp. 305–15.

24. Rodgers, "Regionalism and Burdens of Progress," pp. 3–6. Two other notable titles from the anthropologists working in the delta are: Hortense Powdermaker, *After Freedom: A Cultural Study of the Deep South* (New York, 1939), on Indianola, Mississippi (as was Dollard's *Caste & Class*); and Allison Davis, et al., *Deep South: A Social Anthropological Study of Caste and Class* (Chicago, 1941) set in Natchez and Claiborne County, Mississippi.

25. Rodgers, "Regionalism and Burdens of Progress," p. 9.

26. C. Vann Woodward, "The Search for Southern Identity," *Virginia Quarterly Review* 34 (Summer 1958): 321–38. Southern historiography flourished in the thirties as much as did social science—witness the establishment of the Southern Historical Association in 1934, the appearance of *The Journal of Southern History* in 1935, the inauguration of the Walter Lynwood Fleming Lecture series at Louisiana State University in 1937, and the publication of such notable studies as W. J. Cash's tour de force, *The Mind of the South* (in 1941), Douglas S. Freeman's massive set of books on Robert E. Lee and the Civil War, and C. Vann Woodward's biography of Tom Watson. All this activity can be related to the quest for the South in the thirties that I am concerned with, but I reluctantly limit discussion of the matter to this note and to the comments on Woodward in the text. Woodward's recent retrospective view of his life and work, *Thinking Back: The Perils of Writing History* (Baton Rouge, 1986), contains a captivating essay on his graduate school days at Chapel Hill in the 1930s, where he encountered some of the people and felt (and absorbed some, rejected some) of the climate of opinion that I have discussed in the pages above.

Bibliographical Essay

For overviews of the South since the Civil War see John S. Ezell, *The South Since 1865*, 2nd ed. (New York, 1975) and Idus A. Newby, *The South: A History* (New York, 1978); both C. Vann Woodward, *Origins of the New South, 1877–1913* (Baton Rouge, 1951) and George Brown Tindall, *The Emergence of the New South, 1913–1945* (Baton Rouge, 1967) are authoritative accounts by master historians. Charles P. Roland, *The South Since World War II* (Lexington, 1975) is an adequate introduction that needs to be brought up to date. Among the more important state studies are Albert D. Kirwan, *Revolt of the Rednecks: Mississippi Politics, 1876–1925* (Lexington, 1951); Sheldon Hackney, *From Populism to Progressivism in Alabama* (Princeton, 1969); and Numan V. Bartley, *The Creation of Modern Georgia* (Athens, 1983), an insightful look at the processes of "modernization."

For political history see V. O. Key's classic, *Southern Politics in State and Nation* (New York, 1949); Robert Garson, *The Democratic Party and the Politics of Sectionalism, 1941–1948* (Baton Rouge, 1974); and Numan V. Bartley, *The Rise of Massive Resistance: Race and Politics in the South During the 1950s* (Baton Rouge, 1969). Among biographies of political leaders, two stand out as models of scholarship: C. Vann Woodward, *Tom Watson: Agrarian Rebel* (New York, 1938) and T. Harry Williams, *Huey Long* (New York, 1969). The following biographies are also useful: Francis Butler Simkins, *Pitchfork Ben Tillman, South Carolinian* (Baton Rouge, 1944); Dewey W. Grantham, Jr., *Hoke Smith and the Politics of the New South* (Baton Rouge, 1958); William Anderson, *The Wild Man from Sugar Creek: The Political Career of Eugene Talmadge* (Baton Rouge, 1975); and John A. Salmond, *A Southern Rebel: The Life and Times of Aubrey Willis Williams, 1890–1965* (Chapel Hill, 1983).

The best overview of southern religion remains Kenneth K. Bailey, *Southern White Protestantism in the Twentieth Century* (New York, 1964). It should be supplemented with David Edwin Harrell, *White Sects and Black Men in the Recent South* (Nashville, 1971) and Harrell's splendid biography, *Oral Roberts: An American Life* (Bloomington, 1985). For the relation of religion to social reform see John Patrick McDowell, *The Social Gospel in the South: The Women's Home Mission Movement in the Methodist Episcopal Church South, 1886–1939* (Baton Rouge, 1982). The standard books on the evolution controversy in the South are: Willard B. Gatewood, Jr., *Controversy in the Twenties: Fundamentalism, Modernism and Evolution* (Nashville, 1969) and Gatewood's *Preachers, Pedagogues and Politicians: The Evolution Controversy in North Carolina, 1920–1927* (Chapel Hill, 1966). Liston Pope, *Millhands and Preachers: A Study of Gastonia* (New Haven, 1942) remains an undisputed classic. George M. Marsden, *Fundamentalism and American Culture: The Shaping of Twentieth Century Evangelicalism* (New York, 1980) is a sophisticated analysis.

For women's history, Anne Firor Scott's pioneering work, *The Southern Lady: From Pedestal to Politics, 1830–1930* (Chicago, 1970) should be supplemented with Jacquelyn Dowd Hall, *Revolt Against Chivalry: Jessie Daniel Ames and the Women's Campaign Against Lynching* (New York, 1979) and Jacqueline Jones, *Labor of Love, Labor of Sorrow: Black Women, Work, and the Family from Slavery to the Present* (New York, 1985), two first-rate studies. Ann Goodwyn Jones, *Tomorrow is Another Day: The Woman Writer in the South, 1859–1936* (Baton Rouge, 1981) intelligently places selected women writers in perspective.

Southern intellectual history has come of age in the past two decades. Paul Gaston, *The New South Creed* (New York, 1970); Bruce Clayton, *The Savage Ideal: Intolerance and Intellectual Leadership in the South, 1890–1914* (Baltimore, 1972); and Jack Temple Kirby, *Darkness at the Dawning: Race and Reform in the Progressive South* (Philadelphia, 1972) focus on the New South's first generation of intellectuals. For selected figures in the next generation see Michael O'Brien, *The Idea of the American South 1920–1941* (Baltimore, 1979). Morton Sosna, *In Search of the Silent South: Southern Liberals and The Race Issue* (New York, 1977) and John T. Kneebone, *Southern Liberal Journalists and the Issue of Race, 1920–1944* (Chapel Hill, 1985) document the centrality of race in southern thinking. Much broader in scope are George M. Fredrickson, *The Black Image in the White Mind: The Debate on Afro-American Character and Destiny, 1817–1914* (New York, 1971) and Fred Hobson, *Tell About the South: The Southern Rage to Explain* (Baton Rouge, 1983), the latter a challenging interpretation of the South's compulsion to analyze and defend itself. Daniel Joseph Singal, *The War Within: From Victorian to Modernist Thought in the South, 1919–1945* (Chapel Hill, 1982), is a path-breaking analysis. Richard H. King, *A Southern Renaissance: The Cultural Awakening of the American South, 1930–1955* (New York, 1980) is brilliantly provocative as is Joel Williamson, *The Crucible of Race: Black-White Relations in the American South Since Emancipation* (New York, 1984) which subtly (if quixotically) explores the psychological complexities of racial thought. Not to be overlooked are the brilliant essays in C. Vann Woodward, *The Burden of Southern History*, rev. ed. (New York, 1968).

C. Vann Woodward's *The Strange Career of Jim Crow*, 3rd rev. ed. (New York, 1974) remains the starting point in any discussion of southern race relations. See also the relevant chapters in Woodward, *Origins of the New South* and Tindall, *The Emergence of the New South*. Louis R. Harlan, *Separate But Unequal: Public School Campaigns and Racism in the Southern Seaboard States, 1901–1915* (Chapel Hill, 1958) remains the standard source. Louis R. Harlan's, *Booker T. Washington: The Making of a Black Leader, 1856–1901* (New York, 1972) and *Booker T. Washington: The Wizard of Tuskegee, 1901–1915* (New York, 1983) supercede all previous biographies of the great black leader. Dan T. Carter tells the story of *Scottsboro: A Tragedy of the American South* (Baton Rouge, 1969) with humane insight.

The industrial evolution of the South has received intelligent analysis in selected chapters in Woodward, *Origins of the New South* and Tindall, *The Emergence of the New South* and most recently in James C. Cobbs' perceptive synthesis, *Industrialization and Southern Society, 1877–1984* (Philadelphia, 1985). For a cogent analysis of the powerful Duke dynasty see Robert F. Durden, *The Dukes of Durham, 1865–1929* (Durham, 1975). Broadus Mitchell, *The Rise of the Cotton Mills in the South* (Baltimore, 1921) remains the standard source but David Carlton cogently explores the social tensions brought about by the emergence of a mill labor force in *Mill and Town in South Carolina, 1880–1920* (Baton Rouge, 1982). For the circumstances that kept poor whites poor in the age of industrialization see Wayne Flint, *Dixie's Forgotten People: The South's Poor Whites* (Bloomington, 1979). The standard source on the labor movement in the South is Ray F. Marshall, *Labor in the South* (Cambridge, 1967). Pope's *Millhands and Preachers* is the indispensable source for understanding the South's most violent, controversial strike. See also Dan McCurry and Carolyn Ashbaugh, "Gastonia, 1929: Strike at the Loray Mill," *Southern Exposure* 6 (Winter 1974): 185–203. For a broader perspective see Jacquelyn Dowd Hall, Robert Korstad, and James Leloudis, "Cotton Mill People: Work, Community, and Protest in the Textile South," *American Historical Review* 91 (April 1986): 246–86.

Southern agriculture has been perceptively analyzed in selected chapters of Woodward, *Origins of the New South* and Tindall, *The Emergence of the New South* and comprehensively in Gilbert C. Fite, *Cotton Fields No More: Southern Agriculture, 1865–1980* (Lexington, 1984). Pete Daniel, *The Shadow of Slavery: Peonage in the South, 1901–1969* (Urbana, 1972) explores a neglected topic. Pete Daniel, "The Transformation of the Rural South, 1930 to the Present," *Agricultural History* 55 (July 1981): 231–48, explores some of the changes in agriculture in an era of expanding industry.

Index

Agee, James, 191–93
Ainsworth, William N., 162
Albright, Mayne, 43
Alexander, Kelly M., 39
Alexander, Will, 15
American Federation of Labor (AFL), 73, 79
An American Epoch (Odum), 176
Anti-Saloon League, 158–59
Artist, Russel, 142
Ashurst, Senator Henry, 54

Banks, Ann, 197
Baptist Challenge (Moser), 140
Barden, Representative Graham A., 42
Barkley, Senator Alben, 16, 33, 40
Bayard, Thomas, 56
Becker, Carl, 172
Bennett, Bruce, 141
Bennett, Lura, 162
Bird, Wendell, 143
Black, Senator Hugo, 55, 61
Blackwell, Robert E., 157
Blease, Coleman L., 10–13, 22
Bogard, Ben, 131–32
Borah, Senator William E., 51, 56
Bourke-White, Margaret, 191–93
Brann, W. C., 173

Brownell, Herbert, 43
Bruce, Senator Walter, 56
Bryan, William Jennings, 52, 57, 59; and antievolution, 125, 127–28
Butler, Marion, 57
Byrnes, James F.: early life of, 3–4; legal career, 4–5; as secretary of state, 21; seeks vice-presidency, 18–22; senatorial career of, 10–17; and Supreme Court, 17–18; and white supremacy, 6–12

Cabell, James Branch, 173
Caldwell, Erskine, 191–92, 197
Calhoun, John, 12
Cannon, James A., Jr.: absences abroad, 154–55; assessments of, 152–56, 163–66; and election of 1928, 159–61, 174; friendship with H. L. Mencken, 161–63; personality of, 151–52, 156; and temperance movement, 157–59; trial of, 161–62
Cantwell, Robert, 188
Capper, Senator Arthur, 56
Caraway, O. Thaddeus, 55, 58–59
Carolina Israelite, 162
Cash, W. J.: and antievolution, 128, 144; early life of, 172–73; and Freud,

177–78; health of, 174; journalistic career of, 174–76; and Marx, 177; *Mind of the South, The*, 171, 177–82; and modernism, 171–72, 179, 182–83
Cason, Clarence, 145
Caste and Class in a Southern Town (Dollard), 198
Catts, Sidney J., 78
Chandler, Warren A., 154, 158
Civil Rights, 32, 34–39, 107, 114–15. *See also* Negroes, Racism, Segregation
Cleveland, Grover, 50, 52, 57–59
Collier, John, 193–94
Communist Manifesto (Marx), 177
Congress on Industrial Organization (CIO), 15, 19–20, 107–8, 113–17
Coolidge, Calvin, 50, 56
Costigan, Edward, 110
Couch, W. T., 197
Council of National Defense, 109–10
Criswell, W. A., 132
Culbertson, Senator Charles, 55, 58

Dabney, Virginius, 130, 152–53, 162, 197; *Dry Messiah*, 152–53
Daniels, Jonathan, 195
Daniels, Josephus, 58, 155, 161, 163
Darrow, Clarence, 125
Darwin, Charles: and antievolution, 125–31, 133–37, 139–44; mentioned, 173, 178, 182
Davidson, Donald, 176, 191
Davis, Jefferson, 164, 176
Davis, John, 60
Davis, Watson, 133
Dean, Braswell, Jr., 140
Delano, Jack, 193–94
Democracy in America (de Tocqueville), 187
Democratic party, 7, 11–17, 19, 31–33, 38–40, 49–52, 54–58, 115, 159, 161, 174–75
Denny, Collins, 154, 161
Densmore, John B., 70–71, 75–76, 78
Department of Labor, 70, 73–74, 76, 80, 112
Department of War, 70–71

Depression, the, 32, 94, 164, 175–76, 187, 190, 195–96, 198
Dewey, John, 177
Dewson, Molly, 111–12, 118
Dial, Senator Nathaniel B., 10, 56
Dill, Senator Clarence, 50
Dillard, James H., 72–73
Division of Negro Economics, 74–75, 78
Dixon, Amzi C., 127–28
Dollar, John, 198
Douglas, William O., 17–18, 20
Dry Messiah (Dabney), 152–53
DuBois, W. E. B., 8–9, 75, 180
Duke, James B., 175
Durr, Virginia, 117

Eastland, Senator James O., 138
Edens, Bessie, 92
Edge, Senator Walter, 52
Edwards, Kaola, 91
Eisenhower, Dwight D., 41–42
Elliott, Grace, 87, 92
Elliott, Ralph, 140
Ellwanger, Paul, 143
Epperson, Susan, 141–42
Evans, Walker, 190–94
Evolution. *See* Darwin, Fundamentalism, Scopes Trial

Falwell, Jerry, 137–39, 142
Farley, Jim, 14
Farm Security Administration (FSA), 190–91, 193–95, 197
Farm tenancy, 191–92
Faubus, Orval, 141
Faulkner, William, 174
Federal Writers' Project (FWP), 188–89, 195–97
Feminism, 108, 117. *See also* Women
Finley, Vesta, 85, 87
First Person America (Banks), 197
Fletcher, Senator D. U., 55–56, 58, 60
Flood, Henry D., 158
Flynn, Edward, 19, 21
Fosdick, Harry Emerson, 37
Freud, Sigmund, 177–79, 182
Fundamentalism, 126–32, 137–39, 141,

INDEX 211

144, 172. See also Darwin, Scopes Trial

Gardner, O. Max, 30, 174
Garner, John Nance, 58
Genesis Flood, The (Morris), 139
George, Senator Walter, 59
Georgia Nigger (Spivak), 190
Gerwick, Katherine, 110, 118–19
Glass, Carter, 56, 160–62
God's Little Acre (Caldwell), 191
Golden, Harry, 162
Goldmark, Pauline, 110
Gompers, Samuel, 72–73, 75
Gone with the Wind (Mitchell), 182, 189
Graham, Billy, 131, 137
Graham, Frank P., 36

Ham, Mordecai F., 128, 131–32
Hancock, Gordon B., 111
Hannegan, Robert, 20
Hardwick, Representative Thomas, 50
Harlee, William C., 13
Harrell, Costen J., 162
Harris, Senator William, 54, 61
Harrison, Senator Pat, 56, 59–60
Haynes, George Edmond, 73–76
Heflin, Senator Thomas, 55, 59
Hillman, Sidney, 20–21
Hine, Lewis, 190
Hirsch, Jerrold, 197
Hoey, Bess, 30
Hoey, Charles Aycock, 30
Hoey, Clyde R., Jr., 30
Hoey, Senator Clyde R.: appearance of, 29, 43; beliefs of, 29, 43–44; and Fair Employment Practices Commission (FEPC), 37–39; legal career of, 31; and North Carolina politics, 30–32, 174; personal life of, 29–31; and segregation, 32–35, 38, 40–41, 43; as senator, 33, 36, 43
Holland, Rosa, 86
Holland, Senator Spessard, 38
Hoover, Herbert, 159, 174
Hopkins, Harry, 18–19
Horton, Myles, 115

Hull, Cordell, 18, 51
Hux, Martin Luther, 129

I'll Take My Stand, 176, 191
Industrialization, 85–86, 98, 136

In This Proud Land, 193

Jackson, Giles B., 74–76
Jacobs, Vera, 134
Johnson, Louis, 40
Johnson, Lyndon B., 12, 43
Jones, Brownie Lee, 119
Jones, Eugene Kinckle, 73
Jones, Thomas Jesse, 73
Jung, Theo, 193

Kazin, Alfred, 188
Keating, Representative Edward, 55
Kelley, Florence, 110–11
King, Nolia, 97
King, Senator William, 52
Kirkby, John H., 79
Kitchin, Representative Claude, 50, 58
Ku Klux Klan, 11, 34, 55, 125, 160, 176

Labor: and CIO, 108, 113–15, 120; and National Consumers League, 112; and politics, 14, 19–21, 52; and strikes, 97–98; and women, 87–89, 92, 97; and World War I, 69–80
La Follette, Senator Robert, 50–51
Lang, Walter, 139, 141
Lange, Dorothea, 190–91, 193–94
Lee, Robert E., 43, 108, 195
Lee, Russell, 191, 193–94
Lerner, Max, 138
Leslie, J. A., Jr., 152
Let Us Now Praise Famous Men (Agee and Evans), 191–94
Lewis, John L., 14, 113
Lipscomb, Bernard F., 156, 164
Lodge, Henry Cabot, Jr., 42
Lomax, John A., 196
Long, Huey, 61
Lorentz, Pare, 188

INDEX

Loyalty Leagues, 77
Lynching, 8–12, 36–37, 176, 181

McAdoo, William Gibbs, 56
McCallum, Helen Hawley, 162
McClellan, Senator John, 138
MacDonald, Lois, 85, 99, 116
McGrath, Howard, 42
McKellar, Senator Kenneth, 33, 54–55, 61
McLaren, Louise, 116
McLean, Senator George, 52
McLendon, Baxter F., 128
Marshall, John, 108
Martin, Senator Thomas, 75, 158–59
Marx, Karl, 177–78, 181
Mason, George, 107–8
Mason, James Murray, 108
Mason, Lucy Ambler, 108
Mason, Lucy Randolph: and CIO, 107, 113–16; and Consumers League, 111–13, 116; early life, 108–9; family background, 107–8; personal life, 118–19; and the South, 115–17, 119, 183; and spiritualism, 119–20; *To Win These Rights*, 116; and YWCA, 109–14
Massee, Jasper C., 127
Masters, Victor I., 126
Maxey, Robert E. Lee, 135
Mayfield, Senator Earle, 54–55
Mellon, Andrew, 50–51
Mencken, H. L.: and Bishop Cannon, 151, 160, 162–63; and fundamentalism, 136; and Scopes Trial, 125; and W. J. Cash, 123, 175, 182
Message of Genesis, The (Elliot), 140
Mill villages, 85, 89, 93, 96, 98–100, 107, 114, 174
Mind of the South, The (Cash), 171, 178–82
Mitchell, Margaret, 182
Modernism, 171–74, 176, 179, 181–83. *See also* Cash, W. J.
Monroe, James, 164
Moore, George Ivey, 134
Morris, Henry M., 139, 141
Morse, Senator Wayne, 39

Moser, M. L., Jr., 140–42
Moton, R. R., 73
Mouzon, Edwin D., 154
Murphy, Edgar Gardner, 181
Mydans, Carl 193

National Association for the Advancement of Colored People (NAACP), 8, 16–17, 37–39, 41–43, 73
National Consumers League (NCL), 110–13, 115–17
Negroes: attitudes toward, 4, 31–34, 58, 180–81; and civil rights, 36–37; and the Courts, 4–6; and Democratic party, 15, 19, 21; and labor, 72–79, 88, 93, 114–15; and lynching, 9–11, 37; and segregation, 40–42, 95; slave narratives, 196–97; support for, 110–11; and white supremacy, 6–9, 15. *See also* Race issue; Racism; Segregation
New Deal, the, 12, 14–15, 31, 49, 61, 112, 187–88, 195
New South, 55, 69, 86, 109, 111, 181
Niebuhr, Reinhold, 177, 183
Nietzche, Friedrich, 171, 173
Norbeck, Senator Peter, 56
Norris, J. Frank, 127–28, 131–32
Norris, Senator George, 50–52, 54–56
Nye, Gerald P., 161

Oates, Mrs. Gordon, 135
Odum, Howard, 175–76, 178, 182, 197–98
On Native Grounds (Kazin), 188
Overman, Senator Lee, 55, 57–58
Overton, William R., 143
Owen, Senator Robert, 51

Page, Thomas Nelson, 182
Page, Walter Hines, 57
Parrish, Beulah, 89
Peay, Austin, 133
People of Plenty (Potter), 187
Pepper, Senator Claude, 44
Perkins, Frances, 112–15
Pollard, John Garland, 158, 161
Pope, Charlisle, 90, 92

INDEX

Populism, 31, 57–60
Porter, Polly, 118
Post, Louis F., 73, 75–77
Poteat, William Lewis, 173
Potter, David M., 187
Price, Lille Morris, 97
Prohibition, 58, 151, 153, 158–61, 163–64, 174

Race issue, the, 4, 12, 14–15, 17–19, 21–22, 29. *See also* Negroes; Racism
Racism, 7, 9, 33, 57–58, 125, 138, 175, 179–81, 198
Randolph, A. Philip, 40
Ransom, John Crowe, 44, 176, 183
Raper, Arthur F., 181
Raskob, John J., 159–60
Reconstruction, 4, 7–8, 52, 80
Reed, Murray O., 141
Religion, 30, 87, 99–100, 126–27, 137–38, 173, 176. *See also* Evolution; Fundamentalism
Republican party, 7, 9–10, 13, 31, 33, 35, 39–41, 49, 51–52, 54–55, 58
Rice, John R., 131, 137
Riis, Jacob, 190
Riley, William B., 127
Roberts, Oral, 137
Robinson, Senator Joseph, 12, 56, 58–60
Roche, Josephine, 112
Roosevelt, Eleanor, 20, 112, 115–17
Roosevelt, Franklin Delano, 12–14, 17–22, 37, 40, 49, 51, 117, 163, 182
Rothstein, Arthur, 191, 193–94
Rovit, Earl, 188–89
Rozzell, Forrest, 140–41
Russell, Richard, 41

Scopes trial, 125, 128
Scott, Emmett, 75
Scott, Gary, 140
Segregation, 4, 7, 21–22, 32–33, 36, 38–44, 60, 136–37. *See also* Negroes; White Supremacy
Shahn, Ben, 193
Sharecroppers, 10
Sheppard, Senator Morris, 54, 61

Shields, Emma, 94
Shillady, John R., 73
Shipley, Maynard, 144
Simmons, Senator Furnifold, 55, 57–58, 60
Smalls, Robert, 7
Smith, A. Coke, 155
Smith, Alfred E., 159–60, 174–75
Smith, Lillian, 118
Smith, Senator E. D., 13, 55–56, 58
Smith, Senator Hoke, 58
Smith, Senator Willis, 36
Smith, William Waugh, 156
Smoot, Senator Reed, 60
Snell, H. H., 79
Snelling, Paula, 118
Southern Conference for Human Welfare (SCHW), 117
Southern Regions of the United States (Odum), 176, 198
Southern School for Women Workers in Industry, 85, 116–17, 119
Southerner Discovers the South, A (Daniels), 195
Spivak, John L., 190
States' rights, 32, 36–37, 43, 125
Stephens, Senator Hubert, 59
Stoney, Thomas P., 13
Straton, John Roach, 127
Stryker, Roy, 190, 193–94
Such as Us (Hirsch and Terrill), 197
Swanson, Senator Claude, 55–58

Talmadge, Senator Herman, 138
Tate, Allen, 174, 176, 183
Terrill, Tom E., 197
These Are Our Lives, 197
Thurmond, Senator J. Strom, 25
Tillman, Senator Benjamin, 5
Tindall, George, 60, 69, 72, 79
Tinkham, George H., 31, 61
Tobacco Road (Caldwell), 191
Tocqueville, de, 187
Tom Watson: Agrarian Rebel (Woodward), 198
To Secure These Rights, 36
To Win These Rights (Mason), 116
Tragedy of Lynching, The (Raper) 181

Truman, Harry S., 18, 20–21, 33–42
Tumulty, Joseph P., 75
Tyler, John, 164

Underwood, Senator Oscar, 52, 56, 60
United States Employment Service (USES), and World War I, 70, 73–80

Vachon, John, 193
Vance, Rupert B., 195
Vardaman, Senator James K., 49, 59–60
Victorianism, 171–73, 181
Violence, 4, 8–9, 18, 37, 59, 175
Virginia Conference, the, 155, 157

Wagner, Senator Robert, 54
Wallace, Henry, 16, 18, 20
Walsh, Senator David, 54
Walsh, Senator Thomas J., 56, 58
Warren, Earl, 138
Washington, Booker T., 74
Watson, Senator Tom, 52
Webb, E. Yates, 30
Webb, James L., 30
Wheeler, Senator Burton, 50
Wherry, Kenneth, 40
White, Walter, 16, 19, 22
Whitehead, Paul, 155, 157

White supremacy, 4–6, 10–11, 16, 21, 23, 29, 31, 52, 128. *See also* Racism
Wiggins, Ella May, 98
Williams, Cliff, 77
Wilson, William B., 70, 72–76
Wilson, Woodrow, 7, 22, 49–51, 58–59, 69–70, 127, 159, 181
Wise, Henry A., 164
Wolcott, Marion Post, 193–94
Women: assaults on, 8, 11, 34; and church, 99–100; and industrialization, 85–89, 100–101; and labor movement, 108, 115–16; and marriage, 91–93; and mill villages, 98–99; and personal relationships, 118–19; and poll tax, 37; and reform, 108–9, 111–12; and strikes, 97–98; and tobacco factories, 93–94; and textile industry, 90–91, 94–97; and YWCA, 91, 116. *See also* Feminism
Woodrow, James, 127
Woodward, C. Vann, 172, 198–99
Works Progress Administration (WPA), 188

You Have Seen Their Faces (Bourke-White, Caldwell), 191–93
Young, Isabel (Hoey), 30
Young Women's Christian Association (YWCA), 91, 109–11, 116, 118

About the Editors and Contributors

WILLIAM J. BREEN is a senior lecturer in history at LaTrobe University, Melbourne, Australia. His publications include *Uncle Sam at Home*, a study of the Council of National Defense during World War I, and several articles in historical journals.

BRUCE CLAYTON is the Harry A. Logan, Sr. Professor of History and head of the department at Allegheny College, Meadville, Pennsylvania. He has published *The Savage Ideal: Intolerance and Intellectual Leadership in the South, 1890–1914* and *Forgotten Prophet: The Life of Randolph Bourne*. He is at work on a biography of W. J. Cash.

WILLARD B. GATEWOOD, JR., is Alumni Distinguished Professor at the University of Arkansas. Among his nine books are *Eugene Clyde Brooks: Educator and Public Servant; Preachers, Pedagogues and Politicians: The Evolution Controversy in North Carolina 1920–1927*; and *Black Americans and the White Man's Burden, 1898–1903*. He has also published more than fifty articles and reviews in scholarly journals.

SUSAN TUCKER HATCHER is a part-time assistant professor of history at Elon College, North Carolina. She has published articles on North Carolina Quakers and is currently working on a biography of Clyde R. Hoey.

ROBERT A. HOHNER is associate professor of history and head of the department at the University of Western Ontario. He has published numerous articles and is currently completing a biography of Bishop James Cannon.

WINFRED B. MOORE, JR. is associate professor of history at The Citadel. He has coedited two books of essays on southern topics, and is currently writing a biography of James F. Byrnes.

BURL F. NOGGLE is Distinguished Alumni Professor of History at Louisiana State University. He has published three books, *Teapot Dome: Oil and Politics in the 1920's, Into the Twenties: The United States from Armistice to Normalcy, 1918–1921* and *Working with History: The Historical Records Survey in Louisiana and the Nation, 1936–1942*, and several articles. He is currently writing a cultural history of the 1930s.

ERIK N. OLSSEN is professor of history at the University of Otago, Dunedin, New Zealand. He has published extensively in the history of both the United States and New Zealand. His most recent book is a history of the province of Otago.

MARION W. ROYDHOUSE teaches history at St. Joseph's University in Philadelphia. Her dissertation was entitled "The 'Universal Sisterhood of Women': Women and Labor Reform in North Carolina, 1900–1912," and she has published articles on several aspects of women's history.

JOHN A. SALMOND is professor of American history at LaTrobe University, Melbourne, Australia. Among his books are *The Civilian Conversation Corps: A New Deal Case Study* and *A Southern Rebel: The Life and Times of Aubrey Willis Williams, 1890–1965*. He has recently completed a life of Lucy Randolph Mason and is currently working on a biography of Clifford J. Durr.